DAVID LYNCH

Michel Chion

Translated by Robert Julian

BFI PUBLISHING

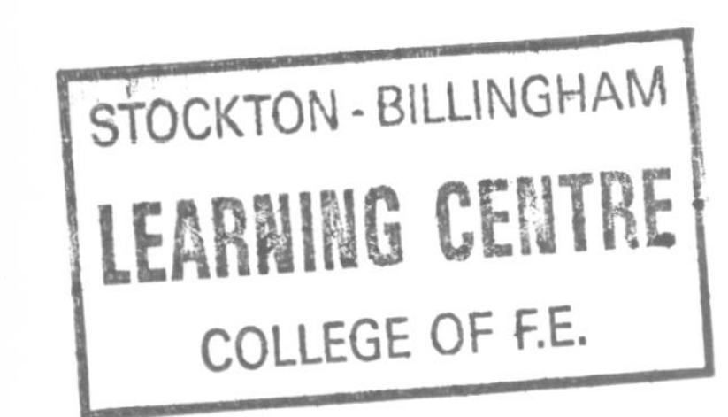

Published in 1995 by the
British Film Institute
21 Stephen Street
London W1P 2LN

Reprinted 1995, 1996

The British Film Institute exists to promote appreciation, enjoyment, protection and development of moving image culture in and throughout the whole of the United Kingdom.
Its activities include the National Film and Television Archive; the National Film Theatre; the Museum of the Moving Image; the London Film Festival; the production and distribution of film and video; funding and support for regional activities; Library and Information Services; Stills, Posters and Designs; Research, Publishing and Education; and the monthly *Sight and Sound* magazine.

British Library Cataloguing in Publication Data
A catalogue record for this book is available
from the British Library

ISBN 0-85170-456-5
0-85170-457-3 pbk

Cover design by Matthew Losasso
Cover still: Isabella Rossellini in *Blue Velvet*

Typesetting by D R Bungay Associates, Burghfield, Berks
Printed in Great Britain by Page Bros Ltd, Norwich

For Anne-Marie

Sometimes a wind blows
and the mysteries of Love
come clear.

CONTENTS

FOREWORD AND ACKNOWLEDGMENTS

The first section of this book presents the work of David Lynch in a straightforward chronological order so as to combine an account of the circumstances in which the films were made, an analysis of their themes, and a highlighting of constant technical and stylistic aspects together with their development, all viewed within the context of the history of cinema. In the Lynch-Kit (see pp. 145–182), a composite portrait of the director is given in the form of alphabetically organised entries in an order which is both logical and alphabetical, that is to say, Utopian. (Note: For this English edition, the Lynch-Kit's ingredients have been rearranged in accordance with the English alphabet even though such an arrangement infringes the sequential logic of the kit's organisation in the original).

In mixing two levels which one tends to find treated separately in other works, I wished not only to account more completely for a creative artist who himself believes in the plurality of levels of meaning and reality; my aim was also to show that a book on the cinema can, and in certain cases must, perform at least two things at once: to inform and to provide matter for reflection, and to transmit and to take a position (thereby resisting the 'specialism' which, here as elsewhere, tends to be the rule).

Similarly, because I feel that the theory of the film-maker as auteur is wasting away because of its refusal to consider the multiplicity of collaborators (in particular, the actors) in a film, I have dealt with the latter somewhat more than is customary in a book of this kind. To justify this action, I refer the reader to my book *Le Cinéma et ses métiers (The Cinema and its Professions)* which attempts to rethink the theory of the director/auteur without relinquishing what that theory has taught us. Here, for instance, the politics of the auteur is brought into a dialectical relation with the politics of the work, especially in my discussions of *The Elephant Man, Dune and Twin Peaks.*

Having decided that this will be my last work on the cinema to appear directly in book form (my other projects involve collecting articles which have, for the most part, already been published), I have sought to make this study of David Lynch as multiform and complete, and also as concrete, as possible, so that the cinema, defined as ontological realism by the theories of André Bazin, would itself be viewed in a realistic but not reductive fashion. That our view is focused on a young film-maker at the height of his career carries with it certain risks (particularly that of seeing future works which may refute some of our propositions), and this too is significant: the film-lover's passion must be turned towards living objects and the most recent cinema.

As David Lynch is a creative artist who impassions and surprises, there could be no better choice for the present undertaking. It is my hope that some of the pleasure and emotion which I felt in travelling for a few months through the realm of his work will be communicated by this book, encountering and enriching the pleasure and emotion of Lynch's many admirers.

In this work, my frequent recourse to the writings and theoretical formulations of Françoise Dolto has left an unmistakable imprint, which I in no way wish to deny. My warm thanks go to Anne-Marie Marsaguet for her help and, for our Lynch-ological discussions and the documents which they supplied, to Stephen Sarrazin, Nicolas Saada and Antonio Peña.

All stills reproduced here are courtesy of their respective production companies (see Filmography). The prints were obtained from BFI Stills, Posters and Designs.

Michel Chion, 10 October 1992

Throughout this work, footnote numbers in the text refer to the bibliographical references in the 'Lynch-Doc'; an asterisk refers to an entry in the 'Lynch-Kit'.

Lynch during the production of *Wild at Heart*

CHRONO-LYNCH

From *Six Figures* to *Fire Walk with Me*

'When you begin to treat an unbearable child, you can be sure that the mother will be risking depression and suicide. An unbearable child is truly, chronically, the electroshock of the poor. All day long such children prevent their mothers from lapsing into depressive fantasies. By being aggressive, they give their mothers the chance to be aggressive in turn, and thus to stay afloat.... We know that the newborn child is the mother's first psychotherapist.'

Françoise Dolto, *Séminaire de psychanalyse d'enfants, I (Seminar on the psychoanalysis of children, I)*, Paris: Le Seuil, 1982.

I

A FILM THAT STAYS WITH YOU

(Six Figures, The Alphabet, The Grandmother, Eraserhead)

1

In the beginning, there was not an author, just a film: *Eraserhead.* Grim and awful, definitive about the human situation, one of those films you cannot get over. And along with this film, claiming it, was a name you did not always pay attention to, even when you went to see it a number of times at the Waverly Theater in New York or at the Escurial in Paris.

In a word, the film was perfect; it still belonged completely to its public, and the shadow of the author had not yet fallen on the screen. Later came another film signed by the same person, then a few others (all too many for the purists who were already in attendance) and *Eraserhead* finally became just one more film in the *opus* of David Lynch.

It is true that, from a certain perspective, the author always represents to some extent the work's downfall. But because this director has kept faith, he continues to allow his films – or at least some of them – the chance to break free of him. The paradox is that the films can do this only if the director proves himself to be better each time.

There is nothing more common nowadays than an auteur. Auteur films (which *create* their auteur) are rarer stuff. Fortunately, Lynch has produced two or three. His particular and dramatic situation is that people expect him not to do 'a Lynch'. A film buff disappointed by *Wild at Heart* did not hide his anger in an interview in *Starfix:* Lynch is doing Lynch.[21] He is going to give us more of the same every year! It is almost an honour to disappoint in this way – even if the work in question, in my view, is not a formula film, a dish which can be cooked up at any time.

In a moment of self-infatuation, Lynch spoke of *Eraserhead* as a 'perfect' film, one he could see again and again, like a Hopper painting. He should be forgiven: a film which took years to come to fruition cannot be spoken of reasonably. Afterwards, from this poetic and horrible creation, he too had to find a way back.

2

Who is David Lynch, and what kind of man has such visions? These questions began to be aired after his second feature, *The Elephant Man,* was widely acclaimed. Was he English, as his strict clothes and reserve seemed to imply? A young member of the New York avant-garde? An urban type, in any case, born in a hot, smoky city whose scenery he transfigured in his films? The questioners were not even warm.

'I'm from Montana, and that's really middle America! But it is true that many people in the United States think I am European.'[5] Montana is a wooded state in the north-western United States, on the frontier with Canada and partly in the Rocky Mountains. Coniferous forests are among the state's major resources. David Lynch was born on 20 January 1946, under the sign of Capricorn, in Missoula, a small Montana town of 30,000 inhabitants situated in a valley and surrounded by mountains, lakes and an Indian reservation.

He was the eldest of three children. His brother John, whose presence Lynch mentions in some of his childhood recollections, was born in Sandpoint, Idaho. His sister Margaret, who 'was afraid of green peas because they were hard on the outside and soft on the inside',[3] was born in Spokane, Washington. Lynch's paternal line came from Montana, where his father grew up on a ranch in the wheatfields. His father's profession reflected his origins, for he was a research scientist for the Department of Agriculture. He frequently moved 'to experiment on tree diseases and insects. He had huge forests at his disposal to experiment on.'[5] Lynch has described how he would accompany his father into the forest for his work: 'He loved his job,' he added in another interview, 'and he was already interested in his work when he was a boy. Like I always say: if you cut my father's leash, he would go into the woods and never come back.'[37] It is well known that wood and forests have an important place in Lynch's work.

In his interviews, Lynch is always more guarded in speaking about his mother. She was a housewife, he has explained, originally from Brooklyn. She was also a language tutor (from the beginning, there is a privileged relationship in his films between women, writing and the alphabet). Her father, a tram driver, left school at an early age to work as a docker: 'He lived with a pile of dictionaries,' Lynch recalled, admitting he was impressed by his

Eraserhead

grandfather.[37] It is worth noting that Lynch the director expressed his rejection of school on a number of occasions, and devoted his first short film, *The Alphabet*, to 'a satire on education'.

In contrast, Lynch enjoys telling how his parents first met, that is to say, the circumstances that led ultimately to his conception: 'It was at an outdoors biology class, when they were both at Duke University.'[5] Lynch was born under the sign of the outdoors and biology! His parents never argued, he has said, nor did they drink or smoke (which would have bothered him). He got along well with his brother and sister; all of his grandparents got along well too (he parodied this in the ending of *Blue Velvet*), and when they came to see the family in their handsome Buick they brought gifts. His first experience of the city, going to see his maternal grandmother in Brooklyn, proved memorable for the boy. The New York subway, the wind, the smell and the sound left a strong impression. It is strange how, in other interviews, Lynch associates Brooklyn with visiting his mother (unless the journalist erred in the transcription). Is one to conclude that his parents separated? In any case, these impressions based on a comparison between the easy environment of his childhood and the noisy metropolis, furnished Lynch with the very paradigm of differentiation: 'The contrast when I went to see her led to my fascination with big industrial cities.'[10] 'I think what happened was that I went to a big city and it scared me. It was real frightening.'[2] Lynch always uses contrast to structure his films: 'Contrast is what makes things work,' he said when explaining how he conceives his film projects. And he had this bizarre answer to the question of what his parents were like: 'People differ according to place.'[37] Was he thinking about his father's world of nature and his mother's urban, machine world?

3

At some unspecified date, the family moved to Boise, Idaho, where Lynch lived until he was fourteen, then on to other agricultural and wooded states: Spokane, Washington; Durham, South Carolina; and Alexandria, Virginia, where he entered high school. Lynch identified the atmosphere at the beginning of *Blue Velvet* as that of Spokane: an idyllic, protective world which is a bit unreal, a world which he always delights in describing in the same way, with just a slight change now and then. For example: 'In the mind of a kid, everything seemed peacefully beautiful. Airplanes passed by slowly in the sky. Rubber toys floated on the water. Meals seemed to last five years and naptime seemed endless.'[5] The sky, water (the idea of surfaces and floating), extreme contrasts (airplanes and toys), the dinner table and the bed: Lynch fits in almost everything with which his films are obsessed! Another version: 'It was a dream world, with a blue sky, planes droning overhead, fences, green grass, cherry trees.... But, on the cherry tree, there's this pitch oozing out – some black, some yellow.'[18] He speaks, too, of 'blue skies, red flowers, white picket fences and green grass, with birds chirping in the trees and a plane droning overhead.'[2] Such 'dronings' are present in his films from his second short, *The Grandmother*, onwards, and they constitute 'an enveloping sound'.

The unreal precision of these evocations suggests that they may be reconstituted from a book. Lynch has referred to a primer used in those days to teach American schoolchildren to read, *Good Times in Our Streets:* 'It was about happiness, the environment, good neighbours. You learned to read by following the adventures of Dick, Jane and their dog Spot.'[5] He has often made reference to his childhood with comic-strip type editing and highly contrasting shots: 'I saw life in extreme close-ups. In one, for instance, saliva mixed with blood. Or long shots of a peaceful environment.'[5] 'I had lots of friends but I loved being alone and looking at insects swarming in the garden.'[21] There is always a contrast, here between the human mass (his friends) and the mass of insects on the ground. If we are to believe Lynch, he did not read much as a boy (except for Kafka), and he watched very little television. He drew, swam and played baseball, but most of all he daydreamed.

He has also mentioned an early resistance to school and words, and his difficulty in using words. In particular, he had always liked drawing, and so he began to take Sunday painting lessons: 'For me, back then, school was a crime against young people. It destroyed the seeds of liberty. The teachers didn't encourage knowledge or a positive attitude. The people who interested me didn't go to school.'[37] In Lynch's logic, and in his highly personal way of using certain terms – for example, the word 'abstract' – there is something of the autodidact or, at least, of someone who has created a separate, coded language.

The cinema, too, belongs to Lynch's early memories, though in the form of a neighbourhood movie-house. The first film he saw, in a drive-in with his parents, was *Wait Till the Sun Shines, Nellie* (1952). This melodrama by Henry King recounts a barber's life in a small town, from the time of his marriage to his retirement, and is punctuated by a few family tragedies: 'There was a scene that struck me very much of a button going down a little girl's throat. I'm sure that it was very short and that you couldn't see much, but I still remember the impression I had of this button stuck in the girl's oesophagus.'[5]

In Boise, the neighbourhood movie-house at the end of his street was called the Vista Theater (the name reoccurs in *Blue Velvet*). Films of science fiction and the fantastic (*The Thing*, 1951, by Nyby and Hawks, *Creature from the Black Lagoon*, 1954, by Jack Arnold, and *The Fly*, 1958, by Kurt Neumann) were shown there, along with the Elvis Presley films which Lynch gently parodies in *Wild at Heart*. The Vista also presented Delmer Daves's *A Summer Place* (1959) with Sandra Dee and Troy Donohue, the story of some teenagers' romantic summer adventures on an island: 'It was fantastic to see this kind of soap opera with your girlfriend. It made us dream!'[5] These teenage tastes would surface again in *Twin Peaks*. It was only after he had become acclaimed and more self-assured that Lynch would confess to these teenage memories. Previously, he had always treated interviewers to the more respectable show of a cinema buff listing the great (and mostly European) films which he had discovered in Philadelphia as a young graphic arts student.

4

Originally, David Lynch wanted to be a painter. This was a childhood desire which he could not see how to fulfil since he thought all painters belonged to the past. One gathers that his parents did not enlighten him about this, and so did not especially encourage and cultivate his artistic ambition, at least at the outset. Then, one day, a high school friend named Toby Keeler introduced Lynch to his father, Bushnell Keeler, who became one of Lynch's favourite painters. It was then that he realised one could be an artist. As to the subjects he painted, they were 'Street scenes, in a bourgeois style' if we are to credit what he told Paul Grave for *Cinéphage*. Perhaps he was already under the influence of a painter for whom he felt a lasting admiration, Edward Hopper. Another key high school friend was Jack Fisk, who would become a well-known set designer and sometime director. He made the lovely *Raggedy Man* (1981), directing his wife, Sissy Spacek, who would also help in the production of *Eraserhead*. Lynch has always referred to Fisk as his best friend in high school, along with another youth who died in a car accident (the dramatic nature of the road accidents in *Wild at Heart* may look back to this painful experience).

Lynch began to attend the Corcoran School of Art in Washington DC and, along with Fisk, rented a studio in Alexandria to paint. 'We were competing all the time,' Fisk has said, recalling how he became interested in abstraction since Lynch was drawing realistic scenes.

After graduating from high school, Lynch left his family home to go to the Boston Museum School, where he studied for a year. Disgruntled with the poor quality of the classes and their uninteresting fellow students, Lynch and Fisk laid out a gigantic itinerary for study and travel in Europe, which was to last for three years, including a planned visit to the Austrian painter Oscar Kokoschka (who died in 1980). Salzburg was the first stop, and the disoriented Lynch was anything but ecstatic. With a line that has become proverbial while feeding his image as 'an American', he later described his disappointment: 'I remember contemplating that I was 7000 miles from the nearest McDonald's.' Fisk and Lynch then returned to Paris, where they had arrived in Europe, and drew lots to decide whether they would go to Portugal (Fisk's choice) or Athens (Lynch's choice, and he won). They arrived in Athens by the Orient Express but disliked the city and so, after days and nights on the train, they returned to Paris and flew back home to the United States.

When his family baulked at paying for his studies, Lynch went to work in a picture-framing shop, only to be fired for not being able to get up in the morning. He then performed various odd jobs, including doorman. Fisk spoke to Lynch about the Pennsylvania Academy of Fine Arts in Philadelphia, on the East Coast. The two friends went to look at it and enrolled in 1965. Lynch had found what he needed, the study environment he had dreamed of: 'Schools have waves and it just happened that I hit on a really rising, giant wave.'[2] Here he was to discover the works of action-painters such as Jackson Pollock, Franz Kline and Jack Tworkov (later he would admire Francis Bacon, Edward Hopper and Le Douanier Rousseau). It was also at the Pennsylvania Academy that he met the woman who became his first wife, Peggy.

5

In the course of his studies, Lynch went through a series of pictorial 'periods', and traces from all of them would appear in his later creations. After street scenes, he went on to a series which he called 'industrial symphonies'. Later, in 1989, he gave the same title to a musical spectacle that he

Eraserhead

created with Angelo Badalamenti. This early series was composed of complex mosaics in geometric shapes. 'I also did a series of "mechanical women", women who turned into typewriters.'[7] That is another Lynchian idea: remember how the victims of the mad killer in *Twin Peaks* are found with letters of the alphabet stuck under their nails, as if the author had a fantasy about secretaries. After all, don't they have letters at their fingertips?

In fact, Lynch the painter and sculptor, already fascinated by electric shocks and shock-inducing juxtapositions, began very early on to enjoy manipulating the subject of women to elicit a reaction: 'One year I made a kind of electric pool table, in which you dropped a ball-bearing which went down a ramp, setting off a whole series of contacts that first struck a match on a scraper to light a firecracker, then others opened the woman's mouth, lit up a red bulb and made her scream when the firecracker exploded.'[12]

Then silhouettes began to emerge from the dark.... And, one day, something clicked, though he could not have known that this would be a definitive turning point. He decided to make 'film paintings': 'When I looked at these paintings, I missed the sound. I was expecting a sound, or maybe the wind, to come out. I also wanted the edges to disappear. I wanted to get into the inside. It was spatial ... '[21]

At some specific point, the possibility of penetrating into the painting became real as he looked at a painting he had just finished: 'As I looked at what I'd done, I heard a noise. Like a gust of wind. And it came all at once. I imagined a world in which painting would be in perpetual motion. I was very excited and began to make animated films which looked like moving paintings, no more and no less.'[25] One notes that it is a cross between painting and sound, and a typical Lynchian sound like a gust of wind, that provides the decisive impetus which set him in motion, as if the image could not come alive by itself.

During his second year of study at Philadelphia, Lynch produced his first film, lasting one minute. It appears in his filmography under the title *Six Figures*. The film, which is the only film of Lynch's that I have not seen, was made to be projected on a special sculpture-screen, the surface of which contained reliefs in the shape of heads (modelled after Lynch's) and arms at precise points. The film, which also showed heads and arms, was projected on to the screen in such a way that some of the filmed heads appeared on the heads in relief and thus became deformed: 'In the course of the projection, the heads were transformed into stomachs and it looked like the stomachs caught on fire. Everything started to move, contract and vomit. And then it started up again. For the soundtrack, I used a siren.'[12] Lynch shot this small loop of film himself, one frame at a time, with a non-reflex movie camera which he bought second-hand. This led him to make some instructive errors (for example, he shot from too far away and so the field was wider than his drawings). The work was shown at a school exhibition in the spring of 1966 and received a prize.

At this time, Lynch earned a living as a graphic artist (a job he would later assign to the hero in *Eraserhead*), working for a painter friend named Roger La Pelle, in the company of La Pelle's mother-in-law, Dorothy McGinnis, who was also a painter. With her robust, reassuring physique, McGinnis seems to have been important for Lynch. He gave her the title role in his second short film, *The Grandmother*.

6

David Lynch's first child, Jennifer, was born in April 1968. Since then he has had two more children by two other women: Austin from his marriage with Jack Fisk's sister, and Riley in 1992 with Mary Sweeney. Peggy and David Lynch lived fairly modestly in 1968. Lynch would later create a veritable myth about this Philadelphia period, to the point of describing *Eraserhead* as an expression of the fear and tension he felt in that city during his five years there: 'I have said it before and I will repeat it again: Philadelphia is the most violent, run-down, sick, decadent, dirty and dark city in America. To go there is like entering an ocean of fear. Its motto is "the city of brotherly love".'[37] No doubt, because this motto is merely the translation of the Greek word Philadelphia. Lynch appears not to know it, which allows him to be all the more struck and seduced by the unusual contrast. The question of brotherly love remains rather obscure in Lynch's work. As the eldest of three children, he must have experienced the first-born's drama of being deprived by an intruder of the exclusive love of his parents. The dreadful baby in *Eraserhead*, whom everyone wants to kill and get rid of, represents what a first-born child can feel as it sees the wrinkled, screaming thing which comes to the family and steals its place.

This is all very commonplace, of course, but it is Lynch's particular gift to remain close to some very atavistic experiences which everyone shares but which we habitually overlook. At this time, Lynch lived in a scarcely inhabited industrial area in south Philadelphia, near the mortuary. Legends sprang up very quickly about this building being the source of his inspiration. Years later, he felt the need to point out that he had been inside the building only once, out of curiosity, though he did pass in front of it every night on the way to dinner. Outside, the bags used for corpses were opened and set out to dry, a detail that would inspire the 'smiling bags' of *Twin Peaks*, a mysterious phrase which is one of the clues given to Dale Cooper by a giant in his dreams.

Needing more room for their painting, David and Peggy rented a twelve-room house in a poor neighbourhood. Racial tension, violence, fear and burglaries became their daily lot. 'One day I said to some people, "The only thing protecting me from the outside is a brick wall" and they started to laugh and said, "What more do you need?" But this brick wall was really like a sheet of paper.'[2] At night, this industrial area of narrow streets and large, dark, abandoned buildings was almost deserted, and only occasional footsteps or a passing car were heard.

As a student, Lynch lived the life of a hippy. Four years later, in photos taken during the shooting of *Eraserhead*, he still had the typically long hair. One day it prompted a man on a bicycle to threaten him as he passed by: 'The 24th Street gang is going to kick your ass.'

Perhaps none of this is particularly serious, but the threat of such violence was not imaginary. If one considers the marks left by violence on someone such as Scorsese, who lived with it on a day-to-day basis throughout his childhood, then what is one to think of people who were raised in a protective environment only to discover violence suddenly as they left the security of the family?

7

Lynch's first 'film painting' masterpiece cost him two hundred dollars. He considered this expensive and was not thinking of continuing in that vein. But a millionaire named H. Barton Wassermann saw his work and offered to buy a film painting for a thousand dollars. With this extraordinary sum, Lynch bought a brand-new camera. He did not know that it had a defective focus. He then began work on a new piece based on the same principle, with a sculpted screen to receive images from a loop of animated film. He spent two months making the animation frame by frame, but when the film came back from the laboratory, it was blurred. Lynch called his patron to explain what had happened and Wassermann told him simply to keep the money and do with it as he liked. Lynch then requested support from his father. The result was his first real film, a four-minute colour short.

The very brief credits of *The Alphabet* state proudly: 'A film by David Lynch, Production H.B. Wassermann'. Lynch has described the film as 'a little nightmare about the fear connected with learning'.[1]

It is dense, abstract and disconcerting as well. In the first image, a woman lies on a bed with a large white pillow, against a black background. This is followed by a close-up of the woman's face, cold and hidden behind dark glasses. The face is joined to the left side of the frame by an abstract line, like a thread. The sound is that of a children's choir relentlessly chanting '*A, B, C*' over and over again. A stylised world then appears in cartoon form: a bare floor drawn in perspective, and a sky in which the sun fits in a frame like a flag. The sun and a vigorous male voice, which sings the letters of the alphabet up and down the scale, appear as one and the same, a generative force making shapes and lines (and sometimes a tube from which letters pour in disarray) grow on the floor, while a cloud spreads over the sun. A joyful creative arbitrariness seems to govern the apparition of the letters (a *K* falls from the sky), until we see two rows from *l* to *t* and from *u* to *y*. *Z* is missing. Then there is an abstract image: the woman's face behind a circle and grillework. A small circle advances in a vertical corridor. A big *A* with roots (which looks like part of a rebus, a form which may have inspired the film) expels an oblong feeler that turns into a tubular shape and spits two small, wailing *a* letters out on to the ground. Next, a woman sits on the edge of a bed in an abstract room, connected to a cord. Her face and body constantly form and reform in an inextricable mixture of geometric and organic shapes. The face then stabilises as an asymmetrical mask and near it, a rectangular red surface fills in, swallowing empty space like a video Pacman. It too is connected to the ground by a cord. A heart emerges from the rectangle and grows hairy. The heart releases seeds and little *abc*s which pour into the open skull of the seated woman. The mask-face opens its mouth, as a real woman in a nightgown does at the same time. The drawn woman thrashes about as her body and organs disintegrate. A close-up of a grotesque face says menacingly, in synch: 'Please, remember you are dealing with the human form.' The children energetically resume their chant of '*A*, *B*, *C*' while the image shows red particles in motion. These run down like drops on to the woman lying bloodied in her bed and on to the sheets. To finish (and this is the most seductive part of the film), a series of rapid, almost still shots presents the woman in the nightgown lying in different positions and reaching towards the letters of the alphabet which loom up in different parts of the space, like animals she would like to catch or, quite the opposite, aggressors she would defend herself against. We do not know which.

In parallel, a soft, submissive woman's voice recites the alphabet to the tune of the alphabet-song and concludes, 'Now that I have said my *ABC*s, tell me what to do.' She then writhes in her bed as if in pain and covers her face with her hand. The end. And all this in four minutes.

The most striking thing about *The Alphabet* is how unpredictable and unstructured it appears to be. The mixture of techniques, forms and rhythms is disconcerting, and no immediate connection can be drawn between the film and a particular idea or concept. The sound has a pressing, intense character which is rare in 'artistic' animated films (where, in general, the sound is simple and airy). This is paradoxical in view of the film's theme, which would lead one to expect a formal exercise. Here the letters quickly proliferate through time and space in obvious disorder. In fact, after seeing the film several times, it is possible to reconstitute a kind of symbolic script. There is an opposition between the man's voice which effortlessly chants the alphabet song in a single flow and the woman who painstakingly assimilates the first three letters of the alphabet and then runs up against the others which are discontinuous and piecemeal, and ends by reciting the alphabet like a nursery rhyme she has been forced to learn. There is likewise a confrontation between a fecund, celestial power and a parthenogenetic force (the *A* giving birth). The woman thus seems to suffer a pedagogic violence; at the same time, she is on the side of piecemeal discontinuity and her relation to letters is more than ambiguous (do they come from her?). We shall return later, especially in the Lynch-Kit chapter, to the way Lynch uses a motif of this kind.

It is, of course, difficult to imagine the effect this film might have had on its first spectators, as difficult as resisting seeing all of Lynch's later work foreshadowed in it. But one is first of all struck by a certain violence in the film and, second, by the fact that it resembles nothing else and works according to no logic we have ever encountered.

8

The Alphabet aroused some interest in Lynch's entourage, and when his friend Toby Keeler spoke to him about the American Film Institute, Lynch applied for and received an AFI grant to make another short film. This time he went into high gear: he had a script and a number of actors; most of the images were to be shot directly and, above all, this short film would be substantial in length (34 minutes). The cast of *The Grandmother* consisted of friends. The father was played by an engineer who had previously recorded vocal effects for *The Alphabet*. A painter friend played the mother and a little neighbour played the child (Lynch was very satisfied with his performance), while the key role of the grandmother went to Dorothy McGinnis.

The film's technique was highly composite and contrasted, uniting cartoons, pixilation shots (a stop-frame technique for live subjects which McLaren had used in *Neighbours*, 1952) and direct, normal-speed shooting. There was apparently no live sound recording. Even the parents' barking seems to have been post-recorded. All the synchronised noises were redone in an unreal, stylised way, sometimes reminiscent of Jacques Tati. For the sound production, Lynch discovered Alan Splet, who would prove to be an important collaborator in his first full-length films. A technician and sound inventor, Splet worked in a small post-production company re-recording the sound of industrial films. He had been recommended to Lynch by the sound engineer of *The Alphabet*. The sound production required two months of full-time work, seven days a week, and help was received from Bob Chadwick and Margaret Lynch in creating sound effects.

I shall give a detailed description of *The Grandmother* for three reasons: first, because the film is a kind of highly compact, spontaneous eruption of the Lynchian problematic, but in which nothing seems as yet to have been ordered and censured, so that it is a mine, a veritable compendium; next, because the film is not available on video cassette and so the reader may not readily have the opportunity to see it; lastly, because the summaries one reads now and then do not adequately convey the sense of a film whose complexity and speed often lead one to miss the essential points.

The film opens with something like a symbolic film painting which represents a stylised portion of the world in a sectional view: a sort of underground water-table with a layer of earth above it. Three pockets dug into the earth seem to rest on the sheet of water. The left and middle pockets are extended by a vertical column which opens out on the air, whereas the right pocket is closed. From beneath the water-table, a sort of submarine periscope rises and takes form, making a detour by way of the right pocket then curving back towards the middle pocket. A red, phallic mouth develops on the periscope, and this tube-mouth spits a seed into the middle pocket followed by a stream of white substance which fills it. A human body, drawn as a long shape with unseparated legs and long arms, emerges from the substance. Ejected by the substance which rises with it, the body arrives at the surface of the earth by way of a column while remaining connected to the underground by a cord. This is followed by a live take of a strong man in a T-shirt who appears in the country, on leaf-covered ground. He is the Adam of this creation.

A cartoon: a column-tube tunnels from the male middle pocket towards the female pocket on the left which fills in turn (it is worth noting – and I shall return to this later – that the column-tube connecting the male and female matrix-pockets does not fill with the substance; the column-tube expresses more of an abstract contact). Another body, this time a woman's, issues from the left pocket. Once in the open air, Adam and Eve (fully clothed) stretch their arms out horizontally like wings, then drop them simultaneously. A house setting is drawn around them, with a starry sky above. The man and woman, still connected to the underground water-table by the white substance, twist about, joining their heads and arms.

A live take: the torso of the woman, in a rather ugly print dress, and the man in the T-shirt emerge from the ground. They embrace, vibrating electrically like insects in rut.

The next sequence returns to animation: two drop-like seeds fly from the underground pockets filled with the substance. Both have the same shape and size, but the man's is red and the woman's white (these are the film's dominant colours). The seeds settle in a new underground pocket where they blend to create a white egg while the male seed forms a red kernel.

A live take: in close-up, the man's face moves as if he were startled, and the woman's face remains immobile.

The red kernel turns black, then produces a dark substance which gives birth to a child with a long thin neck who is brutally expelled by the white substance. A live take shows him emerging at the surface: first by the head, then the body which seems to lie lifeless. The father panics and barks. The mother vainly tries to hold him back and despairs (did she not want a child? Would she have preferred a girl?), as he crawls towards the child rolling on the ground.

Lynch returns to film painting for the next sequence. Stretching and stretching, the father begins to grow like a plant in time-lapse photography. He passes over the mother who is between the child and himself. When he reaches the child he hits him, the child screams twice, then grows even bigger than the father. Below them, the mother waves her wing-arms. All three remain connected to the white substance.

At no time during the engendering and birth has there been any bodily relation between child and mother. These scenes are more like the reconstitution of a lived experience in an almost polemical and (with respect to the mother) vindictive form. The man's role in birthing is shown, along with the child's rejection by a mother who has succumbed to post-natal depression.

All this occurs with such dizzying speed that it is impossible to make it out unless you see the film many times in slow motion. As a result, some critics of fanatical honesty and precision have missed this key moment, even after seeing the film repeatedly. One cannot help but think that Lynch wished to show something important here even as he concealed it. Is it a kind of stormy negation of the fate whereby one is born of a mother and connected to her organically?

The next sequence is shot in an interior. The boy looks like a miniature Pee-Wee, with very white make-up, red lips, a dinner-jacket and bow-tie. The handsome little fellow looks ahead to the little magician in *Twin Peaks* and, most of all, to Dale Cooper, impeccable as a gleaming, black duck. We discover the boy's home setting: a room with stylised walls, a bed covered with a white sheet and pillow, and a dresser. He moves to the bed and sits down as if dejected. Then he picks up a potted plant from his bedside table and inspects it.

Outside, his parents crawl about excitedly on all fours. At first sight, one would think they were looking for their vanished child. But in fact, the crawling mother turns upon herself with small cries of distress, and the father approaches her with an inquisitive look. Then follows a cartoon: the inevitable white substance spreads like shaving cream and hurls the couple into the air. For the first time, they separate from the primal matter from which they were made. This is followed by a live shot: the parents's sordid life in their stylised interior. Slumped in a chair, the father drinks while the mother combs her hair, sometimes slowly, sometimes nervously.

The passing of time is represented by a short cartoon in which a bright yellow sun rises rapidly in a frame. To the trickling sound of a stream, the

Eraserhead

boy lying in bed in his pyjamas looks under the sheet. In the next shot, he is up and dressed in his dinner-jacket while the lowered white sheet reveals a large, yellowish-red circle in his bed, as if the child had peed a bright sun! When the father sees what has happened, he barks and carries the child, struggling like an animal, back to the bed and rubs his nose in his dirt. Confronted with the stain, the boy stiffens to the sound of a scream (the film is punctuated by a number of similar still frames). Slovenly and neglectful, with a low-necked dress, the mother takes a more ambiguous attitude. Pointing her finger towards her exposed breast, she signals to the child to come. When he does, she caresses him and puts her hands on his shoulders as if to kiss him, then shakes him and puckers up her lips lustfully, brings her mouth to his neck only to have him draw back (as Mother X does with Henry in *Eraserhead*), and rubs her face with the parted fingers of her right hand (an obsessive motif in Lynch's work, denoting an atavistic female auto-eroticism), and so on – with all of this again happening so fast that one's conscious impression at first viewing is simply that of a child being reproved. But it is easy to understand the good faith of the critics when they remove the sexual ambiguity of the sequence: the mere thought of the sequence is disturbing, not because it depicts parental seduction, but because the depiction is ugly, vague and brutal.

The boy goes back to his room and sits on the edge of his bed (as Henry Spencer will later). As in the days of silent film, a shot of a drawing shows what he is thinking about: the white substance he has been separated from. A three-note whistle calls him and he goes up a stairway towards the attic where there is another bed, but with a metal frame. Here too the critics who have undertaken to describe the film in detail confuse the attic and the bedroom, and take the two beds for the same. Whether consciously or not, the film was clearly made in such a way that these confusions occur. And yet this attic is the first expression in Lynch's work of a parallel world, a world culminating in the Red Room of *Twin Peaks*. After trying, in the unfinished script of *Gardenback*, to rework the idea of the attic as a mental space, Lynch would find other ways of making us enter other worlds, different from the vertical symbolism governing the world of *The Grandmother* which is built of superimposed layers.

9

Next to the bed in the attic, the boy finds a big sack marked 'Seeds'. He takes them out one at a time, shakes them at his ear and listens, discarding those which make a rattlesnake sound. When a seed produces the three-note whistling which first attracted him, he smiles and puts it under his pillow. Next, he spills buckets of earth on to the sheet until a little mound has formed. He scoops a crater from the top, plants the seed and waters it abundantly (though Lynch does not show him collecting the earth and water).

At this point, one hears sounds from the natural world: crickets and thunder, edited together, establish a sense of cosmic time in this abstract setting, as if nature were co-operating with the work under way. Above the mound of earth, a long, mushroom-like shape appears. After being watered, it becomes a large, velvety trunk growing branches. At the base of the trunk, there is a hole; the child lewdly carresses it over and over again. He has an extremely tactile relationship with the plant, whereas he avoided physical contact with his mother. He is also shown lying on his back next to the plant, moving his head like a woman in sexual ecstacy. This is followed by another animated sunrise, then a rapid series of live shots of the mother rubbing her hand on the ground, an image which returns in the brief evocation of the couple formed by Leo and Shelly in *Fire Walk with Me*, and the furious father carrying the boy back to his room and holding him over the stain on the bed, and another frozen scream from the boy. This scene is not a literal repetition of the previous one, but a variation with shots from different angles. Being associated with the sunrise, the variation implies a relationship between the days succeeding one another and a repeated staining of the bed. The dirty sheet never seems to be changed or washed.

When the child in his bedroom hears a gurgling noise, he goes upstairs and witnesses, in a wash of liquid and repugnant sounds, something like the birth of a large body emerging head first ... and shoes at the end. A gigantic woman's face appears, and the grandmother of the title is seen sitting on the ground like a giant, expressionless doll. The boy gives her his plant and the present makes her smile. This in turn makes him smile (compare the scene of the mirroring smiles between Laura Palmer and Bobby Briggs in *Fire Walk with Me* and the song which accompanies it). The sound of something collapsing makes them both turn around: emptied of its content, the placenta-plant has collapsed.

A new family sequence follows. The father and mother stuff their gills in silence; the child is not hungry. When the boy reaches for a bottle, the father becomes violent. The mother's finger points excitedly towards the child and she screams (we don't see her face). The boy runs away from his parents, who bark like animals, and, upstairs, he finds his grandmother asleep in bed. There is food on a table and he eats with relish. At night (denoted by a drawn moon), the grandmother sitting in her rocking-chair calls out, whistling with her hands. The child dresses so he can go to her. At the bottom of the stairs leading to the attic, the parents seem to want to hold the child back. In a strange and fleeting trick image, something like red spaghetti emerges from the boy's mouth.

We now return to a cartoon sequence of an apparent execution. In a small theatre, a figurine (the boy) tugs on a cord which brings a body (the father) lying in bed out on to the stage. A triangular hat falls on to the child's head. When the child again tugs on the cord, there is the sound of flushing water and a triangle with the apex facing down falls on the father-body, decapitating it. The same game is played with the mother-body, but this time the cord brings down a cannonball which cuts her in two. Later, a drawn man and woman are, as it were, reinflated by pipes which grow towards them. This time the drawn father has two separate legs, while the mother is on a triangular red mound like a dress. The father's torso expands horizontally and the mother's legs expand lengthwise. A tubular object in the form of a *Y* rises from the ground between them and connects them by their arms. As soon as they are connected by the *Y*, the man's torso and the woman's legs break apart into puzzles. Particles from these fly into the air!

A long, silent sequence, shot live, shows the boy and the grandmother in the attic to the sound of a woman singing unaccompanied in the poetic style of the 1970s. As the grandmother watches, the boy falls on to the bed, where the plant (for which he is mourning?) still lies. She calms him, smiling and speaking softly. They touch fingertips and one after the other repeat the gesture which was so violent and fragmenting when the mother performed it: that of pointing the index finger at different parts of the other's body. This scene could almost be from a documentary on the rehabilitation of traumatised children through bodily contact – except that a totally incestuous kiss on the mouth, in a still shot, ends this exchange. Planted by the boy and unknown to his real parents, the grandmother thus seems to represent another mother, an extra one, with whom he can have humanised communication in heart, body and speech. Physically, too, she is a single round mass, whereas the parents are out of joint, full of disorderly agitation. And where she represents a bodily whole without grasping or menacing feelers, the parents' arms are squeezing and aggressive.

The next cartoon is full of obscure symbolism and a mad complexity. A flying grandmother-shape (a wide-hipped body, with an articulated lower section) is joined to an underground wheel which turns like a pump. An oblong extension grows from her. A small child with its arms spread like a cross falls to earth from the sky. A giant tree grows on the spot where the child fell, then forms a mouth like a megaphone or a flowercup and an extension, like a shower attachment, from which particles fall making a little pile. An oblong white shape flies out of the pile and enters the flower mouth. Then a flying creature leaves the cup and heads for the sky. It is night. Under the ground, a dead plant directs a feeler towards another plant which releases pollen. In short, here is a series of ecological exchanges, though it is not clear how the different levels communicate and join to form a closed system.

At last, the great dramatic moment arrives. The grandmother's hands go into spasm. She tries to produce her whistling sound, then grasps her neck as if she began to suffocate when she tried to call out. The boy, asleep in his soiled bed, hears and comes up to her. When he sees that she is suffocating or emptying (the two contradictory interpretations are both suggested by the sound, the image and the postures), he shakes her by the shoulders as his father did to him earlier. When he goes downstairs for help, the grandmother stands up. In some impressive pixilated shots, she trips and spins like a mad top, knocking over the furniture, to the sound of a high-pitched whistling which suggests that her vital substance is leaking out. Downstairs, the child pulls in vain at his father to make him come. The father and mother are cruelly mocking. When he goes back upstairs, everything seems to be over though the grandmother's death is not shown. We return to the exterior country setting of the first live takes. Sad and pensive, the boy walks into a kind of cemetery amid the vegetation. There he finds the grandmother seated with her hands on her knees, again a great 'bodily mass'. She leans over, shakes her head 'no', then abruptly reclines and stiffens, with her mouth open – and the child stiffens too, with a despairing look. The last images show the boy standing on his bed in his room. He turns round and round, and the film ends as he falls, while in the background a vague tree-shape continues to rise.

The end is as disconcerting as the rest: is the grandmother of the cemetery the real one or her ghost? In any case, the important point is that she is rooted now, not in the stylised and abstract setting of the attic, but on the ground, among plants, localised. Now she is connected to the earth and water which engendered the other characters, whereas the child had brought her to life in the artificial space of an attic bed, the 'parallel bed' to the one in his bedroom which he impregnated with his urine.

In *Eraserhead*, earth is also brought into the artificial spaces of a bed-side table and a stage. How does earth, dug up and carried away, retain its creative properties? This is one of the film's many questions. Indeed, the film can be understood only as a series of questionings formulated in sound and images. Thus, the film should not be taken as saying, 'This is the way things work,' but rather, 'Have I really understood? Are things really like this? Tell me what is missing' – a child's questions about the mystery of life, fashioned from bits and pieces of parental answers, a fabulous theory which the child knows to be incomplete.

10

I have asked the reader to bear with this laborious effort to recount in detail an un-narratable film which is, first of all, a series of images, sounds, gestures, bodies and actions which must be grasped literally before any attempt at interpretation, because I wanted to start the evocation of David Lynch's cinema by illustrating what this disconcerting world is based upon: a very peculiar logic requiring us to renounce all *a priori* interpretations of behaviour and facts, whether taken separately or in succession.

Taken one at a time, the gestures and images of *The Grandmother* already have a vaguer meaning than their immediate appearance allows. In fact, the strangeness of this short film results from the gap between the aggressively Manichean logic of the script, where the parents are described (anticipating Ettore Scola's *Brutti, sporchi e cattivi*, 1976) as ugly, dirty and mean and the grandmother as good, and the far less simplistic treatment which imbues each image with a host of contradictory meanings. This is why summaries of the film can easily prove misleading. When the mother seems to be molesting her son, she is also attracting him. When the boy shakes the grandmother to help her feel better, he is also attacking and strangling her. The mean, vulgar mother, with her ugly scowls as she eats and brushes her hair, also caresses her child, whereas the sweet granny (not all that old, wrinkled or 'desexed' by age) bestows an utterly incestuous kiss on the boy's mouth.

When the actions and images of *The Grandmother* are taken in succession, they form unusual cause and effect chains defying the first law of thermodynamics (according to which, nothing is lost and nothing is created). This law is internalised by all of us as we learn the cycles of nourishment and excretion, growth and death, transfers between inside and outside. But in Lynch's work, there seems to be no link between food and growth, as if one could increase in volume and density without feeding on some foreign substance. Pipes come from the ground, grow, develop and divide without seeming to derive from anything but themselves the substance and energy needed for their development – unless they derive from the *ex nihilo* movement of the artist who draws, creates and erases them.

Indeed, many of the film's cause and effect relations are presented as mysterious. Why does tugging on a cord cause a triangular mass to fall from the ceiling? Why do two beings rubbing against one another cause a third to grow out of the earth? It would seem that everything is linked by a kind of magical flux, as when a child asks about electricity: why does pressing a switch on the wall make light fall from the ceiling? More than once, the world of *The Grandmother* deals with organic and cosmic matters according to an 'electro-magical' type of logic, the kind which would be used by a twentieth-century child which had been summarily taught about electrical energy and had then deduced from those vague notions the way the world works. According to this logic, everything occurs by abstract transmission. Bodies are not in themselves whole entities made from perishable matter (itself moulded out of other bodies which have been absorbed and transformed) but rather wires, transducers, conductors of an inexplicable, abstract energy. Whence the almost demonstrative, stylised character of many of the film's animated images.

The Grandmother thus presents us with an abstract theory of the world: life, for Lynch, is like an electrical assembly. But this theory knows that it cannot explain, connect or sublimate everything. It knows that the organic world of teeming matter and bodies grappling together remains outside its reach, and that the final account of the energies exchanged does not balance out. And so it cheats. With its meticulous reconstruction of a child's logic, *The Grandmother* is a stunning film which has the honesty to avow its trickery literally, plain to see for anyone who opens his eyes. Thus, at the beginning of the film, the hollow tube which connects the paternal to the maternal pocket fills the latter with the former's substance somehow *without that substance going through the tube itself*. Which amounts to refusing to choose between a theory of electrical flux (the abstract transmission of energy) and a theory of substances (the world as a series of communicating vessels through which one unitary substance seeks to diffuse itself).

However, *The Grandmother* is not only the abstract work we have sought to illuminate (and which sheds light on Lynch's recent, unappreciated *Fire Walk with Me*). The film also expresses a form of cosmic lyricism, destined to blossom in Lynch's later films, which does not hesitate to bring the small into contact with the immense, the disgusting with the grandiose. The reddish-yellow puddle which spreads on the immaculate sheet is both a urine stain and the sun. This lyricism, influenced by the atmosphere of the 1970s (the music of Tractor), transfigures a work which is dark, jumbled and brutal, as if it had been thrown together haphazardly, but which is also wild and generous.

From a technical standpoint, one already finds in the dynamic and pleasing disorder of *The Grandmother* stylistic features of the future Lynch: lighting effects created by pools of very localised light, faces in stark contrast to shadows (*Eraserhead*) and especially the sound effects, with extended sounds, sometimes cut off in mid-shot, creating a sense of duration. Other details, it would seem, suggest the influence of directors whom Lynch admires. The close-ups of the grandmother's face, with their sensation of skin and a mask, appear to issue from Ingmar Bergman's *Persona* (1966) or *Vargtimmen* (1967). As suggested earlier, the synchronised sound effects are close to Tati's work. Many scenes in this noisy film are silent: for example, there is no sound for the steps on the stairs. The smiling grandmother speaks words we do not hear, as in a silent film, while the parents bark a monosyllabic 'Mike? Mike?'

The film also has a characteristic style of lively, rapid shots. The camera moves a great deal, the angle of the shots changes constantly and the cutting is far more fragmented than one would expect in so stylised a film. This could almost be a silent film from the 1920s, with sound added on, like a film by Kirsanoff, highly agitated, unable to keep still. *The Grandmother* hardly allows one to anticipate the static impression created by *Eraserhead*, though it expresses the same underlying impetuousness.

11

Lynch requested supplementary aid from the American Film Institute to finish the film. In doing so, he made the acquaintance of one of the AFI's department heads, Tony Vellani, who travelled to Philadelphia to see the almost finished copy and then gave his agreement. After finishing *The Grandmother* (which was to win a number of prizes at festivals in Atlanta, Belleview and San Francisco, and was shown in Europe at Oberhausen), Lynch went to see the director of the AFI, George Stevens Jr, the son of the director of *Giant* (1956), who remarked that it was common to class films into categories – fiction, animations and so on – but that *The Grandmother* was in a category all by itself. George Stevens Jr and Vellani confirmed their active interest in Lynch's work by suggesting that he apply for a grant to the Institute of Advanced Film Studies, the AFI's film school which had recently opened in Beverly Hills, California.

In 1970, Lynch moved to California with Peggy and the young Jennifer. He was particularly impressed by classes with a Czech professor, Frank Daniel, who taught him the importance of script structure and the role of tempo in the cinema, two lessons which he would take to heart. In California he met Terrence Malick, the author of *Badlands* (1973) and *Days of Heaven* (1978). Lynch introduced Malick to Jack Fisk, who later worked as Malick's production designer.

When he began attending classes at the AFI, Lynch abandoned his studies in painting and, for the first time, immersed himself completely in the cinema.

12

Lynch always denied being a film buff, claiming to have a poor knowledge of the history and the classics of cinema. Of course, this does not prevent him from having favourite films and, especially in the days of *The Elephant Man* and *Dune*, he frequently recited an almost unvarying list: a number of Fellini's films (*I vitelloni*, 1953; *La strada*, 1954; *Otto e mezzo (8½)*, 1963),

Eraserhead

Kubrick's *Lolita* (1961), Wilder's *Sunset Boulevard* (1950), the works of Tati, Bergman's *Persona* (1966) and, among contemporary Americans, Scorsese. He would later add Hitchcock's *Rear Window* (1954). Thus, the films are mostly European and many are in black-and-white.

Surrealistic works are notably absent, though he has often been aligned with that tradition. He admitted seeing *Un Chien andalou* (1928), but only after having made *Eraserhead.* He professed to know nothing else of Buñuel. Reacting to being labelled as a surrealist, he protested: 'Why worry about terms and classifications? If surrealism comes naturally, from inside yourself, and you stay innocent, then it is fine. A forced, affected surrealism would be horrible.'[16] Besides, in Lynch's view, his interest in narration also separates him from surrealism: 'The surrealists were only interested in the medium, the texture.'[19]

In contrast, pride of place is granted to Fellini. Lynch eventually had the opportunity to meet his idol in 1986–7. He commented: 'I have a profound admiration for Fellini. I feel very close to him. He may be very Italian ... but his films could have been conceived anywhere.'[25] Lynch and Fellini are connected by a hidden sign: both were born on 20 January. The fate of both film-makers is also linked to Dino de Laurentiis, who produced *La strada* (which made him rich) and *Dune* (the failure of which helped drive him into bankruptcy). After the final showing of *Dune*, de Laurentiis stated: 'When I made *La strada* with Fellini, the Italian critics said: "so what, Fellini ... ", but the French critics claimed it was one of the greatest films ever made. It's the same thing with David Lynch. First he made a dumb little film [*Eraserhead*], then, a little later, he made a real film, *The Elephant Man.* I chose him for *Dune*. Once more I invented a new director.'[11]

It is worth having a closer look at each of the films and directors Lynch cites to see what he may have derived from them directly or indirectly – that is to say, what they may have revealed to Lynch about himself and about what he wanted to do.

Firstly, it is significant that *Persona* and *Otto e mezzo* are the most experimental films of their auteurs, the films showing most characteristically the substance of the auteurs' idiomatic style, discursive structures and rhythm. It is worth recalling this because, since they were first released, the success of these films has tended to make us forget what at the time struck the public most forcefully. In *Persona*, Lynch may have found his taste for disruptions, for rhythms which can be shifty and slow, then suddenly abrupt and scathing, and for monologues and lines which hang in the void (as Bergman's film is based on the muteness of one of the two protagonists, there is almost nothing but monologue). Lynch could not have been indifferent either to the short, experimental sequence before the credits, with its mixture of jumbled and traumatising images made of cartoons, close-ups of a roll of film, animal viscera and a hand with a nail stuck in it. *Persona* also contains disruptions of the level of reality and breaks such as the one in the middle of the film which simulates the film catching fire in the projector, thus revealing a series of stray images ostensibly from another dimension (echoes of this can be found in *Fire Walk with Me*).

In *The Grandmother*, the boy on his bed who 'grows a grandmother' may have been inspired by the sickly boy in glasses from the *Persona*'s prologue: that boy also lies on his bed in a stylised setting, running his hand over a surface, seeming to trace the image of a gigantic woman's face.

The theme of *Persona* would also be an essential ingredient for Lynch: a child and two women (the mother cloven in two), one of whom is depressed. It cannot be a mere coincidence that for both these directors the same theme leads to a kind of dislocation of reality, to the point where it becomes incandescent. Yet, risking blasphemy, although an admirable film, *Persona* seems to leave an impression of being rather headstrong and somewhat aloof, less spontaneous than the best of Lynch's work.

Lynch's selection of the three films by Fellini he lists among his preferences also tells us something: in *I vitelloni*, the evenings drag on for ever, and groups spend the night endlessly knocking about, as in *Blue Velvet*; there is a provincial atmosphere in these petty stories of family and neighbours, a sense of immobility, of the viscous nature of time; *La strada* is sentimental but it also shows an intense feeling for the bizarre, and a sense of cosmic poetry in the nocturnal discussion between Gelsomina and Il Matto. The film's insistence on Giulietta Masina's 'artichoke head' – that strikingly coiffeured head with a whole, unformulated world inside, a head which frequently occupies the centre of the screen like a star or a sun – must also have impressed the future director of *Eraserhead*. And Il Matto's sudden, unexpected death at the roadside is recalled in certain details of the accident by night in *Wild at Heart*. *La strada* is also the story of an unhappy woman looking for reasons to bear up and go on living; having lost these reasons, she fades away as if of her own accord, consuming herself. We shall return later to the form this theme takes in Lynch's universe; *8½*, like *Eraserhead*, is obsessed with adultery, the opposition between the bitter, demanding wife and the sensual mistress. Fellini's harem becomes, in Lynch, the little theatre in the radiator, in keeping with Henry Spencer's timid nature. There is also a remarkable back-and-forth movement between a 'real' world and a fantasy world. In addition, the film's exaggerated black-and-white contrasts may have encouraged Lynch to accentuate the shooting of *Eraserhead* in the same way, even if the explicit reference here is to Billy Wilder's *Sunset Boulevard* with its images by John Seitz.

13

Kubrick's *Lolita* also lends itself to this exercise in juxtapositions. The atmosphere in the small provincial town where Humbert Humbert (James Mason) settles so as to be near Lolita (Sue Lyon), the interminable-seeming evenings and the corny dances, all find echoes in *Blue Velvet* and *Twin Peaks*. The way in which each character is isolated from the others, and the emphasis on breaks in tone and setting, are typical of Kubrick as well as being 'pre-Lynchian'. The cold, disturbing writer, Quilby, played by Peter Sellers, Lolita's enterprising, hysterical mother (Shelley Winters) and James Mason who is observant and sarcastic as Winters goes wild, are characters constantly out of synch with one another, like some of the figures in *Wild at Heart* and *Twin Peaks*. The relationship between Lolita and her mother anticipates Lula and Marietta's in *Wild at Heart* (the weakest part of Lynch's film). James Mason's weeping fit at the end of the film, when he realises that his life with the girl is over, may well have touched Lynch, down to the undefinable distance with which Kubrick films the scene (Lynch would become a great filmer of weeping). It seems to me that *Lolita* is also one of the conscious references in *Fire Walk with Me*, as Ray Wise, in the role of Leland Palmer, evokes James Mason's manner when he speaks to Sue Lyon: they have the same tone of voice, the same lacrimosity and, at times, the same 'mask'. They even look a little like each other. Aspects which might be considered 'faults' in Kubrick's film – its uncertain rhythm, its lack of tempo – are rejuvenated when Lynch takes them on. With the inflections of another temperament, faults can become assets.

It is worth noting that, earlier in her career, Shelley Winters had played almost the same role as in Kubrick's film, a mother seduced by a man who, in fact, is interested in her children: *The Night of the Hunter* (1955), which for a long time I felt must have been one of Lynch's cult films (there are echoes of the film at every turn in Lynch's work). I have never been able to trace any comment by Lynch about that film, and so perhaps I have imagined it. But what of the multiple apparitions in Lynch's films of a woman's face, speaking, outlined against the sky (for instance, the portrait in *The Elephant Man*, Princess Irulan in *Dune*, the good fairy in *Wild at Heart*), recalling the meeting with Lillian Gish at the beginning of Laughton's masterpiece, or the roaring Frank Booth as he hunts in the night in *Blue Velvet*, like Robert Mitchum in Laughton's film, or the night populated by animals and the fairy-tale atmosphere of *Twin Peaks*? Perhaps we should simply call them encounters between the films.

Lynch also admires another of Kubrick's films, *2001: A Space Odyssey* (1968). Could *Eraserhead* and its slow penetration into a micro-universe be described as a bedroom-*2001*? The space stations are replaced by the radiator or, in *Blue Velvet*, by a human ear lying in the grass, which the camera enters with the same solemnity as Kubrick's spaceships. In response to the planet-sized astral foetus at the end of Kubrick's film, Lynch offers a premature birth. Whatever the truth may be about these encounters, the important point is that the two film-makers are concerned with the same questions: the atavistic, man's place in the void and the cloven structure of a world which both film-makers express via razor-sharp cuts.

Lynch frequently cites Tati as one of his film-maker idols, and certain shots from the episodes of *Twin Peaks* are explicitly in the Tati mode (the gags with the Norwegian delegation in the hotel and, in the 29th episode, the scene in the Mibler bank, with the diminutive guard in a disproportionate setting). Both authors are attuned to the secret rhythms which can issue from the cosmos or float through the air (the prologue of *Fire Walk with Me* is like a Tati film, both in its characters and its way of exploring the sky and the surface of the shot). The author of *Mon Oncle* (1958) also had other American admirers: Blake Edwards, one of the rare American film-makers who can be compared to the author of *Blue Velvet* when it comes to matters undecorous and bizarre, with his peculiar sense of rhythm and casting, his metaphysical bad taste and his sense of death (compare *S.O.B.*, 1981).

Rear Window? Jeffrey Beaumont's voyeurism certainly recalls that of L. B. Jeffries in Hitchcock's film. But the young Lynch must also have been interested by the structure of a film which, beneath the linearity of the main plot, is so utterly unconventional. Autonomous characters living out their fate and secondary details abound in Hitchock's film, which also presents a number of parallel worlds. The courtyard of James Stewart's building is like a mini soap opera setting, and the life of the spinster on the first floor, or the young married couple who just moved in across the way, could easily constitute autonomous soap opera episodes or even films. Furthermore, *Rear Window* and Tati's films have common features which also point to Lynch: the sequences focusing on singular characters (all, as it were, encased within their own silhouettes) of whom we know very little and whose words we hear only from a distance. With its courtyard noises, radio music and city sounds, *Rear Window* is also one of the very rare acoustic films of the 1950s, a time when sound in films was generally limited to dialogues in close-up and musical accompaniment. As noted earlier, in Lynch's films noise, clamour and droning are present from the outset, constituting a dimension without which the film might not even have been possible.

However, I disagree with the critics who have attempted to construe a more general filiation from Hitchcock to Lynch, and *Twin Peaks* in particular. The allusions to Hitchcock in the series, about which more later, seem more like conscious citations of an author who is part of a general, shared culture than a homage to a director with whom one feels a deep affinity.

Lastly, Lynch has often expressed his admiration for *Sunset Boulevard* with its expressionistic use of black and white and its morbid atmosphere. In Wilder's film, the hero takes charge of a fallen woman who could be his mother, echoed in the underlying Lynchean theme of assisting a depressed mother. In addition, it has often been remarked that Lynch's work recalls the atmosphere of silent films, even in the way certain actors play their parts. Perhaps the author of *Fire Walk with Me* was marked by the evocation of silent cinema in *Sunset Boulevard* and, in particular, by the stylised, larger-than-life acting of Gloria Swanson.

14

In the course of his film studies at the American Film Institute in Beverly Hills, Lynch worked on a project for a new medium-length film called *Gardenback* (again a story of plant-life). He later summarised the story, which was clearly inspired by Kafka: 'When you look at a girl, something crosses from her to you. And in this story, that something is an insect, which grows in this man's attic, which mirrors his mind.'[2]

Just as the boy in *The Grandmother* had fantasies which grew in the attic, so Henry Spencer in *Eraserhead* lives in an upper storey and the elephant man is lodged, Quasimodo-style, in the garret near a church tower whose sounds resonate as if they were inside his head. However, unable fully to work it out to his own satisfaction, Lynch finally abandoned *Gardenback*. With a $5000 grant from AFI, he began working on another project which he particularly wanted to make into a feature-length film: *Eraserhead*.

The problem was, however, that the AFI had attempted to produce feature films before, with less than happy results, and did not wish to try again. Lynch wrote a script of 21 pages which was highly synthetic and contained little dialogue. The AFI authorised him to shoot a 21-minute film. 'I think it's going to be a bit longer than that,' Lynch warned and the AFI's answer went something like: 'Well, OK, 42 minutes.'

The Grandmother was shot in 16mm colour. For *Eraserhead*, Lynch envisaged shooting in 35mm and the AFI agreed, provided that he made it in black and white, which suited him perfectly. Initial preparations were made early in 1972. At the time, Lynch imagined the filming would take six weeks. In fact, work on *Eraserhead* was to last for five years. The thing that made this possible was that Lynch stumbled upon a treasure trove at the AFI itself: a large number of unoccupied rooms and spaces. The AFI had bought an abandoned summer palace containing several dozen rooms which had belonged to one of the founders of Los Angeles, the millionaire Doheny. Doing much of the work himself, Lynch prepared five or six rooms in the outbuildings – garages, servants' quarters, storerooms – and set up an office, a set and a small recording studio. For almost four years, he was able to enjoy the unexpected prize of a small film complex of his own.

With help from his brother John and from Alan Splet (who had become the head of the Sound Department at the AFI), they immediately started building the sets. Instead of *The Grandmother*'s abstract and stylised sets, or the furniture against a black or a drawn background, this time the walls were to appear real and solid, even if they were made of papier mâché. A number of sets (the pencil factory, the floor of the building where Henry lived, and some others) were built in the same space. Being a handyman and a cabin builder, Lynch personally worked on the constructions. What would turn out to be the film's greatest attraction was also built there at the same time: a monster-baby made from a trunk-like mass (which is always on a table) wrapped in strips of cloth, a long, thin neck sticking out and leading to the skinned head of a rabbit-like animal. With its cries and moaning synchronised to its movements on the screen, the baby's existence was totally convincing. Lynch has always refused to reveal the secret of how the baby was made and animated, even when pressed by questioners, and his closest associates have maintained the mystery, adding to the film's legend.

15

It is clearly easier to tell the story of *Eraserhead*, at least in part, than that of *The Grandmother*, but it is essentially a film which, by and large, one can only describe. Honesty dictates that one narrate only what one sees and hears. Can one really say, for instance, as certain summaries of the film do, that Henry Spencer represents the acme of human misery? In fact, even when it comes to his monstrous baby and his apparently sordid fate, we only ever see him somewhat bothered, preoccupied. To be faithful to the story told by the film, nothing should be added.

Like *The Grandmother*, the film opens with a cosmic prologue, but this time with live shots in a slow, ceremonious rhythm. We see the hero (his head, at any rate) weightlessly floating horizontally, with a planet-like sphere superimposed on his head, suggesting that the world of the film is a mental world. Frankly, you need the help of the film-maker's own statements to understand that this grainy-surfaced mass is a planet, and the setting for the action! We come closer to the sphere and skim its rough surface. Next, a man, whose face is disfigured by hideous burns, is seen seated near a window in an infernal setting. Something like a cord with a head is superimposed on the hero's head.

The seated man shifts a large lever two or three times; the cord runs out, then falls into a pond. We dive into the liquid, into the dark. A hole of light appears, then grows to become a flash of light filling the whole screen. This fade-in leads to the hero, all alone in a vast urban setting. But for his dishevelled hair, he is a kind of Kafkaesque clerk, with a number of pens in the breast pocket of his jacket. With a brown paper bag in one hand, he waddles somewhat comically towards the background of the shot. As he advances to the sound of machines and foghorns, we discover a gigantic, deserted world, a neighbourhood which is partly industrial and partly a port with derelict buildings, empty lots, sordid streets and puddles of water everywhere. The lively music of a theatre organ resonates in the air, unreal.

This bleak atmosphere is extended as we enter the sinister building where Henry Spencer lives. He seems to wait for eternity on a landing of striped tiles, as in the future Red Room in *Twin Peaks*, for the slow lift to arrive and to leave again. There are electrical problems in the lift itself. Famous for their derisive, sinister atmosphere, and long since banalised through more or less successful repetitions and imitations, these shots themselves betray the successfully assimilated influence of Kubrick, Fellini (who, one forgets, is a great lover of empty lots and abandoned places) and, of course, Tati. Henry's next-door neighbour, an attractive brunette, informs him that a certain Mary is at her parents' house and that she called to invite him to dinner. Henry goes into his little room, which vibrates with a range of noises somewhere between the hissing of gas and the sound of a radiator, or between the din of a factory and a cosmic storm, depending on the moment. The room is furnished with the by now familiar large metal-frame bed. Henry performs some small actions like putting a record on the turntable, his socks on the radiator and rummaging through a dresser to find a torn-up picture of Mary. He goes to her house, located in a place teeming with noise and smoke. Mary X (that is her name) is a submissive, fearful young woman, with a harsh, inquisitorial mother and a father who is a former plumber reduced to cursing the degenerating neighbourhood, his former profession and his paralysed arm.

When *Eraserhead* is shown in public, the long dinner sequence at the Xs' always provokes great rounds of laughter through its accumulation of ghastly and bizarre details: the paralysed grandmother in the kitchen reduced to the state of a living vegetable, the meal of dried-up little chickens (more like pigeons) oozing a thick stream of blood when Henry tries to cut them. It is precisely at this moment, in fact, that Mary's mother goes into a trance, races off into the kitchen followed by Mary, then returns to interrogate the young man (as the father, who never left the table, freezes once and for all with a stupid smile): has he had sexual intercourse with Mary or not? For Mary has given birth to a baby, though she is not sure that this premature creature really is a baby. When he hears the news, Henry's nose begins to bleed and the mother

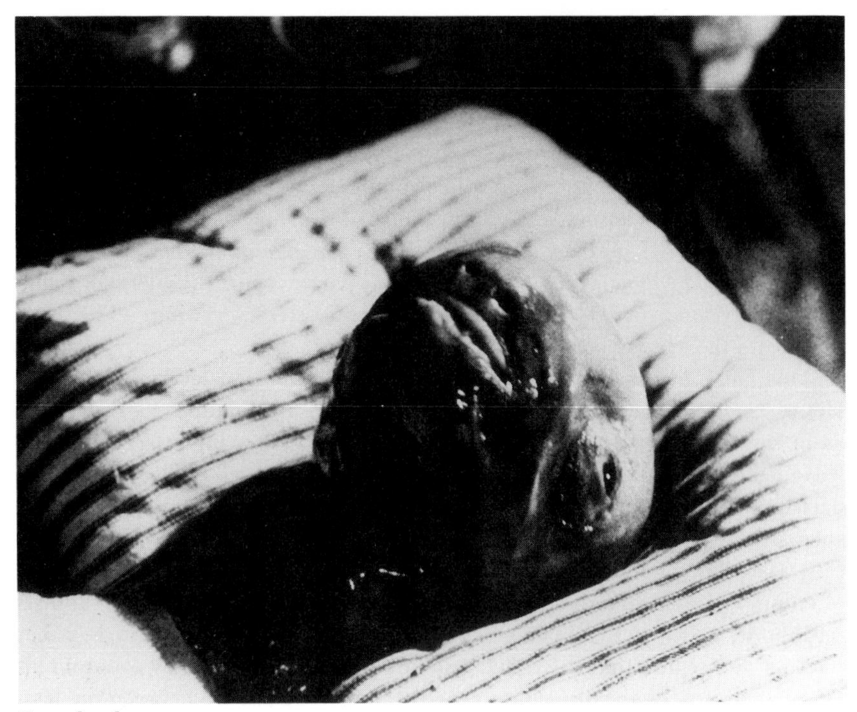

Eraserhead

(half-vampire, half-doctor) approaches to examine him. Later, we find the little family in Henry's room, the father idle and beaming as the mother vainly tries to feed the moaning thing on the table with a spoon. Tormented by the baby's crying, she soon becomes depressed and prepares a suitcase to go to her mother's for 'a decent night's sleep'. The horrible-looking baby turns more horrible still, breaking out into boils and sores, preventing Henry from going to check the mail. (Among the oddities in his room, we should mention a sort of tabernacle-cupboard, in which he carefully places a seed.) At night (interminable night scenes occupy an important place in the film), Henry dreams that the radiator in his room lights up, revealing a miniature theatre inside with a lone player, a little woman with strangely swollen cheeks who dances with little steps and smilingly crushes under her heel a series of organic cords which fall on to the stage. Henry wakes up with Mary at his side (the spectator has not been apprised of her return). Like the women in *The Alphabet* and *The Grandmother*, she thrashes about and rubs herself, makes noises while scratching and gives birth under the blanket to an endless series of cords; Henry gets out of bed to throw and smash them against the wall.

The door of the tabernacle-cupboard opens and lights up like a second stage on which a little worm-shaped thing begins to move and raise little cries. Then, like a piece of intestine, it opens towards the camera and swallows the spectator.

Henry is again alone with the baby. The neighbour knocks. She cannot get into her apartment and asks if she can spend the night in his. She is disturbed by the monster, which Henry tries to calm. In a sacred, magical atmosphere, they make love in the bed, transformed into a bathtub full of milk. The woman's head disappears except for her hair which floats on the surface.

The dream of the Lady in the Radiator now returns, as she sings a canticle about heaven. Henry climbs on to the little stage and draws near to her. When he touches her in passing, the emotion, sound and light become very intense. A large plant is wheeled on to the stage. Henry takes refuge behind the bar of a courtroom (Kafka?), fingering the thing nervously. Suddenly, his head is expelled from his body by something oblong. In a kind of solidarity between all living things (compare *The Grandmother*), the plant exudes a blood-like fluid. The baby's head appears on Henry's decapitated collar and produces a long scream of cosmic distress. Henry's head, lying on the chequerboard stage floor, falls into the surrounding pool of blood as though it has been swallowed up, and finally drops into the outdoor setting of an empty lot, where a child in a cap picks it up and carries it away like a rugby ball. The key sequence of the film occurs at this point (a more detailed consideration of this matrix, which gave the film its title, can be found in the Lynch-Kit), as the child sells Henry's head to a factory where it will be turned into the rubbers at the end of pencils.

Henry wakes up (so this was a dream!), and finds himself alone and increasingly on edge because of the baby who seems to laugh at his misfortune. On the landing he sees his neighbour in the company of a small, ugly man. Henry takes a pair of scissors and cuts the little monster's bandages, undressing it and piercing its body as the head tosses about with a mixture of cries of pain and rhythmic, patently sexual moans. Substances issue from the body in an endless flow, like a thick mush. The lamp 'illuminating' the room flickers and magnifies what follows with stroboscopic flashes. Covered at first with mush, the baby's head emerges at the end of a cord and hovers in the air. It becomes as big as an inflated balloon (resembling a fish-head) and flies towards the lamp which burns out, as Henry looks on helplessly. The planet which is the setting for the story cracks like an egg. The man seated at the lever tries in vain to brake and the strident sound rises to a mystical paroxysm, in which the Lady in the Radiator and Henry (his eyes shut) are seen holding each other closely in a flash of white light. Then everything stops; sound and image are cut, and the credits appear on a black background to the sparse music of Fats Waller. Then, the lights come back on in the cinema for the shaken and mute spectators. Many of them have now seen a film that will stay with them, but to achieve that, Lynch had to go through numerous tribulations.

16

The basic crew of *Eraserhead* was quickly assembled: initially, the chief cameraman was Herbert Cardwell, whom Lynch had met in Philadelphia. But as filming continued, interminably, he left and was replaced by Frederick Elmes, a young documentary cameraman. The production manager and in charge of props (the film required strange objects and substances) was Doreen Small. Catherine Coulson, a woman who was very important for Lynch, worked on the film from start to finish. At the time, she was married to the actor John (later called Jack) Nance. Later she would become known to millions of television viewers worldwide as the Log Lady of *Twin Peaks*.

Coulson, who was already an actress, also played a small part in the film as a nurse disgusted by the baby, but the scene was not shot for budgetary reasons. However, she was a precious and active collaborator, combining the jobs of assisant cameraman, general assistant, script girl and even cook. And hairdresser as well, for she was the creator (in accordance with Lynch's wishes, but going even further than he expected) of one of *Eraserhead*'s other attractions: Henry's famous hairstyle, trimmed short on the sides and standing high on top, extending and lengthening the mass of his head just as an eraser extends the length of a pencil. It is also worth mentioning that, contrary to the AFI's usual practice, Lynch insisted on every member of the crew being paid a salary (however modest) or, when this was impossible, a percentage of the box office receipts.

Everyone worked hard on the film. Crew members loaned props, sheets and make-up accessories, while Lynch and Splet created a highly efficient sound insulation. This collaboration at the most material level between the director and his soundman turned out to hold one of the film's most valuable lessons for Lynch. It is on the basis of this experience that, for Lynch, sound became not some abstract problem to be dealt with as is all too often the case with directors, but something concrete with which he had a direct, intimate relationship.

The first actors approached for the parts were the ones that were hired. Judith Anne Roberts (the Beautiful Girl across the Hall), Allen Joseph and Jeanne Bates (Mary's parents) were members of a theatre company. Charlotte Stewart (Mary) was a friend of the production manager. Physically, she is anything but pampered in the film, always crying and appearing as a woman is in the privacy of her bed, without protective make-up. It is understandable that she was not enthralled by the experience. Nevertheless, she was to work with Lynch again, taking a discreet part as Major Briggs's wife in *Twin Peaks*.

The film's great discovery was John Nance. A Texan of Irish origin, Nance began as a theatre actor in Dallas with a few minor parts in action films. He is a reserved, ironical man, with a slow, drawling voice which may well have seduced Lynch, for whom speech rhythms are essential. Nance has appeared in practically every one of Lynch's films as well as *Twin Peaks*, but, apart from performing in Wenders' *Hammett* (1982), this very fine actor never looked for a prominent career. In *Eraserhead*, his contribution is decisive. In turn distrustful, furious and embarrassed, he forges with great precision a thwarted, human character who at times even physically recalls the wonderful Jack Lemmon (perhaps an echo of Billy Wilder, whose best actor was Lemmon).

As for the photography, black and white was an obvious choice – as well as a reference to *Sunset Boulevard*, which had impressed Lynch with its perfect welding of atmosphere and story. This was the only film which he showed to his crew prior to shooting. Lynch has justly remarked that black and white allowed him to create a more schematic, less distracting image, in which the interiors and exteriors could be connected more smoothly. It also allowed him to draw the viewer more easily into another world (already in *The Grandmother*, the use of colour had been rarefied and stylised). Lynch knew exactly what shots he wanted and he carefully prepared everything with Cardwell (and later with Elmes). However, the laboratories did not immediately recognise their radical intentions: 'The dailies would come back from the lab, and they'd say, "Are you shooting this with one candle in a tunnel?" And David would send them back, saying, "Not dark enough. I want this darker".'[2] Lynch dared to use light which illuminates only in pools, so that parts of the set remained in the shadows or in complete darkness.

Elmes and Lynch asked for advice from special-effects specialists in the major studios, who told them of cheap ways to produce effects. They also proceeded a great deal by trial and error. For reasons both of economy and quality control, optical effects such as multiple exposure, fade-out and fade-to-white were almost never produced by the laboratories, as is generally the case, but rather in the course of shooting, which accounts for their beauty. This also meant that more time was needed for shooting, but time for preparation, testing and filming was the great luxury which the crew had opted for as the price of a much heavier personal workload.

A watchful eye had to be kept on the laboratories because they no longer worked in black and white, except on rare occasions, and did not always have the proper skills or equipment. Actually, in recent years, more and more films and, especially, music-clips and advertising have spectacularly renewed the use of black and white. As it happened, the laboratories which they used in the first year were simultaneously handling Peter Bogdanovich's nostalgic comedy, *Paper Moon* (1973), one of the first neo-black-and-white films of the 70s, so that, fortunately, the right equipment was available.

17

The work with the actors of *Eraserhead* was painstaking but not intellectualised; the whys and hows of certain choices were left unanalysed. Often the actors simply had to walk, open a door, sit down and pronounce the odd word or give a look. Such quasi-silent parts are among the most difficult things to do in the cinema, much more so than long scenes of dialogue which at least provide a framework, a momentum, an orientation.

The evening at the Xs' was the first scene to be shot. Henry is seated apprehensively on a sofa next to Mary (in the same compact, uncomfortable position as Kiefer Sutherland in *Fire Walk with Me*), and he has a conversation with Mrs X. 'What do you do?' she asks, and he replies 'I'm on vacation.' Lynch wanted to give this scene a particularly unnatural tempo, so that the answer seemed disconnected from the question. One take was enough. At this time, Lynch believed in long rehearsals and few takes, possibly also in order to economise on film stock.

From then on, shooting proceeded at a steady pace for almost a year and the directors of the AFI gave their blessing, believing matters were in good hands. As some of the locations were in use or too noisy during the day, the crew worked more and more often at night. This allowed the crew members to lead two professional lives at once, but it also made their timetable difficult. *Eraserhead* is a night film shot at night, even for the interiors, which no doubt was essential for the veracity of its atmosphere and tempo.

Lynch calmly let the conception of the film unfold and, as he could be trusted to maintain the inner coherence of the script, he incorporated fresh ideas as they arose. The most important change to the original script involved transforming into a dream what was a full-scale nightmare at the outset. Indeed, the original plan called for the film to end with the baby's murder and the disintegration of Henry's world. Lynch was anxious and agitated at the time, smoking and drinking a great deal. 'I had everything going for me,' he said, 'I was supposed to be doing the thing I wanted to do most of all, making films. I practically had my own little studio, and we were working, but I just wasn't happy.'[2]

He learned meditation techniques and one day the image came to him of the little lady in the radiator with the foetus falling out of her, an idea he later transferred to Henry's wife. 'The idea came after the filming had started, when I had already filmed the radiator, but it must have been there already in my mind, I think, because one day I ran into Henry's room and looked carefully at the radiator. I saw the perfect spot, a little space like a miniature stage which seemed to have been made for her. Warm and comfortable. She was born there.'[16]

However, serious trouble loomed since the money was now running out. To raise funds, Lynch and Splet edited and dubbed the scene of the evening at the parents' house to show to a producer. The man was furious: 'People don't talk like that! People don't act like that! You people are crazy! What do you think you are doing?'[2] In short, it was a fiasco. After that experience, Lynch refused to show his work to anyone other than the crew, wanting it to be judged only when finished. But the AFI felt that the film was drifting towards feature length and decided to cut off funds and the supply of stock, only allowing some money to maintain the equipment. Production ground to a halt in the spring of 1973 and Lynch faced a difficult year. They were even beginning to take away some of his sets. To finish *Eraserhead* in spite of everything, Lynch momentarily considered building a small marionette of Henry and to shoot the remaining parts frame by frame.

The crew remained in touch, and Lynch performed odd jobs like selling newspapers. In the meantime, Splet and Lynch (with help from Catherine Coulson and Jack Nance) edited the existing footage. Elmes, assisted by Coulson, used the break to shoot John Cassavetes's *The Killing of a Chinese Bookie*, with its daring approach to movement and grain. Nevertheless, *Eraserhead* continued to unite the group which met to consider solutions, make drawings and prepare shots and special effects with a view to a resumption of shooting. Fortunately, goodwill from many quarters came to the rescue. George Stevens Jr obtained the agreement of the labs to print at least the negative; financial support came from relatives and friends. Shooting resumed in May 1974, though under more straitened conditions and for short, intermittent periods only. Divorced and homeless at the time, Lynch was squatting in Henry's room, having found a way of concealing the tracés of his illegal presence outside working hours.

This second period of shooting, again at night, commenced with the scene of the Lady in the Radiator. Lynch frequently had to interrupt work at midnight to go and sell the *Wall Street Journal*. Then the AFI announced to Lynch that he could no longer maintain his sets on AFI premises. The AFI had been pressed by the unions to cease production of non-union short films. New regulations were adopted to limit their production and distribution in the future. Lynch was lucky enough to slip through these regulations while retaining his rights in the film. However, he was given an extremely tight schedule in which to complete it. A number of single-frame and miniature sequences were shot in

Fred Elmes's living room, forcing Lynch to rent an animation stand. For example, the scene with the little worm which crawls and moans on the surface of the planet, sinking and then bobbing up again, required a day to set up the scale model and the scenery, a day to test the animation and another day to shoot.

In spite of all this, Lynch retains an excellent memory of this type of work and in his later career, even when he had more money and a full crew, he would always try to keep his hand in by doing some manual work himself. For instance, in 1992, on *Fire Walk with Me*, he personally calibrated the sound levels when mixing the music.

In 1975, when Alan Splet was able to join Lynch in the garage-studio they had equipped, they worked together for a long time creating the film's sound effects. The equipment they used was fairly standard and many of the film's sounds were achieved acoustically using pipes and traditional instruments, exploring very thoroughly the sound potential of their equipment, adopting the same techniques deployed for *musique concrète* in France. The film bathes in an uninterrupted sound-atmosphere, with the constant rush of boiler sounds, whirlpools, electronic organ chords, and the like. Its great originality lies in the use of brutal and instantaneous cuts into these sounds, cuts which often coincide with a change in shot and have surprising power. They are like image tensors, isolating the shots from one another even as they join them, drawing out the time of each shot in relation to its two boundaries, constituted by the two cuts confining the segment. This phase of the work, which combined Lynch's editing of the images and Splet's sound edit, ran from the summer of 1975 until the spring of 1976. In the final days Splet and Lynch accelerated the pace, hoping to be selected for Cannes. They worked around the clock, sleeping and working in the same room. On the other hand, the mixing done by Splet took very little time because it had been carefully prepared. Lynch arrived in New York with an edited though still rough version of the film only to find that the Cannes selection panel had already left. The film was also refused by the New York festival. However, Lynch's second wife Mary, Jack Fisk's sister, advised him to try Filmex in Los Angeles and here the film was finally accepted

18

It was screened at the AFI for the cast and crew and friends. At that time, the film ran for one hour and fifty minutes. When the lights came back on, there was no applause and nobody said a word, as if they did not know what to make of it. The world première on 19 March 1977 in Los Angeles provoked the same kind of surprise but, according to Jack Nance's recollection, there was also a round of applause. Nevertheless, *Variety* published a negative review of

Eraserhead

the film: 'A sickening bad-taste exercise.... Set, apparently, in some undefined apocalyptic future era, *Eraserhead* consists mostly of a man sitting in a room trying to figure out what to do with his horribly mutated child.... Like a lot of Institute efforts, the pic has good technical values (particularly the inventive sound mixing), but little substance or subtlety ... Lynch seems bent on emulating Herschell Gordon Lewis, the king of low-budget gore' (23 March 1977). The reviewer refers to the marginal director of *Blood Feast* (1963) and *2000 Maniacs* (1964), films often regarded as 1960s precursors of the recent gore wave.

In the light of this experience, Lynch concluded in distress that to keep the audience's attention he would have to cut a large part of the film. No less than 20 minutes of the film would be discarded. How exciting it would be to see today those original scenes which to my knowledge have never been shown again, either reintegrated into the film or separately. At least we know their general drift from the accounts given by Coulson and Lynch. They include sequences of the Xs bringing Mary home from the hospital with the baby, a telephone call received by Henry and Mary's nervous fit in Henry's apartment. In another scene which was cut, Henry hears strange noises from the floor below. When he goes down to investigate and briefly opens the door of an apartment, he has the singular vision of a 'sexual' scene involving two women tied to an iron bed with wire and a man with a black box who advances towards them. The longest cut involved an exterior daytime scene outside Henry's window. As a cloud of dust blows by, a child sees something shiny on the ground, bends down and, as he begins to dig, discovers some coins. Henry wants to go down despite the fact that the baby is crying, but the lift has been blocked by the landlord who has wedged the door open with a broom while he is doing the cleaning. The baby's crying is heard through the open door and it invades the lift shaft. Furious, Henry kicks the armchair in the lobby and is reprimanded by the landlord (this is one of the few direct expressions of aggressiveness in Henry before the murder at the end). Henry returns to his apartment and watches from his window as a number of people begin to dig. Later, at night, he witnesses a fight. A brief glimpse of this last shot remains in the film.

The cuts mainly affect exterior settings, reinforcing, very effectively it would appear, the unity of place, which may not have been as clear in the initial project and thus reinforcing the film's tightness as well as its magic. The presence in the credits of actors and characters who are absent from the work as we know it suggests that the cuts were made on the original negative.

19

However, the Filmex screening did bear fruit: it aroused the interest and enthusiasm of the distributor Ben Barenholtz who, with films like Jodorowsky's *El Topo* (1971), had created the vogue of midnight cult film shows. His strategy was to run films for long periods without spending much on advertising, which might kill the phenomenon, so that the public could discover the films over a period of months relying on word of mouth. In 1977, Lynch and his wife Mary went to New York and spent two laborious month supervising the striking of a decent print, always something of a nightmarish operation for Lynch, as demonstrated later when he was very critical of the quality of the *Elephant Man* prints.

On this occasion, Barenholtz made the acquaintance of a surprisingly well-behaved young man, not at all a New Yorker, who was incapable of an intellectual discussion, went to bed at 10 o'clock every night, perhaps to overcome the accumulated fatigue of the nights spent making the film, and ate only at McDonald's. The film opened in New York at the Cinema Village in the autumn of 1977 to an audience of 25 the first night and 24 the second. Nevertheless, what Barenholtz had expected finally came true. Shown on Saturday nights at midnight, the film acquired an audience and a legend. A badge was made for the *Eraserhead* fan club, simply saying 'I saw it'. Moreover, the director John Waters gave Lynch a boost when, at the screening of one of his own films, he announced that *Eraserhead* was his favourite film. The film later moved to another Greenwich Village cinema, the Waverly, where it ran until mid-September 1981. In 1982, Barenholtz had 32 copies circulating worldwide.

Presented at the Avoriaz festival in 1980, the film received the Gold Antenna and the Jury Prize (the jury that year was headed by William Friedkin). The French critics were either seduced and disgusted or else simply disgusted by a film which they saw as a fastidious avant-garde exercise close to the New York avant-garde or the theatre of the absurd. The film became a unique event, even for those who had not seen but only heard tell of it with surprise and amazement. My own first encounter with the film, before seeing it at the Waverly, was when I heard friends give detailed descriptions of its sordid atmosphere. A rumour circulated that Kubrick, in his English retreat, had viewed the film repeatedly and had sought to penetrate into the mystery of the baby's construction, declaring that *Eraserhead* was the only film he would have liked to have made.

In an article in *Art-Press*, Régis Jauffret summarised the feelings of many fans: 'I would love to end my days inside this film, eternally leaping like a flea from its start to its end, and finally fashion a coffin out of its last scene.'[22] This may seem paradoxical, given that the characters experience such discomfort, but Jauffret is right because the odours, the variety of textures and organic filth, all linked to the idea of warmth and smoke, combine to form a perfect film-bosom or film-nest with an abundance of the kind of mother's milk in which Henry and his beautiful neighbour make love.

It is interesting to note that standard releases of the film (multiple daily showings, and so on), attempted after the wide success of *The Elephant Man*, have always failed. In 1981, the *Cahiers du cinéma* asked Lynch: 'Do you think that you might someday make another film under the same conditions as *Eraserhead*?' He answered: 'No, you can't turn back the clock. I could never make another film over five years and without money. No, I couldn't do it.'[13]

20

For a spectator who is not overly defensive, viewing *Eraserhead* for the first time is generally an experience which leaves its mark, including its mark as a formal structure. However, the film does not seek to revolutionise film language. It operates at a different level. Despite its gaps and incoherences, *Eraserhead* is a narrative film with dialogue, a hero and a linear story. Its syntax (framing, shooting script) is fairly traditional. There are no more shifts into different dimensions here than there are in Fellini's *Giulietta degli spiriti* (1965) or in Kubrick's *The Shining* (1980). Lynch's visual language is simply the personal application of a common language, but the cinema is so strong a system that distending any given dimension of it will endow a work with a wholly different aspect and surprising expressiveness and eloquence.

Compared with what he did in *The Grandmother*, here Lynch no longer relies on obvious technical differentiation – cartoons, shots filmed in abstract, stylised settings versus those filmed in natural locations – to establish drastic demarcations between the worlds which combine to make up the film. On the contrary, he strives to join and unify them, and introduces audible dialogue as well. In short, he is clearly moving towards a more traditional kind of cinema. None the less, there is a genuine strangeness in the cinematography of *Eraserhead*. Though plain as day, this strangeness is not easy to define and cannot be reduced to the use of particular techniques. Unfortunately, it has become such a powerful cliché in cinema to assess originality in terms of the use of specific visual forms (a sort of simplification of the relation between content and form) that certain critics have felt the need to associate *Eraserhead*'s originality with forms 'different' from ordinary cinema, to the point of concocting an imaginary film which no longer corresponds to what is on the screen. Thus, an attentive and often highly relevant defender of Lynch has tried to persuade us (and himself) in a French review that *Eraserhead* is 'composed of long, almost autonomous static shots.'[16] In fact, not all the shots are long and, what is more, they happen to be mobile at times. Furthermore, if there is one thing they clearly are not, it is autonomous. The shots are connected in very precise and generally conventional ways: angle/reverse angle, whole/detail, and so on. Undoubtedly, there is something novel about Lynch's shots, a kind of surprise to be released from the continuity of time and space and still to be alive. But they are clearly related to the shots which surround them and to all the others. Indeed, the force of Lynch's cinema lies in this patent, visible, demonstrative and, again, 'brand-new' quality in the relationship between different shots.

Beginning with *Eraserhead*, his cinematographic style offers something archaic, stiff and frontal which is close to early silent film, a period about which Lynch appears to know little or nothing. It recalls the films of the 1910s which had only just become awake to the possibilities of editing. A literal film-maker, Lynch takes old formulae concerning parallel editing and 'thought-shots' and makes them new. He often connects images with the same sense of freedom in editing reminiscent of the silent film era. For example, in *Eraserhead*, Henry is stuck in his room while expecting a message to be delivered to his letter-box in the building's lobby. His thoughts are expressed by a shot of the letter-box, but it is impossible to say whether this is a mental shot or an objective shot of the letter-box edited in parallel. The insert counts as an idea, a thought, but it is objective at the same time. Another typical editing example occurs in *The Elephant Man* in the solemn meeting to discuss Merrick's permanent admission to the hospital. An unexpected, brief shot of Merrick, inserted into the continuity of the scene, shows us the person being talked about working (at that very instant?) on his model of the cathedral and saying to himself, 'Be careful.' This is a typically Lynchian moment, but also recalls silent films where it was common to have an image of a person alluded to verbally, physically inscribed into the scene. The time taken by such an insert does not affect the continuity of the scene (whence the magical impression in these films of communication at a distance between persons). At any rate, Lynch is close to the kind of cinema which preceded theatrical linearisation established by sound film, even though it was well on its way before sound's arrival.

In Lynch's work, there is no pre-existing rhetoric, that is to say, there is no reference to a coded, closed cinematographic language, no *a priori* connotations related to a given style of filming (static shots, sequence shots, and so on) on the foundation of which sequences are elaborated. If he adopts the traditional, classic type of cutting continuity, he does so for functional and utilitarian purposes. It is a means to which he does not ascribe the value of a language. For Lynch, every shot is in a category of its own. Lastly, it is worth noting that, unlike many contemporary directors, Lynch refuses the kind of continuous camera movements freely tracing arabesques in space, unconnected with any gaze at the characters. This is his classic side.

21

It is also in *Eraserhead*, with the tart music of Fats Waller's Hammond organ and the quivering song of the Lady in the Radiator, that a specifically Lynchian concept of music emerges, although he did not seem able to master it and to make it fully his own until much later. This concept involves the sensation of the instrument or solo voice as bare, fragile, trembling in the void. With the help of Angelo Badalamenti, who would be his Nino Rota, Lynch developed this type of sound in *Blue Velvet* and even more clearly in *Wild at Heart* and in the album *Floating in the Night*. It would become his own particular musical ethos, especially as expressed in the thin voice of singer Julee Cruise. Another interesting, specific aspect of Lynch's music that emerges with *Eraserhead* is the mix of religious and profane styles. The organ sounds of Fats Waller's joyous swing evoke the vaults of a church ceiling and have something in common too with the hymn of the Lady in the Radiator. However, the force of the film's sound concept lies especially in the absence of any separation between the music and its overall atmosphere. The film moves naturally from a surging sound like a storm or a machine to a sustained tremolo which can be melodramatic or ecstatic. For example, when Henry discovers that the baby is sick, one of the film's most traumatic sound-image edits shows its head suddenly covered with pustules and lumps just as an electronic organ sound erupts, continuing seamlessly, without any aesthetic rupture, into the rumbling of a boiler.

Lynch can be said to have renewed the cinema by way of sound. If his visual continuity is classic and transparent (though with a kind of warp which once again reveals the force of cinema, as a slight change in the conventional rules yields a wealth of new effects), his sound continuity is idiosyncratic from the outset. Sound has a precise function, propelling us through the film, giving us the sense of being inside it, wrapped within its timespan. The sound is animated from the inside by a perpetual pulsation. The noise of the machine, its micro-activity of particles, places us in a secure inner space like some bodily machinery, the archaic body which the boy of *The Grandmother* tries unsuccessfully to reconstruct. And yet, bizarrely, this continuum is shot through with discontinuities. Having learned that to join, to build, one must first separate, Lynch began, with ever-increasing clarity, to construct continuities by means of discontinuities, to join by separating. Like many directors, he does this through the image but also, and with far greater originality, through sound. Given its fundamentally temporal nature, sound (far more than the image) is ordinarily likened to a continuum, a flow, and used in this way.

However, in Lynch's work, the pulsation of sound environments does not give rise to a flow which overrides the cuts. The pulsation is perpetually stopped and started by scissors which at once separate and join, often in synch with the visual cuts. The author controls the pulsation like a flow, which he interrupts to distribute and regulate it in spurts. This may be why Lynch denies confusing creation and dream. Dreams cannot be controlled, he has said, which means that for him their flow cannot be cut and put back together again. The result is a paradoxical style of sound editing which, from *Eraserhead* to his most recent films, reaffirms continuity through interruption. Unlike Godard, for example, who cuts sound in the same way as he cuts image and text, prising it out of its temporal specificity, Lynch uses abrupt, often bold interruptions in sound to the opposite effect: his sound cuts are designed to achieve an inscription into time, amounting to a creation of time by the director, like a demiurge. An emblematic example of such a demiurgical gesture occurs at the beginning of *Eraserhead*. Henry is back at home and turns on the phonograph. He places the needle on different grooves of a jazz record, carving out little islands of swing music separated by silence. As the director's *alter ego*, Henry performs live sound editing! Without scissors, just using his hand well before the invention of scratch music, he creates islands of sound time. With sounds in Lynch's work, we are constantly within something. To begin with, we are inside the shot. Synchronising the sound cuts with the visual cuts settles us inside the shot as if in a nest.

In *Wild at Heart*, short scenes are dilated by being chopped into segments which are then edited in parallel. What separates them also perpetually joins them. There is no escape from that. By virtue of the wound which divides it in two, every fragment (of sound or scene) can be felt as part of a whole which it endlessly reaffirms. Lynch's scissors are thus neither destructive (cutting off life) nor abstracting (that is, isolating a fragment lifted out of its context and time). Rather, they create a renewed life, a life which is more monstrous than ever. That is the meaning of the impossible murder at the end. Could *Eraserhead* be about the impossibility of death?

22

Among the commentaries which *Eraserhead* has inspired, it is worth mentioning George Godwin's most interesting comments in *CinéFantastique*.[2] For Godwin, the entire film is placed under the sign of the fear of sex. The baby is a phallic symbol, a penis which in growing independent of its owner, becomes a separate and demanding entity, free of the mind's conscious control. In destroying it, Henry performs a kind of self-castration which at the same time destroys the means of perpetuating the species, and so, the planet explodes. It is undoubtedly true that the baby is something of a partial object, a part of Henry related to the penis, and that it is opposed to the mind as the seat of conscious control. However, one can also see other things and continue the analysis by referring the film to *The Grandmother*, which preceded it and with which it has definite links. *The Grandmother* and *Eraserhead* both contain the idea of a stain, an inscription on an immaculate surface. The boy's gesture in marking the virginal white of the two beds with urine, then earth and water is echoed in *Eraserhead* by the page marked with a pencil stroke. Another parallel involves the Lady in the Radiator who, along with the baby, is the other (mental) fruit born of Henry. Remember how the idea for this character came to Lynch late on in the production. The Lady was born by herself in the warm, empty space of a corner of a central-heating radiator, born from Henry's waiting, rather than issuing like the grandmother from the gardener's active efforts. Like the grandmother, the Lady's body is closed in upon itself, but instead of sitting in a chair with which she seems to merge, she is standing up with her hands and feet joined together. The Lady in the Radiator is indeed a reappearance of the grandmother, representing an escape avenue from the hopeless hell of life on earth. It is worth noting that Lynch began by inventing a universe in which she had no place, but in which she nevertheless succeeded in imposing herself – just as much later, after planning an unhappy ending for *Wild at Heart*, Lynch would introduce *in extremis* the saving apparition of a good fairy.

The Lady in the Radiator is related to perfect love and the dream of incestuous fusion. When Henry comes on to the stage of his fantasy and touches her with his fingertips, a blinding flash and a burst of sound are used to convey the unbearable intensity of this moment. This intensity is strikingly reminiscent of what Françoise Dolto has said about the incendiary character of incestuous physical contacts. Even as the Lady sings her hymn about heaven where, indeed, there is no fusion ('You have your things and I have mine'), her gesture towards Henry at this moment is beautiful. Her hands are clasped over her heart, then she opens them and draws them back in a gesture which ambiguously mixes an offering, a gift and an appeal with a sense of grabbing something, appropriating it – unless it is an outright demand.

Last and most important, in both films the hero finds himself with something he has brought into being and which dies or is transfigured at the end. In the earlier film, the grandmother suffocates in calling out, in an act of communication with cries for help like those of Laura Palmer. In the second film, Henry rips the baby open with his scissors. In both cases, there is an idea of a body emptying. The grandmother is found still seated in her chair in the cemetery, whereas the baby takes on cosmic proportions but does not die.

The erasure referred to in the title of Lynch's first feature thus concerns not only the scene in which a man makes a mark on a page and then erases it with the other end of the pencil, but also Henry's attempt to destroy the baby he brought into being, as an omnipotent creator can efface the work of his creation. Instead, we are treated to a kind of apotheosis, a metamorphosis like the one which later ends *Fire Walk with Me*. To date, four of Lynch's films end with the death of the main character: *The Grandmother*, *Eraserhead*, *The Elephant Man* and *Fire Walk with Me*. None of these four deaths leave us with a corpse which can be buried. They lead us into a beyond which is clearly designated (and it cannot be helped if this seems a truism) as a place where one never dies. Is this perspective exalting or, on the contrary, terrifying? In his first and indelible feature, it is Lynch's strength that he does not allow us to decide between these two alternatives.

II

IMMOBILE GROWTH

(The Elephant Man and *Dune)*

1

'I don't know what would have happened if I had continued to make films like *Eraserhead*. I don't know if I would have been able to go on making films at all.'[12]

Indeed, one wonders, but fate has given the answer to that question. Besides, Lynch did not seem inclined to repeat the experience anyway. He was ready to go on, but under less exceptional circumstances. In short, he was ready to become a director. Thanks to a guardian angel named Stuart Cornfeld, he did not have to wait for another ten years. An executive producer, Cornfeld had seen *Eraserhead* in Los Angeles. He had fallen in love with it and he phoned Lynch to tell him so. Lynch thanked him. 'What are you doing now?', Cornfeld asked. Lynch replied: 'I'm repairing roofs. The reception wasn't very good and I've had no other propositions.' This conversation was the start of a friendship, and Cornfeld undertook to help Lynch direct other films. With Cornfeld's encouragement, Lynch began to write *Ronnie Rocket* and the two men sought unsuccessfully to launch the project. It remains unfilmed to date.

Lynch then decided to read scripts written by others. A few weeks later, a producer named Jonathan Sanger who had taken an option on the rights to a script by Chris de Vore and Eric Bergren called *The Elephant Man* showed it to Cornfeld, who suggested Lynch as director. Sanger found Lynch to be a surprising man and he was seduced by the cinematographic maturity of *Eraserhead*. *The Grandmother*, which he also asked to see, confirmed his judgment.

At the time, there was much talk of a play by Bernard Pomerance starring David Bowie called *The Elephant Man*, inspired by the same true story of John Merrick who had been exploited as a freak before ending his life in a hospital. The play had been optioned for a film independently of Bergren and de Vore's script, much to the dismay of Lynch, Sanger and Cornfeld, who desperately wanted to go ahead with their own production. At long last, after many refusals, the script was accepted thanks to the help of Mel Brooks. Cornfeld had been the associate producer of *History of the World Part I* (1981), the most expensive of the parody-films that Brooks had made his speciality. Cornfeld gave the script to Brooks who decided to make it the first production of his new company. Brooks was invited to a screening of *Eraserhead*. Lynch was afraid this would put an end to the whole plan, but on the way out of the screening, Brooks hugged him and said something like, 'You're crazy, but I love you.' 'I was flabbergasted,' the author of *High Anxiety* (1977) later said, 'It's very clear. It's beautiful. It's like Beckett. It's like Ionesco. And it's very moving.'[1]

We can be grateful to Mel Brooks for having felt moved where many others, including most of the people who liked the film, remained fixated on distasteful details and were unable to get beyond an almost physiological reaction. *The Elephant Man* thus began with a budget of six million dollars in an atmosphere which, according to Lynch, filled him with a sense of confidence and freedom. According to the press book, however, Brooks was closely involved in the editing though not in the shooting. It is not known to what extent the director of *Young Frankenstein* (1974), a poetic parody in black and white in which the monster shows some affinities with Merrick, played an active role in the film. He may well have been responsible for adding a few decisive touches of humanity. In any case, we have the finished product.

2

John Merrick, the hero of *The Elephant Man*, lived at the end of the nineteenth century. We know what he looked like from photos of the period. He had been afflicted since childhood by a rare disease, neurofibromatosis, which made his skin spongy and dangling. His gigantic head was deformed by protuberances. His upper lip curled back in such a way that it resembled an elephant's trunk (whence his nickname) and his right arm and lower members were extremely deformed. As a result of a hip problem, he limped and, to crown it all, he gave off a pestilential smell.

According to Merrick's protector, the surgeon Frederick Treves, whose book was one of the bases for the script, Merrick had been displayed in local fairs for 20 years, wearing a hat proportioned to his giant head. Treves first saw him in a shop in London where he was being exhibited for twopence.

'Stand,' ordered the man who ran the show (this 'stand' inspired a number of scenes in the script), and Treves discovered what in his view was 'the most abominable specimen of humanity which has ever existed'. Outraged, he had the police forbid the exhibition. Bytes, the showman, left England and tried in vain to launch his show in France and Belgium, but he finally abandoned his creature in a train where he was arrested by the police. Treves's visiting card, from the time of the London visit, was found in Merrick's possession. When contacted, the surgeon arranged for two small rooms to be made available to the unfortunate man in the London Hospital in Whitechapel where he worked. To meet the expenses, Treves made the case known and donations poured in. Merrick became a celebrity whom people travelled for miles to see – even the royal family paid a visit. As his shyness prevented Merrick from speaking, he had at first been taken for a half-wit, but in fact he was intelligent and learned. He enjoyed sentimental novels and, according to Treves, fell in love with every attractive woman who came to see him, sobbing over their gestures of friendship and kindness. He died in his bed in April 1890, after his enormous head had broken his neck, for he could sleep only in a sitting position leaning on cushions and resting his head on his knees. Apparently he died because he wanted to sleep like everyone else.

The emotional resources of such a true story are easily imaginable, as is the difficulty of supplying it with dramatic turns, unless one took liberties with both the facts and chronology of Treves's account, which the authors did. A more recent biography by Michael Howell and Peter Ford argues in favour of a less troubling account. The historical Merrick would seem to have earned his living exhibiting himself in the company of his mother, who took care of him until his premature death.

'Chris and Eric's script was very good,' Lynch said, 'but so close to the real story that it started by going up and then it flattened out. We restructured the whole thing and wrote a lot of new scenes. It was a team effort. The beginning and the end weren't in the original script. I learned a lot from this work because I had never done this kind of writing before.'[9]

Though the material was, after all, fairly slight, the script managed to create a kind of progression by counterpointing the improvements in Merrick's condition by day with the increasing degradation of his life by night. This idea of creating two parallel worlds seems to have been Lynch's. The script also invents the owner Bytes's return to regain possession of his creature just when Merrick thinks he has escaped from the condition of being a freak. In addition, two enigmas would be exploited for all their worth to keep the spectator in suspense. Firstly, the physical revelation of Merrick, whom the doctor discovers almost at the beginning, is delayed by some 30 minutes, at which time it is made through the eyes of a nurse. And secondly, Merrick's speaking reveals that he is not a half-wit but an intelligent though extremely scared man. On paper, in the abstract, these strategies might seem forced but, thanks to Lynch's particular style, on the screen the solemn enactment of this double revelation of an appearance and a voice becomes a troubling ritual.

3

For the first time since his unsuccessful European trip, Lynch left the United States for a long stay abroad. The shooting and post-production of *The Elephant Man* required him to spend a year in England, where the drama is set and where most of the cast and crew lived, from pre-production through to the striking of the final release print. Later, he would describe the shoot of *The Elephant Man* as both his 'best and worst experience', because of the fears inspired by his new responsibilities, the pressure which he had never known before of a large crew and a tight schedule, and, lastly, the panic of failing in a project for which he was the last hope. In addition, he would have to direct actors as distinguished as Anthony Hopkins and Sir John Gielgud. It appears that there may have been tension between Lynch and Hopkins, who was already an exceptional actor at the time, but whom Lynch found to be a difficult man who liked to have a drink. However, for Lynch, there was nothing unusual in these tensions: 'I was going to work with really great actors on a true story from Victorian times in a country I didn't know. At first, I thought I wouldn't be able to handle it. I

The Elephant Man

couldn't get into the atmosphere. I couldn't even find the locations I wanted. Then, one day, I was at an abandoned hospital in the East End of London and it clicked. Everything was there: the atmosphere, the rooms, the long corridors.'[16]

Lynch was surrounded not only by great actors, but also by a crew of accomplished technicians. Freddie Francis, who would work on *Dune* as well, was one of Britain's best cinematographers. Moreover, he had already directed horror films for Hammer, showing a flair for creating atmosphere. He was certainly no novice when it came to shooting films for the big screen. When reading the script, Lynch visualised it in black and white, but he was afraid to broach the subject with Mel Brooks. Luckily, Brooks was already thinking along the same lines: 'It was a deliberate choice because of the atmosphere, the industries, the smoke, the dark little streets.'[9] There were precedents for black and white films, such as Woody Allen's *Manhattan* (1979) and of course *Young Frankenstein*, shot during the dictatorial reign of colour. But the black and white of *The Elephant Man* is in no way chic, camp or old-fashioned. On the contrary, it projects the idea of smoke, filth and misery. Throughout the film, a multitude of large and small details, probably introduced by Lynch, recall the energy sources of the period, the equipment used in surgeries, lighting and heating, and the atmosphere these elements could engender. Treves is shown operating on a worker injured by a machine, cauterising a wound with an iron drawn from a fire. In the foggy streets, men work with heavy machines pounding the earth. The flame of a magic lantern burns during Treves's lecture. In the hospital, there is gaslight and a huge boiler. Even Merrick's nightmares are obsessed with images of dark workshops in which men work like slaves. However, on the screen, the force of these images does not derive from the kind of realism one associates with a 'reconstruction'. On the contrary, the flames and the smoke are alive in Lynch's eyes, and so they live for us.

What is more unexpected for a film-maker working for the first time under ordinary studio conditions is the choice of a large-screen format, but Lynch adopted it enthusiastically and would continue using it for all of his later films, with the singular exception of *Fire Walk with Me*. Rather than filling the image with decorative details, CinemaScope has served Lynch well by extending the emptiness around his characters, the inactive zone of the image, and creating a spatial sense of time. That is why, when he was forced to return to a standard rectangular format when making *Twin Peaks* for television, Lynch compensated in the episodes he directed with extemely wide and spacious shots.

Alan Splet is credited with *The Elephant Man*'s sound design. Although Lynch and he did not have the same opportunities for fantasy that they had enjoyed on *Eraserhead*, they succeeded in using the kind of elements of the setting we mentioned earlier to introduce the sounds of dull thudding, the hiss and whistles produced by steam, and even the sound of a soft wind of cosmic proportions. These sounds are signalled to the spectator's ear by the device, already applied in *Eraserhead*, of cutting the sound precisely when the shot changes (as in the scene where night falls in the hospital room). In some scenes, an abstract cosmic murmur can be heard although the setting in no way requires it. This murmur is always in a precise register which is Lynch's own, evoking intimacy, the world's voice speaking in our ear, as when, for instance, Treves leaves the hospital to see the exhibition of the elephant man or when, unable to sleep, he questions his own morality, peering into the night. Another major sound effect in the film involves the insistence on Merrick's laboured, asthmatic, terrorised breathing, well before we have seen his features hidden under a hood, as if there were a continuum between the sensation (conveyed primarily through the sound) of this worn, suffering bodily machinery and the film's rendering of industry.

John Morris's beautiful music highlights the film's melodramatic character. It is almost entirely based on themes in 3/4 time, suggesting an on the spot shuffling rather than a march, and thus the idea of fate. There is the soft waltz as heart-rending as a lament (the elephant man's theme), a cascading, mechanical waltz for a barrel organ at the fair, an implacable scherzo reminiscent of Mahler (Merrick's suffering with his nightly visitors), and the sumptuous, chilling Viennese waltz of the pantomime show. In the counter-melody during the credits one can hear echoes of Nino Rota (a chromatic slide irresistibly drawn downwards), betraying Lynch's liking for Fellini and *La strada* (1954), which, like *The Elephant Man*, tells the story of a confident but immensely vulnerable creature's suffering.

As for Jack Hayes's orchestration, it relates the instrumentation to the idea of childhood and the music box (recorder, metallophones, and the like). John Morris did not have the satisfaction of putting the final moments of the hero's life to his music, for Lynch here employed a neo-classical piece by Samuel Barber, the *Adagio* for strings. That the piece works without seeming to be added on suggests that Lynch filmed the scene on the basis of the grave liturgical rhythms of the music.

The film premièred in New York in October 1980. To date, its worldwide success remains Lynch's greatest public triumph in the cinema (the television series *Twin Peaks* is another matter), and it received eight Oscar nominations and a prize at the Avoriaz film festival. However, this essentially popular success also aroused the suspicion of many high-brow film fans, including that of many admirers of *Eraserhead*. For *The Elephant Man* is outwardly traditional (mistaken for 'conventional'), a sentimental, tear-jerking film which one would not have expected from Lynch and which therefore aroused distrust. Certain critics would go so far as to call the film 'abject', seeing in it a defence of bourgeois self-righteousness and class hate directed against the people, about which more anon. In any case, Lynch did not disown his creation: 'I think I did the best job that could be done. And I didn't compromise except maybe two or three times, but no more than that.'[12] Was Lynch ruined by his commercial film début?

4

After the credits, *The Elephant Man* opens with a series of dream-like images and sounds evoking John Merrick's birth. Large eyes look out at the spectator to the melody of a musical box. A zoom-out reveals that the eyes belong to a photographic portrait of a woman. The atmosphere becomes dramatic as images of elephants, monsters of a deformed, confused texture with their wrinkled skin clearly displayed, advance towards the camera. A woman lying on the ground screams and shakes her head back and forth, and a trumpeting seems to issue from her mouth. A cross-fade suggests the passing of time. Then we hear a baby crying as we see the image of a little, white mushroom cloud of smoke – a strange, expressive visual idea for a life being born.

Suddenly, an explosion of sound and light produces a brutal shock. We are at a working-class fair. An upper-class man is taking a stroll when a curtain

The Elephant Man

attracts his attention. The man enters a gallery of monsters through a door marked 'no entry.' The action is now under way. Throughout the beginning of the film, our curiosity will accompany that of Frederick Treves, the respected, humane surgeon. Does he act out of morbid curiosity, a desire to impress his colleagues by discovering a rare specimen, or compassion for his fellow man? We will never really know and, in truth, the absence of a psychological explanation is not a problem. Anthony Hopkins's lively, concentrated acting provides motives enough. Playing on a certain contrast between his rapid, frank elocution and the perpetually moist, attentive look of his pale eyes, Hopkins conveys a child's avid curiosity before an enigma and a mystery. He is impatient to see a so-called elephant man, a sight apparently so upsetting that the exhibitor, Bytes, is constantly being driven away from fairs. Treves succeeds in arranging a private showing and the sight of the elephant man's features, which until now had been behind a curtain or invisible in the shadows, causes a tear which he hardly notices to roll down his cheek (but we, the spectators, are not yet allowed to see them). Treves has Merrick brought to the hospital for an examination, but does not succeed in getting him to speak. Treves then presents him to his colleagues as an interesting case and sends him back to Bytes. The story could end there.

However, when Treves learns that Bytes has cruelly beaten the creature, he decides to take Merrick away from his tormentor and provide him with a garret room. The hospital's director, Carr Gomm (Sir John Gielgud), is understanding but also fears that it may be wrong to admit an incurable patient. A young nurse sent with a tray of food for 'the patient in the isolation ward' opens the door and screams. A brief shot finally reveals the monster's face to us for the first time, and shows that he is as frightened, if not more so, than those who see him. What we have in fact encountered, with a large, disproportioned head and John Hurt's sad eyes, is not a monster but a child. He is as frightened as a child, he listens docilely to what he is told, and he generally behaves like a child. The script thus seems bound for a prematurely happy ending.

At this point, the hospital's night porter, a rough, cynical man, makes his entrance. The porter realises that there is money to be made in clandestine showings of the monster. As a result, the more the elephant man's official fate becomes settled, the more his nights become tormented as the porter arranges visits for men and women who pay money to get their thrills, including sexual ones, in seeing him and who plunge him deeper into his sense of difference and ugliness.

It is worth noting that Merrick, who in the meantime has shown himself capable of speech, does not mention these nocturnal nightmares to Treves, thus heightening the spectator's sense of day and night as two separate worlds, each with its own laws. Whereas night is the realm of the all-powerful porter with his set of keys, day belongs to decent people. Indeed, the scriptwriters carefully kept the two worlds apart until the scene where the elephant man is snatched from the hospital. In the diurnal world, Merrick is loved by everyone. He displays the delicacy of his feelings and his knowledge of the Bible, and he is invited to Treves's home. He becomes an attraction in London's high society. As a crowning touch, he is offered a royal pension for life. However, at night, his sleep is heavy and fitful, beset by nightmares and the visitors haunting him. This alternation works only because Lynch aggrandises the night porter's apparition in a beautiful silent scene which is both theatrical and operatic. The scene serves as a kind of vestibule through which we enter into this hellish back-and-forth, day–night contrasting oscillation.

Finally, after a night when he is treated in a particularly horrid manner, the elephant man allows himself to be led away by his former master and he vanishes without leaving a word. We next find Bytes and Merrick at a fair in Ostend where the sordid spectacle of the elephant man, sick and abused by a Bytes more drunken than ever, meets with no success. In the face of this cruelty, a dwarf, a lion-man and a giant join together to free Merrick and to pay his ticket home. Wearing his pilgrim's garb once again (a cape beneath which he limps, his cowl with a single square opening, a shapeless, laughable cap on his head and a staff), Merrick is harassed by a band of children at the London railway station, then chased by the crowd for having knocked over a little girl as he fled. In the toilet where he is finally cornered, he screams for the first time in revolt. It is a terribly moving roar: 'I'm not an elephant! I am not an animal! I am a human being ... '

Treves is informed of the incident and recovers his friend. The elephant man is back at home but he does not have long to live and his friends seek to make his last hours easier. He attends a pantomime which actress Madge Kendall dedicates to him, is applauded by the audience and then, at peace after a final conversation with Treves, decides to sleep lying down for the first time. We know that this will be his death, and he carries out the ritual of his last rest to the sound of Barber's *Adagio*.

The script thus presents a classical construction in three acts: the discovery of the elephant man; his stay in the hospital and his gradual, not unambiguous admission into a society which craves, as Serge Daney[9] put it so well, to look at itself in his eyes; then, after his last torment, he dies. These stations of the cross are punctuated by three occasions when he is asked to stand up: first as the freak at the fair, then as a medical phenomenon before an amphitheatre full of doctors and, lastly, at the theatre where he is summoned to receive the crowd's acclamations. The last occasion is the most troubling, for no one knows exactly why or what they are applauding!

Lynch with John Hurt during the filming of *The Elephant Man*

5

For what could the film be taken to task, from the moral standpoint? To begin with, one might object to the fact that Merrick is not only passive but that, instead of accepting his monstrousness, he aspires to one thing only: normality, right-thinking, bourgeois normality. This aspiration drives many scenes animated by a special kind of humour. For example, when Merrick finally leaves behind his filthy rags and the hospital gown, he parades in a handsome suit with a waistcoat and a watch, receiving the nurses' compliments and, once he is alone, miming a genteel conversation, brimming with the pleasure of being respectable. This zeal for being like others, to sleep like everyone else and to take tea like everyone else, is overwhelming. Though Merrick's submissiveness may be frustrating, we cannot criticise him for not revolting or, rather, for being someone who, in his only moment of revolt, screams his desire to be like everyone else, 'a human being.' Particularly in countries where racism is rife, this is the legitimate claim of millions of people who aspire to the right to be considered ordinary men and women. Merrick's case is moving not because it is morally exemplary, but because it is true.

Some viewers have been disturbed by the film's portrait of the lower classes with their coarse laughter at the hero's deformity, their excitement at seeing him, and so on. However, the film makes no judgments. The lower classes with their uncouth, rough characters, are treated in a Dickensian vein. The people who go to see the elephant man are not especially bad; they are like us. They are us. The distinguished but morbid curiosity of right-thinking people is constantly paralleled in the script by the more direct curiosity of others, and both reactions are shown to be of the same nature. In a beautiful scene, showing once again, through Wendy Hiller's performance, how in the West only the English cinema manages to offer a decent image, neither bland nor demagogic, of the popular classes and of ordinary folk, the nurse protests to Treves, with all the good sense and compassion she can muster, against the unseemly flow of distinguished thrill-seekers in search of sensation. In fact, all the women employees at the hospital are depicted with humanity and tenderness. Later, when a furious Treves goes to find the porter in search of information about Merrick, we are not presented with a conflict between good and bad, but between two men of different social classes, one of whom, the surgeon, is so sure of being in the right that he refuses to hear what the other has to say. It should also not be forgotten that on the hospital board there is an unpleasant figure who argues against Merrick's admission.

Nevertheless, if the film creates the impression of looking down on ordinary folk and of aspiring to smug bourgeois normality, an impression shared even by the film's admirers, and if this is not based on the script's literal content, where does it come from? The reason may be that Lynch is clearly interested in the story's potential for contrast and parallelism on mythical and symbolic levels, which leads him to make maximum use of, and thus perhaps to ratify, social difference as a divisive force. At the same time, however, his vision does not bespeak any moral condemnation.

In any case, *The Elephant Man* does not make John Merrick into a sacrificial victim like, for instance, Quasimodo, since he dies in bed. Nor is he presented as a Promethean rebel. Perhaps this is the troubling point: Lynch's lack of respect for the rather questionable tradition which refuses to those who are not like everyone else the right to ordinary anonymity.

6

The Elephant Man is also a great film made collectively. It would be unjust to overlook the contribution of the actors, especially John Hurt. No doubt there are those who, reasoning like some of the film's characters, will see only appearances and object that an actor wearing layers of moulded plastic on his head, with two holes for his eyes and another for his mouth, is closer to a walking special effect than a competitor for an Oscar. However, such an attitude overlooks the actor's main resource in sound films: the voice! Without any technical artifice, Hurt gives Merrick an astonishing falsetto which combines the laboured speech of the handicapped, the plaintive intonations of a whiny child and, once the elephant man has become fashionable, the accents of high society. The unusualness of this mixture contributes greatly to the film. In addition, the naturalness and rhythm of Hurt's gestures are impressive.

Anthony Hopkins's remarkable performance in the role of Treves is simple and transparent enough to provide a neutral point of identification for the spectator. When Freddie Jones shows him the monster, Hopkins's intense gaze and protruding tongue express his childlike fascination very well. Speaking in short, dry sentences, pausing in between as if thinking all the time, his speech rhythm focuses all attention on what he sees. It is via Hopkins that we construct our own look at the elephant man. Freddie Jones (whom Fellini would soon afterwards employ again as the showman-narrator of *E la nave va*, 1983) plays an epic Bytes, making him into a Micawber-like character. His way of keeping on his feet like a dignified drunk is grandiose.

All these characters have something in common: they seem prey to an inner trembling, making the likes of Mrs Kendal, Carr Gomm and the porter seem cold and serene by comparison. Merrick trembles with terror, convulsed by fear of his master and the porter. Treves trembles with morbid curiosity and juvenile fascination; Bytes from drink and nervousness. This intense, compacted agitation, enhanced by the rigorous simplicity of the frame and the ineluctable rhythm of the shooting script, gives the film the Lynch touch. It is more visible and characteristic here than in *Eraserhead*: it is the art of filming with great intensity someone who just stands there, riveted.

7

The simplicity of the shots, which some could mistake for stiffness and classicism, is thus a way of preserving a mythic dimension. In *The Elephant Man*, Lynch creates an atmosphere of ritual theatre frozen to the spot. Of course, he is helped by the acting of John Hurt who, underneath his make-up, is reduced to a kind of talking marionette recalling the Japanese puppet theatre, with Treves and Bytes as his manipulators. Thanks to the actors and the space they create through changes of vocal register and their judiciously timed pauses, we remain glued to the show throughout the film. Freddie Jones sets the tone by theatricalising all his scenes, even those in which Merrick alone forms his audience, as in the scene in which he recovers Merrick and emphatically announces, with dramatic pauses, that they are to leave. The film's dramatic high points are also presented 'straight' as *coups de théâtre*, underscored by the rhythmic pattern of the scenes, leaving the spectator the time to react and to become aware of his or her reaction. This oscillation between the film and the audience seems to have disturbed some cinephiles, as if it were an undue constraint on their sensibility. However, *The Elephant Man* forms part of popular cinema, using techniques which are akin to a kind of theatre in close-up. What might be called discomfiture shots are especially important here, for they emphasise a character's undoing simply by holding a shot of his or her reaction, making the character into a public target, as in the shot of the dislikeable Broadneck.

The editing is totally literal. There are no ellipses. What is spoken about is shown. What a character sees either appears or is clearly designated as not shown. All the procedures are openly presented. *The Elephant Man* is also a film with timing; it breathes. Pathos is maintained by the concatenation of numerous short sequences ending with fade-outs, often in the middle of a situation, rather like finishing scenes with questioning suspension points. Given the continuous emotional tension maintained by the film, compensating for the slightness of the script, these fade-outs are deployed as if to coincide with the spectator's rising tears, as when one seeks

The Elephant Man

out a dark corner to weep in. An example of this is the scene where Merrick is invited to his protector's house and Treves's wife is on the verge of tears (one might consider such weeping as a cheap appeal to the spectator's emotions, but it is consistent with the sensibilities of the period). When Merrick speaks of his mother and of her chagrin at his birth, Treves's wife breaks down. Merrick offers her a handkerchief and says, 'Please.' A fade-out rapidly closes the scene on this word, as if the spectator had been offered a handkerchief for comfort. Another example is Merrick's nonplussed 'I am?' when the coquettish actress calls him a Romeo; or when Treves in a fit of conscience asks, 'Am I a good man or am I a bad man?' To each question, the shooting script answers with a fade-out which works like a dark mirror, deflecting the question back on the spectator.

The experience of many spectators, and my own as well, confirms that *The Elephant Man* is one of the most effective tear-jerkers since the invention of the cinema. I think this is due less to the use of cheap trickery (Merrick experiences fewer calamities than many other characters in the film) than to the fact that Lynch and his actors succeed in working us over, using rhythms, glances and tones of voice which capture the cruel gentleness of childhood. From the very first image after the credits, the woman's eyes which strike us to the quick, *The Elephant Man* is a film of faces, down to its very object of suspense: we are impatient to discover the elephant man's head, anxious to read something in his eyes. Many sequences of the film end with questioning, surprised, altered faces and, by way of the many low-angle shots, we become like children clinging to the faces which represent all the power and wisdom available to us, and whose tensions affect us directly. These faces are portraits in which the cameraman has captured a change that disturbs us. By virtue of its subject, the film contains many faces reacting to the sight of Merrick, faces at a loss, excited, illuminated or even ecstatic with fascination. When Anne Treves, deeply disturbed at the sight of the elephant man, turns towards her husband like a little girl calling for help, we too become children overwhelmed by the sight of their parents in difficulty. In this sense, Lynch's use of reaction shots, rather than being upsetting or transgressive, seems unaware of the implicit code of honour adopted by a certain form of modernism which rejects such shots precisely because they are seen as inviting an unwelcome complicity between the screen and the audience.

8

What may appear paradoxical is that Lynch made a popular film with extremely sophisticated actors. On the basis of *The Elephant Man* and especially the films which followed, it seems that after his initial, difficult encounter with a new way of working, Lynch learned an enormous amount from his actors. Their sense of stylisation and distance, their exploration of different vocal registers (English actors are not afraid to speak in falsettos), offered Lynch a precious model. He came away with an interest in non-naturalistic, Shakespearean forms of speech, a style of speaking mobilising a wide range of types of articulation, idioms and vocal textures which he explored in *Dune*, with the coaching of Maggie Anderson, and in *Blue Velvet*.

The special alchemy of *The Elephant Man* lies in its marriage between a subtle, advanced acting style and an archaic cinematographic language. As for the direction, regardless of how much Freddie Francis and Mel Brooks contributed, its profound wisdom resides in the decision to construct a resonating box for this acting style, to provide a frame which is open and flexible enough not to stifle it yet resistant and taut enough to make it resound and lift it to another dimension. Indeed, what one might call the 'frame' of this film is more than just the frame of the image on the screen: it takes in the entire scene, bounded by the above-mentioned fade-outs. The sound edits, the actors' pauses between certain sentences or gestures, everything in the film contributes to this taut frame-effect, so that the performative idioms and the situations resound like beats on a membrane stretched to just the right tension, creating pure tones. With *The Elephant Man*, a film mercifully devoid of auteurial effects, Lynch confirms his status as a genuine artist in the sense that his choices are not inflected by a concern to appear intelligent and that he shows himself muture enough to listen to his subject and his instruments (the actors), making himself passively receptive to his theme so that the film may transcend him. *Eraserhead*, *Blue Velvet*, *Wild at Heart* and *Fire Walk with Me* are all films which Lynch actively sought to make. *The Elephant Man* and *Dune* were films which circumstances foisted upon him. Does that make them less interesting? I do not think so.

9

The considerable, worldwide success of *The Elephant Man* made Lynch into a popular figure. Interviewers were struck by his rosy-cheeked, well-behaved exterior and his studied dress sense. His taste was discovered for baggy tan trousers and white shirts buttoned at the neck without a tie (in the days of *Eraserhead* he wore only three ties!). He would later enhance his style by adding a cap with a long beak like the one Sailor and Lula's boy would wear in *Wild at Heart*. The cap gives him the profile of one of his mascots, the duck.

Stories made the rounds about his known pastimes and his innocent eccentricities: building cabins and dissecting animals, collecting dead flies tacked on panels, amassing piles of rubbish (including used chewing gum) for use in sculptures, and so on. Mel Brooks's description of him as 'a

Lynch during the production of *The Elephant Man*

James Stewart from Mars' was widely repeated. Several years later, another side of Lynch would come to the fore: the protective, reassuring big brother, very kind while shooting. As a joke, he started adding 'Eagle Scout' to his birth date on biographies, so that critics mistook it for his place of birth. His actors appreciate the way he trusts and counts on them, not contenting himself with the technical side of directing while leaving them to fend for themselves. This mutual attachment, institutionalised through his Bergmanesque taste for using the same actors over and over again, goes beyond the conventional compliments which actors and directors pay one another in press books and promotional appearances. All of this is worth recalling in so far as it offsets the media image of Lynch as obsessed with style and pyrotechnics, deflecting attention from his films, as it did most notably at the release of *Fire Walk with Me*, when it overshadowed the most exciting aspect of the work: the Bergman-like solo for one character and its performer.

10

Given both the critical and the worldwide public success of *The Elephant Man*, one may wonder why Lynch did not continue with Brooksfilms. Did Mel Brooks keep too close an eye on the editing of the film? Or did the public failure of *History of the World Part I* lead Brooks to reduce his production plans? In any event, Lynch next considered projects with fellow independent film-makers George Lucas and Francis Ford Coppola. In 1981, Lucas proposed that Lynch direct the third episode of the first *Star Wars* trilogy, *Return of the Jedi* (1983). This was a sign of esteem and confidence, in view of the financial as well as the emotional stakes riding on this third episode which would have to match the global success of the first two. Lucas's choice may seem surprising, because in *Star Wars* (1977) and *The Empire Strikes Back* (1980), the emphasis had been on the brio with which scenes were linked to each other and on the light-heartedness of the overall tone. Judging by his first two features, these two qualities were the opposite of Lynch's. Before Lucas, science-fiction films (there had been excellent productions in the 1950s) always waxed solemn as soon as the action moved into space, as if film-makers were afraid of trivialising space travel. *Star Wars* broke with this pattern by making spaceships throb like Formula One racing cars. But Lucas's proposition suggests that along with the obligatory purple passages, he wished to give the third episode a graver tone in line with the mellowing of the characters and the trials they had undergone. In the event, Lynch refused and the third episode was finally directed by Christian Marquand. The reasons given by Lynch were perfectly clear and lucid. To begin with, he did not care to direct a sequel, which would require him to use and respect characters who had already been defined. Furthermore, it would not have been his film but, in large part, Lucas's.

This was the period when Francis Ford Coppola, riding high on the success of *The Godfather* (1972), *The Godfather Part II* (1974) and *Apocalypse Now* (1979), sought to revolutionise the process of shooting films and to draw all of the most interesting directors into his company, Zoetrope. In this extraordinary period, Wim Wenders, Hans-Jürgen Syberberg, Werner Herzog and Dusan Makavejev all crossed paths in Coppola's Napa Valley home near San Francisco. Coppola invited Lynch as well, who proposed his *Ronnie Rocket* project, the story of 'a little three-foot guy with sixty-cycle alternating current electricity and physical problems.' When Zoetrope Studios went bankrupt in 1981 after the flop of the beautiful *One from the Heart* (1982), Coppola had to abandon all these projects. However, it was at Coppola's home that Lynch met Sting, known at that time mainly as the lead singer of the Police though he had already acted in films.

Several months after the Coppola episode, news broke which was of great moment to fans of *Eraserhead* and *The Elephant Man* as well as to the devotees of the most famous and widely sold science-fiction novel. David Lynch was to direct *Dune*. Lynch subsequently hired Sting for the role of Feyd Rautha in the film.

11

The unfinished projects concerning *Dune* could furnish a novel in themselves, and their cost would have been enough to make three films. The American author of *Dune*, Frank Herbert, certainly could not have foreseen this fate when he began publishing his saga in three episodes in the science-fiction magazine *Analog*. He later developed and expanded the narrative for publication as a book and the film is generally faithful to this later text, millions of copies of which were sold throughout the world.

The novel is set in a distant future when humanity has spread throughout space. The Emperor of the Known Universe, Shaddam IV, has to contend with the powerful Guild navigators. Dune, also called Arrakis, is a desert planet of considerable importance both to the Guild and to the inhabited universe because its sandy soil contains a wondrous spice which confers the gift of foresight on its users ... along with perfectly blue eyes. Another attraction is the presence of 'sandworms' which can be several hundred metres long. A proud, unsubdued people called the Fremen live on Arrakis and they believe in the coming of a Messiah who will restore them to their rightful place and re-establish the true faith. However, and this is where *Dune* criticises the Messianic myth it deploys, this belief was implanted on Dune by Bene Gesserit, a secret women's order, to manipulate the native population. The goal was to use genetic selection to produce one single perfect male with fantastic psychic powers, the Kwisatz Haderach. As the novel opens, we learn that Jessica, the wife of one of the clan chiefs, has violated the rules of the order's Reverend Mother by not giving birth to a girl. Out of love for her husband Duke Leto, Jessica has a boy. The way the sex is controlled is not explained. It is clear that the young man conceived in violation of the rules, Paul, who receives the finest physical and psychic training, will become the famous Kwisatz Haderach after enduring many trials.

Paul is pursued by the Harkonnen clan. With the help of a traitor, they kill his father and he is abandoned with his mother on the planet of the spice. Thanks to his special training and Jessica's advice, Paul is recognised by the Fremen as the Messiah. He leads them in war against the Empire by sabotaging the spice mines, the basis of the galaxy's commercial system. In the end, he becomes part of the imperial family by marrying the Emperor's daughter, Irulan, who writes the account of the epic, but not before Paul, renamed Muad'dib by his Fremen troops, undergoes the experience of the spice and develops hidden powers. He also receives a little sister, born in the spice (rather like Obelix falling into the magic potion when he was little in the *Asterix* comic books) and who risks being far more powerful and bloodthirsty than he is.

Dune's success cannot be explained merely by its heroic plot. After all, heroic fantasies narrating legendary Knights of the Round Table-type tales set in a distant past or future, or on other planets, is a flourishing genre which has known a great many brilliant authors and ambitious stories. *Dune*'s originality lies, first of all, in its obsession with ecology. Arrakis, the planet of sand, is so lacking in rain and water that this life-giving element becomes both a vital, daily preoccupation and an important religious and symbolic motif. To keep from drying up and perishing in the desert, the Fremen wear special clothes, 'stillsuits', which use a system of taps and pipes to recover, filter and recycle bodily discharges.

A second virtue is certainly the book's echoing of themes from the 60s and 70s. The spice puts one in mind of oil on account of its economic implications, and likewise drugs, especially LSD. This is why, when the film was released in 1984, some people naïvely wondered if the story was dated, as if drugs and ecological concerns were an invention of the 60s and had ceased to be relevant.

A third (and in my opinion the most profound) reason involves Herbert's masterful and magical use of names in blends which are both familiar (issuing from known, especially Muslim, cultures) and strange. Even the idea of giving two different names to the planet of spice, the one providing the book's title being the one used less frequently, is an ingenious stroke which

Dune

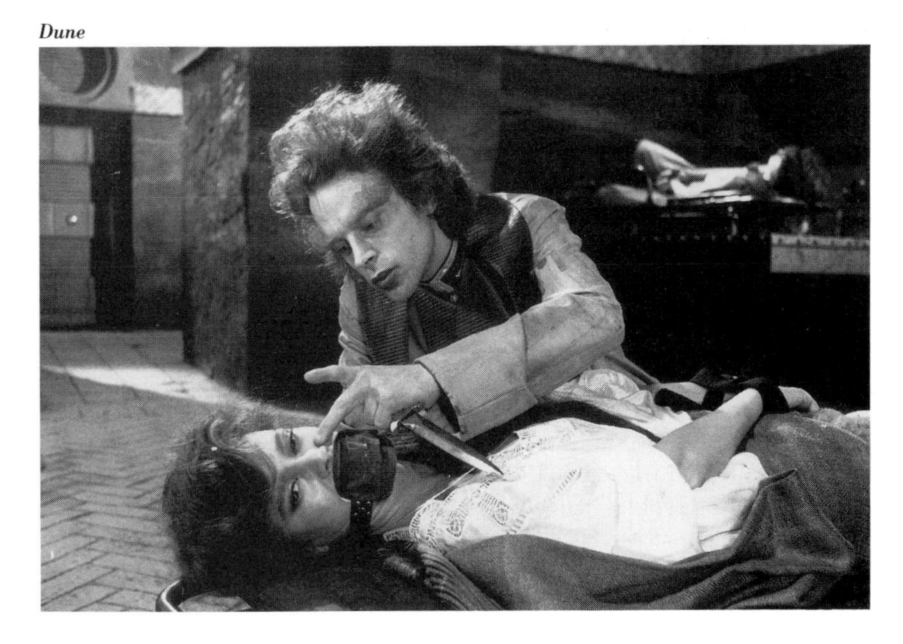

sparks the imagination. For the human mind, the distance between two names for the same thing or the same person is a far greater space than all the light-years between galaxies.

12

The success of his first novel, which was long in coming but then turned out to be global, allowed Frank Herbert to write a number of sequels, *Dune Messiah* and *The Children of Dune*. Had Lynch's film been a success, these works would have provided a *Dune II*, *Dune III*, and so on. In 1975, after a first attempt at an adaptation failed, the director Alejandro Jodorowsky, much in vogue at the time, began work on a project with the French producer Michel Seydoux. Jodorowsky had big plans. He wished to hire Dali to design the sets and to play the emperor. He also wanted to cast Orson Welles, Gloria Swanson, Mick Jagger and Alain Delon. Artists who would later be involved in Ridley Scott's *Alien* (1979), such as Möbius and the sculptor Giger, were also contacted. Two million dollars were spent on the project but Hollywood then dropped out and Dali quarrelled with Jodorowsky.

In 1978, Dino de Laurentiis acquired the rights to the novel. He contacted Ridley Scott to direct the film, and Scott set Randolph Wurlitzer, who had written Monte Hellman's *Two Lane Blacktop* (1971), to work on the script. Rumour has it that Wurlitzer's adaptation thickened the plot by adding incest between Paul and his mother. In the official account, the project was scrapped because the script was never completed, and Ridley Scott began work on *Blade Runner* (1982). Raffaella de Laurentiis, the producer's daughter, took over the project for her father's company. She had discovered *The Elephant Man* which moved her so intensely that she conceived of a *Dune* that would be utterly different from the large-budget science-fiction films which flourished in the wake of *Star Wars*'s success. *Dune* would be a film with characters and feelings.

Lynch claims that when he was first contacted, he did not even know the title of Herbert's novel and when he heard the name for the first time, he mistook it for the woman's name 'June'. He negotiated a contract binding him personally to direct three successive Dunes, with the proviso that de Laurentiis help him produce *Blue Velvet* and *Ronnie Rocket*. The producer seems to have been in an optimistic mood, signing Kyle MacLachlan, the actor cast in the role of Paul, for no less than five films.

Pre-production started in 1981 and Lynch began work on the script with his two associates from *The Elephant Man*. A number of versions were drafted, but recast each time for being too long, or because Bergren and de Vore's conception differed from Lynch's. Lynch produced the next three drafts himself, and the last of these was accepted at the end of 1982. At the time, Lynch was also working with producer Richard Roth on a project which he would only direct, later written and directed by Michael Mann: an adaptation of Thomas Harris's thriller *Manhunter* (1986). This film had the distinction of presenting for the first time the serial killer of *Silence of the Lambs* (1991), the cannibalistic psychiatrist Hannibal Lecter, whom Anthony Hopkins would portray in the film by Jonathan Demme. According to some sources, Lynch was initially to have made *Blue Velvet* with Roth.

It may seem surprising that a novice scriptwriter and a young director like Lynch were left to work by themselves on a project as risky as the high-cost adaptation of a world-famous bestseller. It would appear that all the shenanigans around the novel had induced a kind of lassitude, while at the same time Lynch's personal charisma encouraged people to put their trust in him. 'I'm doing this film for David Lynch' was a line heard more than once in interviews of the period.

13

Lynch has always said that, in order not to disappoint its fans, he aimed to condense the essentials of the novel into the film. Nevertheless, in his adaptation a certain number of the book's important elements are treated rather allusively. Some have been attenuated or have simply been transposed. These changes reveal much about his approach to the story. The most important one of these modifications is what might be called the 'anti-machine taboo'. *Dune* is set in a society where thinking machines (computers) have been banned after being destroyed in the course of a long-ago holy war. This is the justification for the mission of Bene Gesserit: man must be led to develop certain powers so as to become a 'human computer'. The second modification relates to religion. In the novel it is made very clear that religion is an invention designed to manipulate the masses. However, in the film, this notion that the religious myth has been manufactured is passed over in silence. Everything suggests that Paul and the Bene Gesserit are themselves believers, which makes all the difference. When Paul haughtily declares (in a line borrowed from the novel but to which Lynch accords pride of place, at the end of the film), 'God created Arrakis to train the faithful. One cannot go against the word of God', the film makes his statement sound like an article of faith.

What makes this statement particularly surprising is that there has been little question of God previously. Given the symbolic importance of speech in the film, the use of the word God *in extremis* turns it into a sort of *coup de théâtre*, a clap of thunder with most disturbing reverberations. We suddenly realise that these people are fanatics and that we do not know Lynch's opinion on this. We do not even know whether he has one. In fact, there is every reason to suppose that Lynch has a religious sensibility, though to my knowledge he has never openly expressed it. Religion is present in many ways, directly or indirectly, in *Eraserhead*, *The Elephant Man*, *Dune*, *Blue Velvet* and *Fire Walk with Me*.

A third aspect which has been attenuated in the film is Bene Gesserit's genetic programme with its obvious racist connotations. One understands the reasons for this omission. When a novel presents such characters, it can also disclose their logic and offer a critique of their actions. The cinema, on the other hand, relying on strategies of direct identification with the characters, inevitably simplifies matters, which means that extra caution is required. In the same way, the complex economic and political system imagined by Herbert was reduced in the film to its simplest expression.

As for the characters, the biggest change involves the young hero's mother. In the novel, she is a pitiless, resolute woman with an influential voice. She is also the book's second most important character, present in a great many scenes narrated from her point of view. She does not hesitate to reprimand, advise and toughen her son. In the film, through a radical reversal, Jessica becomes a gentle woman, a sollicitous mother and wife, and finally a docile and discreet companion in flight.

Consciously or not, on his own or under pressure from a film genre which requires that heroes be raised by men, Lynch played down the key role of women in the book. Symmetrically, he valorised the roles of Paul's father and those of his male teachers. This change is made clear from the outset in the opening scene. The novel opens with women at Paul's bedside deciding his fate (which provided Lynch with a beautiful scene later in the film) whereas the film opens with a summit meeting between the emperor and a mutant navigator. The women are confined to the margins. Lynch did indeed entrust the narration to a woman's voice, even to a woman's face, as if taking up where the last image of *The Elephant Man* left off. However, this discreet narration follows the storyline rather than guides it. And if the film presents with great intensity the trial which the Reverend Mother inflicts on Paul, it is to show all the better that men have again gained the upper hand.

Where Lynch has been most audacious is in the structuring of the story. He devised a kind of spiralling structure, described by him as circular, in which all the information needed to understand the story is given from the start rather than being doled out progressively. Via the voice of the narrating princess we are bombarded straight away with facts and names. Only later, little by little, are the facts allowed to find their meaning and the names their faces. Prior to *Wild at Heart* and *Fire Walk with Me*, *Dune* is thus Lynch's first effort at feature-length, non-linear narration.

In fact, Lynch runs up against the limits of cinema. In *Dune*, the words never quite manage to find an adequate incarnation because they are too laden with symbolism from the outset. For example, the word 'spice' never quite attains and joins with the concrete, recurring image of the black liquid which is its visual equivalent, maliciously compared by some to a coffee advertisement. Lynch took an enormous but admirable risk when he banked on the encounter between words and image-symbols.

The central axis of what, in an interview on the film's release, he called his circular construction is indicative of his highly abstract reading of the novel. No one else would have thought of it quite in this way: 'In *Dune* there is a basic question: what makes the universe function? What exactly are the relations between people and what connects them to Paul? The emperor wants to get rid of Paul and Paul finds out about this. He is surrounded by spies who relate to various people. The spies provide the unity linking up all the parts. They are responsible for the conspiracy and also for Paul's ascent and awakening.'[10] The idea of linkage is interesting and totally Lynchian, even though it must be admitted that the film hardly achieves it. In any case, Lynch's construction is based on a desire to make literal use of the cinema, with recurring images, sentences and words which obsess Paul without his knowing what they mean and which he will discover only as his destiny unfolds: an open hand (an image added by Lynch), the second Moon of Arrakis, a drop of spice and faces speaking mystery-sentences to him (the beautiful Sean Young says to him, 'Tell me of your home world, Uzul,' when he does not know that one day he will have to use that name). The main risk of such a procedure, actually rather adroitly overcome, is that it comes close to something that has always posed grave dangers to cinema because it evokes the structure of trailers, and that is the literal reuse at different moments of the film of one particular image or micro-scene, as if shots, regardless of their surfeit of concrete details, could function as the equivalent of words or notes of music.

Another major innovation, missed by practically all the critics when *Dune* opened, lies in the recurrent use of a generalised inner voice. In general, cinema uses a voice-over to provide part of the narrative in the past tense, to comment on or to call forth other images. It is less common for the inner voice of a character visible on the screen to be audible to us alone, as in a soliloquy or in a theatrical aside, revealing thoughts as he or she acts. It is almost unique for an inner voice to be shared by a number of characters, though this convention is frequently found in comic strips. Why has this procedure never been transferred from comic strips to the screen? The main reason is probably because, in cinema, the voice speaking over images always seems in some way to be guiding or generating them, making the images appear 'subjective' in some cases. Consequently, such a voice tends to be reserved for key characters. Again revealing his primal genius for cinema, Lynch savours and exploits an ambiguity from which others shy away: that of making scenes, shots and faces which are both subjective (meshed in

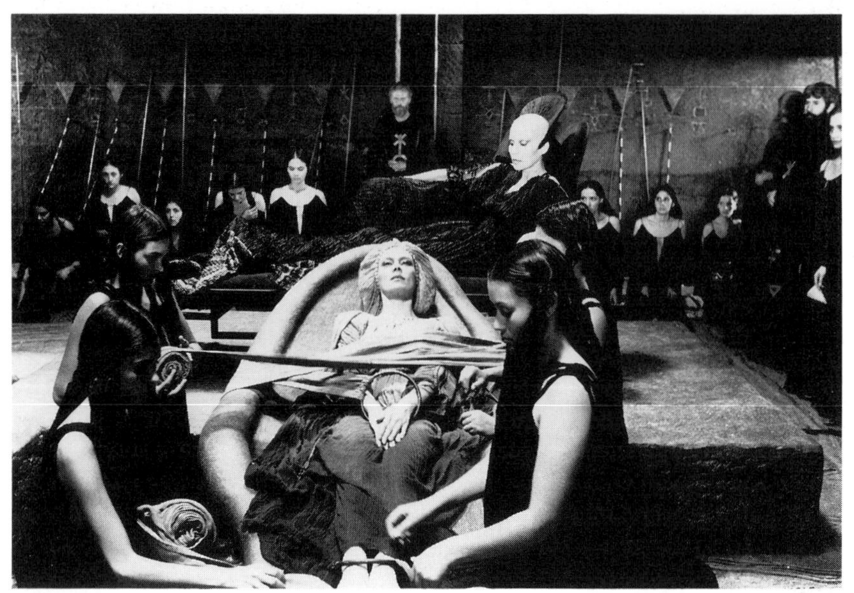

Dune

a character's speech, generated by his or her words) and objective (existing for the senses themselves). He appreciates the vertiginous nesting of levels which arises from the generalisation of narrative voices and, in this case, of thinking voices. In cinema, this generalisation does not have the same resonance as in the homogeneous, purely verbal universe of a novel or a poem, because cinema both generates and destroys elements which are themselves concrete (images, sounds).

Thought-sentences are attributed to characters in Herbert's original novel, but they are distinguished from the rest of the text through the use of italic print. In the film, there is a continuum between the sentences spoken aloud and the inner reflections, without any corresponding sound code to distinguish them. The film's inner voices, often spoken softly, belong to the same space as the externalised voices, thus blurring our relation to reality. The reality on show rests on a discourse proffered as if in a dream. Lynch's intention was indeed to make a dream-film, though this is not to say that he wholly mastered the project. The problem with such a flock of mental voices is that they jam the other voice-over, the traditional narrative voice of Princess Irulan, so that she seems like an intruder, out of place, when she returns an hour after the beginning of the film. The many diegetic voices in *Dune* function as a litany, an incantation and a leitmotiv more than as a plot element. These voices tell us nothing which we could not guess (such as:

'He's going to kill me' or 'I'd better be careful') and often they repeat what we see. The impression of saturation experienced by many spectators when seeing and listening to the film is thus not due to some informational excess since important things are repeated over and over again. On the contrary, what is at issue is a saturation of registers of discourse, a saturation of concepts, not so much because of the quantity of words but their weight. There are simply too many important words. And yet, here, even more than in *The Elephant Man*, Lynch again showed his taste for experimentation within the framework of popular cinema. That is to say, he brought something to the cinema which greatly enriched it.

14

After making his personal adaptation, Lynch needed to actualise it on the screen. As is almost always the case with films of this genre, the contributions of a great many specialists were required. Special effects would be crucial to the film. Raffaella de Laurentiis hired noted artists to construct the sandworms, the various creatures, vehicles and sets. They included Carlo Rambaldi, famous for his work on *E.T.* (1982), Kit West for the mechanical special effects, and the famous Al Whitlock, the veteran creator of mattes, paintings on glass which simulate a gigantic set. He had worked on Hitchcock's *The Birds* (1963). There would be no major problems in any of these departments. On the other hand, the visual effects were a source of many problems. As the crew of Industrial Light and Magic had its hands full with *Return of the Jedi*, the job went to John Dykstra, who had his own studio. After three months of shooting, Dykstra resigned, though the reasons for this are rather unclear. The official explanation was that Raffaella wanted direct control of where money was being spent. She decided to contract with the firm of Van der Veere and, what is more, against the advice of many of her colleagues, to have the special effects produced directly in Mexico where the film was shot. The result was that the film's visuals were not as good as they could have been. From a strictly technical viewpoint, one of the film's weaknesses lies in the often unsuccessful insertion of characters into sets and scale models: the backgrounds are too grainy, the outlines of the inserted characters are too visible, as in the scene where Baron Harkonnen is hurled into the mouth of a sandworm, and so on. Such moments undermine the film's credibility and give rise to a disturbing visual discontinuity when juxtaposed with the chiaroscuro interiors shot by Freddie Francis.

Anthony Masters, an English designer, was assigned the onerous job of production designer. The job was particularly difficult because his instructions amounted to nothing less than a total remodelling of the imagery of the science-fiction genre while avoiding a high-tech style. After much research and an inspirational study trip to Venice, Lynch and Masters decided to create the unknown from a novel combination of the known. They relied on four styles: Venetian, Egyptian, Old German and Victorian Baroque, the latter appearing on the planet of Giedi Prime with the smoky industrial landscape Lynch loves so much. These often attractive sets were a problem not because of the mix of styles but because of construction difficulties. For better and for worse, this problem was to have repercussions on the very aesthetics of the film.

When Freddie Francis arrived at the studio in Churubusco, he discovered to his horror that the sets had been constructed as solid, whole pieces rather than as structures that could easily be taken apart. This meant that they could not be moved to allow for the positioning of cameras and lights. Francis's solution was to light the set as if it were a natural location, using less light and a greater diaphragm opening. Then came the second stroke of bad luck. When the cameras arrived at the studio, it turned out that they could not be used in that way, so that it became necessary again to deploy a full lighting plan. Given the way the sets had been constructed, this created enormous problems for the positioning of the lights, for moving the cameras and for changing the angles of shots. The result is obvious from the very first scenes. Even lay spectators must have been intuitively aware that, for instance, the throne room and its crowd of actors is constantly filmed from ground level, without any advantage being taken of the set's volume or expanse. This unexpected obstruction was not entirely negative. It did affect the film's success but it also contributed to the film's stylistic originality. In many scenes, the sets necessitated a frontal, static filming style, endowing the shots with a certain archaic force recalling Egyptian wall paintings, even if that kind of stylised stiffness was the last thing the public expected to see in such a film. To be honest, it is unlikely that Lynch managed to transform these last-minute problems into a deliberate and coherent style, though it is safe to assume that, had the sets and the equipment allowed him to do so, he would have filmed certain scenes in a less monotonous manner.

The Rembrandt or Caravaggio style of lighting was also criticised for being incompatible with a film for wide audiences, yet, largely thanks to the talent of Freddie Francis, the golden, warm and glowing tonalities of *Dune* make it a splendid film to see. Its pictorial quality was based on the use of a technique which was a Francis's speciality: 'Lightflex', which endows shadows and low lighting with a distinctive colour and unifies the image as a whole, as if covered by a layer of varnish. The facial close-ups are especially beautiful because Lightflex frees them from the harshness which current shooting techniques and film stock often inflict.

As for the costumes, which are a jumble of known historical and military styles, their design was essentially that of Bob Ringwood, who had worked on John Boorman's *Excalibur* (1981). Ringwood followed Lynch's sketches while Lynch himself took responsibility for a major and perhaps unfortunate although coherent choice. The Fremen were deprived of the noble, flowing robes which Herbert had imagined on the basis of nomadic peoples' mode of dress. Their stillsuits were instead conceived as close-fitting costumes, like a second, dark skin displaying the equivalent of exposed muscles. The stillsuits give the Fremen as a group a rather unspectacular appearance. They look like clumsy, helpless grub-worms, shrunken by the dark shades of their outfits which are hardly in keeping with the requirements of a warm country. The stillsuits are likewise unattractive for the women, despite the efforts made to adapt the costumes to the curves of breasts and long flowing hair. It was as though Lynch, by refusing to use robes, had sought to exaggerate these warriors' virility, as if any hint of a cape or cloth would necessarily connote femininity.

15

Finding an actor to play Paul who would satisfy *Dune*'s millions of readers was as crucial an affair as finding a Scarlett for *Gone with the Wind* (1939). The choice made by the creator of *Eraserhead* was a great surprise, for he chose neither a punk nor a hippie, nor even a muscular hero, but a young

Dune

man with a clean, smooth, all-American face, a face which had not yet become an emblem in the role of Dale Cooper. Kyle MacLachlan had read and loved *Dune* when he was fifteen, identifying himself with the main character. Having been noticed by a casting agent, he was the only actor selected from the western United States, while the other headhunters were busily shuttling between New York and Chicago. MacLachlan had played in repertory companies and small-town theatres for six years. *Dune* was to be his first film. It was a good choice. Moving beyond his 'respectful son' looks, MacLachlan excellently and accurately plays the role of Paul, being juvenile when he needs to be or hard and imperative, with a deep understanding for his physique and an unemphatic quality.

Lynch apparently regretted at one point that MacLachlan had not been cast in the right role. However, the casting did suit the story. Paul is not a rebel but a youth who carries out a programme for which he has been chosen and conditioned. Much was also made of a certain physical resemblance with Lynch and there was talk of MacLachlan being his *alter ego*. The rest of the numerous cast is so full of famous names that the star value of any one of them gets lost in the crowd if not by the brevity of their appearance. Big names such as Max von Sydow or Sylvana Mangano were reduced to cameo roles. There are also survivors from *The Elephant Man* and *Eraserhead*, such as Freddie Jones and Jack Nance, both also underemployed. Lynch's habit of using actors in roles which contrast with their earlier appearances in fact dates from *Dune*, his third feature. The role of Dr Yueh, the pathetic traitor who is also the victim of the story, was to be played by John Hurt, except that this time his face would be visible. When Hurt proved to be unavailable, he was replaced by Dean Stockwell, who was then to reappear in *Blue Velvet*, and so on.

The most striking male role, apart from the hero, is that of Baron Harkonnen (Kenneth McMillan), not only because of the suspension harness which enables his obese body to float in mid-air and paradoxically endows him with a lightness envied by the other actors, but also because of the horrible acts which Lynch has him commit, the disgusting skin diseases which afflict him and the excessive, thunderous, Falstaffian register of his acting. He is Lynch's first gleefully bad guy, preceding Bobby Peru in *Wild at Heart*, Bob in *Twin Peaks* and perhaps even the darker and more tormented Frank Booth in *Blue Velvet*. The film excellently plays on the contrast between the character's physical and moral horror, and the liveliness of his clear, human eyes. He is thus the only (or almost the only) character which avoids being a melancholic, distant 'animated portrait', a condition besetting the film's other characters, including that of the young lead's doomed father.

16

In March 1983, demonstrating his support for the project, Frank Herbert in person operated the clapper board for the first shots of a film that would take a year to shoot. The Churubusco studios in Mexico were chosen for the production because labour and extras were cheaper than in the United States, and because it was a large studio with six stages which would have closed down but for the simultaneous production there of *Dune* and another de Laurentiis film, Richard Fleischer's *Conan the Destroyer* (1984). In addition, the desert landscapes required for the scenes on Arrakis were only an hour and a half's drive from the studios. A Mexican stadium and a natural wall of lava also served as locations for some scenes. The budget for the film was between $40 million and $45 million, a record at the time but which has been broken since.

The disadvantages can be guessed: local problems (bribery, extortion of money by customs officials) and the infamous pollution of a city located at an altitude of 2000 metres, inflicting various illnesses on cast and crew during the shooting. Lynch had the idea of making many of the costumes out of rubber, a material which fascinates him. They were heavy to wear and very warm, causing extreme discomfort and numerous bouts of indisposition. There were also the usual problems for this kind of large production: a complex shooting schedule, the organisation of the ten thousand extras obtained from the Mexican army, and so on.

Relations between the young Raffaella de Laurentiis and Lynch were not always smooth. She would later describe them as 'a three- or four-year marriage with a serious argument every three or four months'.[3] She took pleasure in the simultaneous shooting of *Conan the Destroyer* and *Dune*, though it disturbed the respective directors, veteran Richard Fleisher and the young Lynch. 'For one scene, on a dune to the right, there was Arnold Schwarzenegger on his horse, horned barbarians and a mammoth's skeleton, while to the left a whole troop of Fremen in their stillsuits were climbing up and racing down the dunes.'[12] According to other sources, such as MacLachlan, simultaneous shootings in the same part of the desert had less picturesque aspects: 'They always needed the lights from one set for use on the other, when it wasn't cameras or things like that. It was a madhouse.'[2]

'What caused the most problems', Raffaella revealed, speaking with less discretion than usual about Lynch, 'was keeping my balance between the two directors, especially with David who was very jealous. If I said to him, "Wait a second, I've got to take care of Richard," he turned blue.'[12] Dino de Laurentiis gave his side in an interview[11] in *Première*, affirming that he had only one conflict with 'his' director. When he requested that a scene be filmed again (the scene was not specified), the story goes that Lynch at first

Dune

refused, then gave in and ended up going to the producer's office to thank him in person.

17

There is a question about how much freedom Lynch actually enjoyed in this enterprise. He has stated that he had every latitude in the casting. He also made the choice of the rock group Toto, which at the time was considered *passé*, a product of the 70s. It should be noted, however, that his choice is in line with the other heroic fantasies for wide audiences which de Laurentiis produced. For instance, the pop group Queen did the music for Mike Hodges's lovely, semi-parodic *Flash Gordon* (1980). The music for *Dune* takes as its leitmotiv an original theme 'purchased' from Brian Eno. The theme is in a minor key with a dark tonality recalling the atmosphere of legends, deliberately devoid of any triumphal overtones. Toto's contribution is uneven. While the group is sometimes given to stereotyped symphonic rock, here the work contains some good floating passages, but the orchestration lacks polish and is insufficiently varied in the course of the film.

Dune's soundscapes and effects are again curiously disappointing, in spite of Alan Splet's collaboration. Although sound plays an important part in the story (vibrations are used to lure the sandworms, and a magic voice to paralyse the enemy), the soundscapes accompanying the action offer nothing out of the ordinary. The sounds are often realistic and concrete, suited to the film's visual style, with its emphasis on concrete, tactile materials like leather, wood, stone, ceramics, and so on. The masterful sound atmosphere of *Eraserhead* and of parts of *The Elephant Man* is lacking, though fortunately the music and the actors' voices generate a grave, peaceful atmosphere. Here too, however, one may wonder whether Lynch was not yielding to external restrictions. As the film was aimed at a fairly general audience, Lynch was forced to cut some gory scenes such as Dr Yueh plunging his hand into a corpse. Among the horrors which he was permitted to keep, one may mention the (homo)sexual immolation scene when Baron Vladimir Harkonnen descends like a vampire on his trembling prey. The heaviest burden, however, seems to have been the restricted length of the film: 'We are trying for two and a half hours. Two and a half hours is a long time for an American movie. I sort of like the European way of making films. I like films like *2001*, too. I like long scenes. I like silences. Stuff like that. It's going to be really tough for me to condense the movie I see into two and a half hours.'[3] *Dune* would bear the mark of this restriction in the form of rhythmic irregularities from one part to the next.

Indeed, it is this bandy-legged construction which the critics attacked when *Dune* was released, describing it as a royal failure, unbalanced in favour of the story's opening, accelerating absurdly in the epic part. Unfortunately, they did not at the same time take stock of the film's narrative originality, failing to distinguish between the scope of the film's ambition and the occasional failure in its implementation. They likewise maintained that the film did not have enough action scenes, and that the form was too esoteric and badly cobbled together.

The much-awaited release of the film took place in the United States around Christmas 1984, and in France in February 1985. The advertisements made great play with the name and image of Sting. From a commercial point of view, it was dangerous to focus the billing on what was after all a minor role, a guest performance of a rock star. Lynch played this trick again in 1992 with David Bowie's brief part in *Fire Walk with Me*. On the whole, *Dune* was both a critical and a commercial failure and thus, in view of the film's cost and the expectations it had aroused, a disaster. Very few critics defended the film or pointed out its unique tone and beautiful passages. In France, however, the film formed part of a science-fiction tidal wave that included John Carpenter's *Starman* (1984), James Cameron's *Terminator* (1984), Peter Hyams's *2010* (1984) and George Miller's *Mad Max II* (1984), all released in the same year. Though *Dune* had the reputation of being a flop, it nevertheless became a major box-office success in France. Given that the novel had not been very widely read in France, that the film had been badly treated by the media and that the supply of films in this genre was quite abundant, it remains a mystery why

600,000 Parisians paid to see the film. In comparison, *Blue Velvet* and *Wild at Heart* drew a far smaller crowd. The inescapable conclusion is that the film's charm worked its own magic.

Later, Lynch expressed some regrets about *Dune*, which he would never defend as a work entirely his own. In particular, he would regret not having made it longer and more abstract, in black and white and with overall artistic control. Henceforth, he would require such control on his films, accepting smaller budgets and a smaller salary in exchange. However, would the film have been better if he had been totally free while making it? Only rank idealists would claim that artistic freedom always results in better art. Every work of art has its own life, which is not necessarily identical with that of later works nor with the views of its author. It can be a sublime, universal work which is beyond its author, who often rejects it and refuses to acknowledge it, especially if the work does not meet with immediate public success. Undeniably, this is the case with *Dune*, at least to some extent.

One thing is certain: Lynch lacks the skill to make pure action scenes. Scores of other film-makers would have been effective. This clumsiness is one of the obvious reasons for the film's public failure throughout the world. The group scenes are often a little absurd, and the stately Fremen look like a troop of extras hired on the spot, clustering in front of the camera with big smiles. Their entrance makes for the only passage in *Dune* which is downright bad. Poorly filmed and hastily edited, the scene shows us these fearsome warriors immediately pledging their allegiance to Paul after a mere semblance of opposition. Similarly, the treatment of the planet Dune and its myth does not work properly. Filming acres of sand did not convey the presence of a true, mythical planet. The basic themes of the book, the heat, the overwhelming force of the sun and even thirst, remain too abstract. The crowning touch is that the functions for which the cumbersome stillsuits were designed are never put to narrative use. There are fine long shots of each planet but the interiors to which we are then taken, for reasons outlined earlier, reek of the shooting set.

Just as the film's defects are obvious, so the film's beauty is hidden, which makes one want to defend it all the more, especially since the kinds of beauty involved are extraordinary. To begin with, the film is suffused with a noble, unpretentious gravity which is not exactly the tone of average films, whether they are made by auteurs or not. Lynch resisted the temptation to introduce self-mocking nudges to seduce the viewers into swallowing the emphases he wanted to get across. He refuses to resort to the kind of self-parody displayed by similar productions of the period, the kind of 'knowing' pastiche of 50s science-fiction films supposedly designed for popcorn-swilling consumers. And he knew it: 'Our villians are very much larger than life. They are not played for laughs, although they obviously enjoy their work. It's easy to get a laugh in a movie like this. There are cheap laughs that destroy the mood and destroy the picture. I don't think there are any of them in this movie. There is a dark sense of humour in it, though.'[3] Lynch helps to infuse the film with a legendary tone, a kind of sacred immobility, an irreducible strangeness. The film achieves the atmosphere of a daydream via the contrast between, on the one hand, the immenseness of the depicted space and the swarm of individuals inhabiting it and, on the other, the feeling of being in someone's head (as also in *Eraserhead*) produced by the multiple inner voices which often speak in intimate, half-whispered tones. This impression is summed up in the shot where Paul harangues the Fremen in a gigantic hall the design of which seems to be inspired by Egyptian temples. As thousands of Fremen chant his war-name (Muad'Dib) in a peaceful, terrifying unison, he speaks to himself in a whisper, like a little boy who feels he is the master of the world. The scene is chilling.

18

In many ways, *Dune* is just like a little boy's fantasy, that of being the chosen one. Paul has indeed been chosen by the women, for all eternity, and he plays his role with the seriousness of a cub-scout in a troop rite. Fortunately, though, the film never becomes moralistic, it never argues for or against Paul and what he represents. Whether it is a matter of distance or of identification, Lynch's own view of his character is impossible to situate or determine. Indeed, he does not even seem to have a viewpoint. Lynch wanted the film to follow the trajectory of an illuminatory experience. On the basis of visual and acoustic mental images colliding in his mind, the film was to show a character who pieces together and masters the puzzle of his own fate. The father, Duke Leto, bequeaths a sentence to the character the meaning of which he comes to understand much later: 'The sleeper must awaken.' However, when Paul has become an orphan and endured the test of the spice, and he screams to the open sky, 'Father, the sleeper has awakened!', we cannot feel much more than a vaguely abstract difference. It is the entire film, from beginning to end, which remains a waking, static dream. The whole film is spoken and acted as if in a dream. It is worth noting that in *Blue Velvet*, Frank, the fantasmatic father, bequeathes a strangely similar yet different message to Jeffrey in a far less gentle manner, that is to say, by repeatedly punching him in the gut: 'We're together in dreams.'

This dreamlike dimension is also fostered by the actors' diction in some of the dialogues, especially in the sequence already mentioned when the two women are talking at Paul's bedside. At first, they stand before the closed door of his bedroom, which does not prevent them from lowering their voices (like Wendy Hiller speaking to Treves about his protégé in *The Elephant Man*). This generates an atmosphere of universal conspiracy and paranoia: everything centres on the chosen one who believes that everything concerns him while suspecting no one in particular. The force of this scene derives from the fact that the women use a speaking tone which suggests proximity. The link between speaking and hearing is such that a certain way of speaking implies a certain way of being listened to. And this speaking-while-knowing-one-is-being-listened-to (while behaving as if it is not so) endows the film with a mythical atmosphere, something evoking origins, perhaps because these sounds are reminiscent of the sounds which a young child perceives when others talk about him in his presence without addressing him, a common occurrence, after all.

The film also includes forms of 'speaking nearby', a hushed kind of speech as in the dialogue with the sacrificed father in front of a sombre ocean, and a tone that is somewhere between speaking and whispering, as in the recurrent shot of Sean Young addressing Paul with a kind of sadness in her voice. Such strategies, largely overlooked, endow the film with a fabulous charm.

19

If the opening scenes are among the most beautiful in the film, it is also because they represent the only portrait in Lynch's work of a united family, the house of Leto Atreides (there would be a fleeting reoccurrence later, in *Twin Peaks*, when Major Briggs returns). There is ample evidence of the importance of family photos, frames and portraits in Lynch's films: the portrait of Mary pieced back together in *Eraserhead*, the 'two mothers' in *The Elephant Man*, the couple Dorothy and Don in *Blue Velvet*, Marietta Pace in *Wild at Heart* and, of course, Laura Palmer in the credits at the end of *Twin Peaks*. Even more than *The Elephant Man*, *Dune* is a film of frozen portraits, continually open to questioning. These portraits are somewhat dated and formal, referring less to a promised future than to some distant past, the time of grand- or great-grandparents. The women wear complicated, flaring dresses while the men, strapped into their uniforms, look like ancestors who fought in the American Civil War. In addition, the presence of small court dogs recalls Velasquez and *Las Meninas*. In *Dune*, the immobility, the hovering in place, of these portraits is striking, especially during the stay on Arrakis. *Blue Velvet* later confirmed this impression, as I pointed out when reviewing the film's release: 'Beyond his visible eccentricities and his cabinet of monsters, the force of this director lies in his knowing better than anyone how to film immobility, which is supposed to be the opposite of cinema. In a country which most identifies cinema with movement, only a David Lynch could invent men who become potted plants or flowers in a garden bed. Frame-by-frame analysis confirms that beneath the apparent non-movement of the plant world, the most awful and violent things are brewing: heart-rending torsions, horrible intertwinings, endless growth. For Lynch, such is Man. No moment is ever as intense as when there is no more outward bodily agitation to hide the infinitesimal speed of an inner movement animating him, which makes him grow or take root. This static quality contains a great deal of violence, and Lynch's films seem able to capture it.'[17] However, in order to well and truly 'plant' his heroes, Lynch needed soil other than a sterile planet of sand. He had to come back to earth and create Lynchtown.

III

WELCOME TO LYNCHTOWN

(Blue Velvet, The Cowboy and the Frenchman, Twin Peaks)

1

Lynchtown is a cute, typically American, small town in the midst of an ocean of forest, marshalling all the resources of its organised comfort and its sense of order to resist an infinitely mysterious environment. It is a town where one is protected from emptiness and a feeling of cosmic darkness by the little restaurant where the young people go to flirt and by the fireman who says hello from his big red fire-engine. In Lynchtown, the high school is full of playful, giggly girls in bunches of three or four, eyed by youths straight out of the *Happy Days* television series. The police department is run by kindly policemen and the houses have gardens bordered by white fences under a blue sky. In Lynchtown, everything is nearby, everything is close, and everybody knows everybody. Starting with *Eraserhead* and the hero's neighbour living across the hall, the neighbourhood acquires an almost metaphysical significance for Lynch.

However, once night falls and the shadows deepen at the doors of the little houses, and the young people wakening to love go strolling under the tree-lined streets, one can hear, not all that far away, the howling of wolves. Lynchtown is the base camp for an adventure of the imagination, a place where you can come and be refreshed with a cup of hot coffee in a familiar place. It is also a surface, but with only one side, not a recto with a verso. It is a façade with nothing to hide, not even nothingness.

Of course, this is a description, endorsed by its own legend, of the small town in *Twin Peaks* and, before that, of Lumberton in *Blue Velvet*.

2

After the financial failure of *Dune*, many of Lynch's projects fell through. The follow-ups provided for in his contract were cancelled and Lynch's project for the all-too-odd *Ronnie Rocket* became harder than ever to carry out. Fortunately, he was able to make a comeback immediately with a film which, once again, was not expected of him (though he says he had the idea for it at the time of *The Elephant Man*): a contemporary thriller with teenage heroes.

Dino de Laurentiis had read the script, which Lynch had written before *Dune*. It was his first original script since *Eraserhead*. They agreed to very special conditions: full artistic freedom for Lynch on a reduced budget of $5 million which could not be exceeded, and a half-salary for the author-director. The other half would be paid only if the film was a success, which happened to be the case. The film was shot under rigorous conditions in Wilmington, North Carolina, a town much like those which Lynch had known as a child.

Lynch has described *Blue Velvet* as a 'story of love and mystery. It's about a guy who lives in two worlds at the same time, one of which is pleasant and the other dark and terrifying.'[12] On the other hand, neither of these two worlds are quite contemporaneous with ours. The author succeeds in mixing the atmosphere of the 50s with that of today, so that we no longer know where we are. For Lynch, the main character also belongs to the earlier period: 'The boy is an idealist. He behaves like young people in the 50s, and the little town where I filmed is a good reflection of the naïve climate there was back then. The local people tended to think the way people did 30 years ago. Their houses, cars and accents have remained the same.'[15]

The action takes place in an imaginary town, Lumberton, located in a forested region where lumber is the main business. The hero, young Jeffrey Beaumont, is a college student called back to his family home because his father has had a heart attack. Back in his home town, Jeffrey runs his father's shop. When out walking one day, he discovers a human ear in the grass, covered with ants. He takes his find to a local policeman, Detective Williams, who tells him not to mention it to anyone. As he leaves the detective's office, he is approached by the detective's only daughter, a blonde called Sandy, who reveals what she has heard in her room, which happens to be right above her father's office. Sandy puts Jeffrey on the track of a dark-haired woman called Dorothy Vallens, who is being watched by the police and was apparently involved in a murder.

Allowing himself to be drawn in, one night, Jeffrey (with Sandy's help, though at first she is reluctant to give it) breaks into Dorothy's apartment. When Dorothy, a cabaret singer at the Slow Club, comes home earlier than

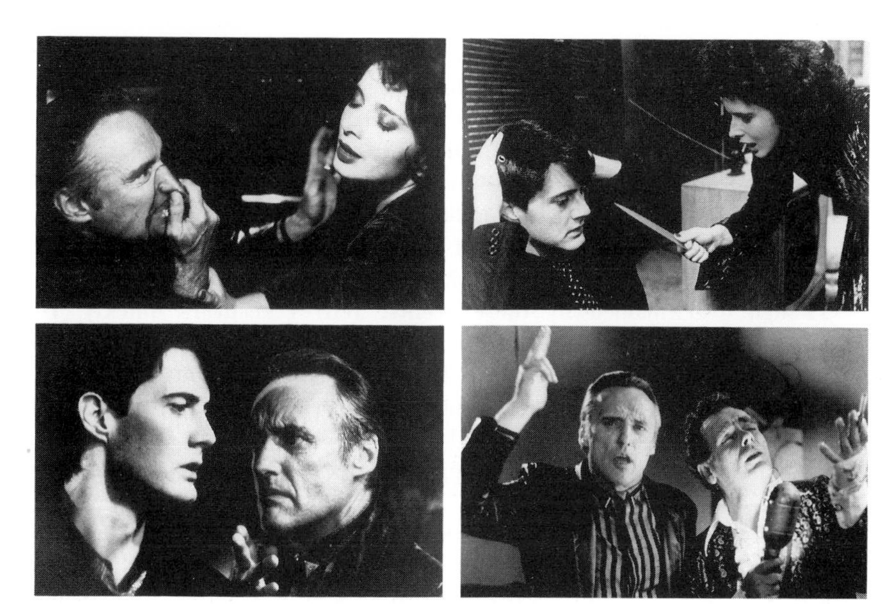

Blue Velvet

usual, Jeffrey has to hide in a cupboard from which he observes and even takes part in a series of strange, terrifying scenes. Dorothy first receives a telephone call from her husband and a little boy who have been kidnapped by a bandit named Frank. She then discovers Jeffrey and, brandishing a kitchen knife, makes him come out and get undressed. She begins to caress him when Frank knocks at the door. Jeffrey goes back into hiding and observes the bandit's frightening behaviour: Frank terrorises Dorothy, and forces her to engage in frenetic intercourse punctuated by insults and punches as he speaks successively in the voices of a baby and a daddy. All this is intensified by unusual accessories such as an oxygen mask through which Frank avidly breathes, and a blue velvet cord. When Frank finally leaves, Dorothy has Jeffrey come out and tries to arouse him. She lets him explore her body and then asks him to hit her. He refuses (later he will accept with visible horror) and leaves, with Dorothy in distress ('Help me!'). She asks him not to say anything to the police.

In spite of this, by virtue of some mysterious force, Jeffrey becomes her secret lover ('He put his disease in me', she says enigmatically) even as he falls in love with Sandy. His relationship with Sandy, arising from their complicity in this shady affair, proves to be one of reciprocated love.

Continuing his investigation, Jeffrey discovers a violent drugs ring involving Frank, a policeman in a yellow suit and a third man whom he calls 'the well-dressed man.' He is caught one night at Dorothy's and forced to go with Frank and his gang for an absurd night out, first to the house of an effeminate friend, Ben, an accomplice in their drug trafficking who is holding the kidnapped husband and child, then in a car racing at breakneck speed. Jeffrey, who wanted to play the white knight in Frank and Dorothy's sado-masochistic game, is badly beaten up but also kissed on the mouth, threatened with death, treated to a declaration of love and asked by the raging Frank 'to dream together', then he is abandoned, bleeding, on some wasteground.

Though overwhelmed by these events, Jeffrey recovers quickly. He passes on his information to Detective Williams while omitting the role played by Sandy. The policeman tells him with a mysterious air that he should stand by for further questioning. On the crucial evening, Jeffrey and Sandy go to a party together, kiss and declare their love for one another. On the way home that night, they catch sight of Dorothy, suddenly appearing as if she were leaving Jeffrey's house. Naked and covered with marks of a beating (Lynch claims to have seen such a sight while out walking one day with his brother), she clutches Jeffrey as Sandy looks on in shock. Dorothy repeats to Sandy, 'He put his disease in me,' and asks Jeffrey to help her husband. Sandy slaps Jeffrey's face (though she will quickly pardon him) and he leaves. At Dorothy's, he finds the man in yellow covered with blood and swaying but still on his feet. The husband lies bound and dead (this is our only image of him). When Frank returns to the apartment, disguised as the well-dressed man (they are the same person), Jeffrey barely escapes with his life. Taking shelter once again in the protective cupboard, he uses a trick to kill the monster with a bullet in the middle of the forehead.

We next encounter Jeffrey in an ideal, becalmed world. His father has recovered, and Dorothy has her child back (there is no hint of sadness for the husband). Jeffrey and Sandy are united in the bosom of their enchanted families. There is a robin in a tree in the garden, like the ones which Sandy described to Jeffrey in an ecstatic dream of love. But the robin has a maybug in its beak. 'The world is strange,' the young people conclude.

This is the story of Lynch's most successful and densest work to date. Its success certainly cannot be attributed to the story being so logical and regular. If the general shape of the story is bizarre, it is even more so in the details. The increasing and seemingly inexhaustible sense of material and psychological weirdness accumulates in the links of the chain.

3

Freer and more experienced after the difficult time he had with *Dune*, Lynch achieved perfect casting for his four main characters. Remarkable as always, Kyle MacLachlan in the role of Jeffrey makes us forget Paul

Atreides. There none the less remains a slight discrepancy. The psychological coherence of the story depends on having a young person who is naïve, with little or no experience of the world, but MacLachlan does not have this appearance: his face expresses too much intelligence. However, he knows how to convey something perverse and disquieting, followed in the next breath by frank directness. Laura Dern, the daughter of Bruce Dern and Diane Ladd, played the part of Sandy after Lynch noticed her in Peter Bogdanovich's *Mask* (1985). By coincidence, *Mask* tells the story of a boy whose face has been monstrously deformed by a disease, and the film has certain traits in common with Lynch's earlier *The Elephant Man*. In *Mask*, Laura Dern plays a young blind girl who cannot be shocked by the hero's physical appearance and falls in love with him. In *Blue Velvet*, she is perfect as a young, apparently sensible but determined high-school girl. Lynch is also said to have chosen her because she and Kyle formed a handsome couple. Lynch likes playing matchmaker and on this occasion he was so successful that the two actors embarked on a real-life relationship. Sandy is particularly troubling when, to the sound of church music, she tells Jeffrey of the dream she had the night they met, simultaneously revealing a hidden, depressive side to her, linking her character to that of Dorothy. In the dream, robins symbolising love bring the light back into a world pervaded with darkness. In the exultation of the moment, she has the eyes of a blind person (there is talk of 'blinding' light), suggesting that her performance in *Mask* had indeed struck Lynch and remained in his mind.

Lynch claims to have met Isabella Rossellini in a restaurant (he often meets people there) without knowing she was an actress. 'I only found out a week later. I sent her the script and she liked it a lot.'[16] Their work on *Blue Velvet* was the starting-point for a relationship that lasted about four years and gave director Tina Rathbone the idea of bringing them together, on the screen. The two act in a saccharine little film called *Zelly and Me* (1988). Unfortunately, its only merit is that it shows Lynch and Rossellini as a couple.

A model and an actress, the daughter of Ingrid Bergman and Roberto Rossellini has an unforgettable, almost traumatising role in *Blue Velvet*. Magnificently beautiful even though she is heavily made-up and looks like a poisonous flower, she marks the film with her carnal presence and a harsh nudity in which the fatigue and fullness of her body are displayed. In fact, her nudity is that of a mature woman marked by childbearing, not that of a youthful 35-year-old. The careless style of her dressing gown, along with details in the set, her behaviour and clothes accentuate the feeling, rare in cinema, of witnessing scenes of genuine intimacy. Her Italian looks are used as an exotic element, not by direct reference to an accent or an ethnicity, but by underlining how foreign a body she is in the neat little world of Lumberton. Isabella Rossellini was supposed to function in a similar way in

Twin Peaks, but the part was eventually changed to that of a Chinese woman and given to Joan Chen. Here she plays her part with great warmth, unconcerned by any fears of damaging her image.

As Frank in *Blue Velvet*, a part made to measure for him, Dennis Hopper achieved a marvellous comeback after Coppola's *Rumble Fish* (1983). He had managed to shake off alcohol and drugs and the shabby condition in which we see him in *Apocalypse Now* (1979). Though on paper the character of Frank is outrageous, thanks to Hopper he is totally alive on the screen. With his striking way of speaking in brutal bursts, matching his contorted, snarling face, Hopper imbues Frank with a sense of anxiety and chaos even as he preserves the larger-than-life quality which Lynch desired.

4

With the help of *Eraserhead*'s cameraman, Fred Elmes, for *Blue Velvet* Lynch again resorted to the screen format to which he was passionately committed at the time, CinemaScope. He was convinced that *Dune* had failed at least in part because it had been shot in colour. He had considered reverting to black and white, but decided against it after some trials. Since the film has become famous for its use of colour, beginning with the title, it may be hard to credit this report, but it appears to be true.

Lynch with Isabella Rossellini and Kyle MacLachlan on the set of *Blue Velvet*

Many of *Blue Velvet*'s shots use a telescopic, wide-angle, slightly curved lens which was new at the time. Cimino is said to have used the same lens in his *Year of the Dragon* (1985). The wide-angle lens allows the screen to accomodate vast rooms, such as the living-room in Dorothy's flat and that of the Williams family. The living space thus created, while virtually coinciding with the frame space, reinforces the feeling that the characters exist in settings which precede them. However, the most important risk assumed by Lynch in this film is, for the first time, that of making images which are no different from those of other American films. Prior to this, from the violently stylised images of *The Grandmother*, clearly influenced by Bergman, to the expressionistic black and white of *Eraserhead* and *The Elephant Man* and the affected pictorialism of *Dune*, the strangeness of Lynch's work was always expressed first of all by a different visual quality. Hence my slight disappointment on seeing *Blue Velvet* in 1987, which caused me to write in *Cahiers du cinéma* that the film was 'a mixed, uneven work in which superb personal scenes alternate with more workmanlike moments'[17] What I had in mind were moments such as Sandy and Jeffrey talking together in the car, the party scene, the diner, and so on. With hindsight, I think I was mistaken. This banality is necessary for the story and, of course, it contrasts with the stylisation of the scenes at Dorothy's. *Twin Peaks* confirmed that Lynch is able to endow the commonplace with an extra dimension, and he has since returned to a more particular visual style in *Wild at Heart* and *Fire Walk with Me*. Be that as it may, *Blue Velvet* exhibits a cinematographic maturity and a mastery of the timing of shots and scenes which cannot but be the result of experience and confidence in what one wishes to say.

The film also marks the arrival in Lynch's coterie of composer Angelo Badalamenti, who does a beautiful job on the credits with a superb, unusually extended theme for strings. It is a sort of long, serpentine motif in a minor key halfway between Brahms and Shostakovich (the main themes in Lynch's films are often set in a minor key). Recurring only once in the rest of the film, the music for the credits is nothing like a traditional leitmotiv. The music accompanying certain intense scenes such as the finale in Dorothy's apartment is more impersonally dramatic. Lynch also includes a compilation of 50s and country and western songs, including the one which gives the film its title. '*Blue Velvet*', Lynch noted, 'is a song by Bobby Vinton from the 50s which I discovered and really liked in the 60s. It put me in a certain mood. As for velvet, it's an extraordinary, sensual, rich, heavy material...almost organic.'[16] The film's other main songs, *In Dreams* and *Love Letters*, are also used for their lyrics. For all we know, Lynch may even have written parts of the script from free associations triggered by the lyrics.

The tandem of Lynch as songwriter and Badalamenti as composer proved itself with their song *Mysteries of Love*, first heard as an instrumental while

Sandy recounts her dream. It then expands with Lynch's lyrics and the voice of Julee Cruise at the party as Sandy and Jeffrey declare their love for one another. A kind of ornamented chorale, this song is the beginning of an original repertory which will have a role to play in *Twin Peaks* and *Fire Walk with Me*. It also fuelled the spectacular *Industrial Symphony No. 1* and generated a record album. Lynch's sentimental side is given free rein here in simple words stamped by a cosmic lyricism. In contrast, Alan Splet's sound effects, groans, explosions and muffled tones are far more confined and localised than in Lynch's first three feature films. Sound effects accompany the descent into the swarming insect world at the beginning of the film, as well as the sequence of shock-images in which Jeffrey relives his frightening discoveries. The rest of the time, however, Lynch creates a normal, peaceful atmosphere, undisturbed by noises from the beyond or winds from the interstices of this world. Such tumult and noise will reappear in *Wild at Heart* and especially in *Fire Walk with Me*, though, by then, they are no longer the work of Alan Splet.

5

Blue Velvet was entered for the Venice Film Festival where it caused a furore, being turned down on the grounds of pornography. When it was presented at the Avoriaz Festival of Fantasy Films, it received a prize, although some purists argued that Lynch's films did not belong to the fantasy genre and thus should not have been shown at Avoriaz. In principle, they had a point, since the film in no way appeals to anything that could be regarded as beyond the laws of nature. In fact, it is more of a psychological thriller. Yet there are so many weird little touches and details that it is hard to deny that it belongs to the fantasy film genre. The most obvious of these weird touches are visual ones, such as the image of 'the yellow man' who, wounded and bleeding, obstinately remains standing before Jeffrey's eyes.

Although at first sight the film's plot may seem watertight, a more logical point of view reveals a number of holes in it. Frank has no clear, rational motive for kidnapping Dorothy's husband and child, no more than Dorothy has for refusing to notify the police (the very idea of doing so simply throws her into a panic), and the confusion surrounding the third man's identity leads nowhere. The massacre at the end is enigmatic. The mysteries which Detective Williams holds up before Jeffrey do not lead to a revelation. Indeed, the way in which the detective is constantly shown implies some frightening secret (incest with his daughter? a general conspiracy?) but nothing transpires in the end. Even the motif of the severed ear obeys no comprehensible logic. Lynch conceals the image of the kidnapped father and child until the very end and then the father is seen dead and the child glimpsed only fleetingly. In addition, lapses in the characters' behaviour add yet another layer of strangeness to the story. Dorothy is moved when she talks to her husband and child on the telephone, but she does not speak about them with Jeffrey, who does not offer to help them, nor does he even ask about them. There are a great many such details.

The bizarre elements do not even stop short at Jeffrey's house. His mother almost never speaks, and she does not show any emotion over her husband's heart attack. Nor do we see her at his bedside. She may seem normal enough, but she constantly watches television programmes without the sound, shown in brief but poignant images, which, anticipating Sarah Palmer in *Twin Peaks* and *Fire Walk with Me*, become fully significant if we see them as signs of deep depression.

The film is a dream, but a structured one. The Sandy/Dorothy parallel encourages us to see the two women as one. Early in the film, when Sandy appears before Jeffrey's eyes one night in a peaceful Lumberton street, she emerges from the disquieting shade of the leaves and a tremor of wind. The music at this moment is particularly unsettling and then who do we see? An ordinary high-school girl and yet, as she will say a number of times, she is the starting-point for his meeting with the other woman. Later, in a diner where the two speak like the adolescents they really are, Jeffrey tells Sandy of all the horrible and fascinating things he has discovered when breaking into Dorothy's apartment. Then, to our astonishment, in the same breath he tells her, rather than the woman who most deserves it, 'You're a mystery.' Sandy and Dorothy incarnate two sides of one figure, each side endlessly leading to the other as in a Möbius strip. Their worlds are divided according to a traditional scheme: the blonde is associated with conventional life and daytime whereas the brunette belongs to the night and a world of shady, fearful characters. If, at the end, Jeffrey takes his place in Sandy's dream, that is to say, in a sugary-sweet world recalling the idyllic paradise she described to him, one may think that he is there to stay ('In dreams you are mine,' says the song Frank plays for Jeffrey) but that he will always find a way (via the ear?) of escaping it, from the inside.

Such an interpretation of fantasy is based on the suspension of our normal points of orientation: in this case, Jeffrey's real parents. It would be wrong to underestimate the way in which Lynch marginalises the parents. Jeffrey's father suffers a heart attack which renders him mute except for a brief moment at the end of the film. As for his mother, there is no doubt that she is present, ever seated on her couch or at the kitchen table, for breakfast and television programmes in the company of an elderly woman identified in the dialogue as an aunt (probably her husband's sister) and who also does not speak. When Jeffrey appears before the women, battered after his nightmarish outing, and his aunt timidly begins to question him, what does he tell her? Simply to be quiet. Jeffrey's parents are silenced by the script while Jeffrey goes through an experience which will end by propelling him into the most absolute conformity. What might they have said? Some advice to be careful ... or something which might have prevented the story from happening?

One readily understands that Jeffrey's father and mother are, so to speak, disconnected for the length of the film, to allow the fantasy parents Dorothy and Frank to emerge from the shadows and play out the primal scene before his eyes. Jeffrey is present as they have sex (is what he sees in fact his notion of sex?), confined in a cupboard like a sort of foetal rival to his father, since Dorothy describes the closet as an extension of her body (when she says in succession, 'I still have you inside of me' and 'I looked for you in my closet'). Or is the film the fantasy of a boy who finds his parents too polite to be other than boring, something which now and again Lynch has suggested in his remarks, and who therefore invents infernal parents with whom life is more intense?

Lynch did not so much state as overstate the foundations for such an interpretation. For example, one of the lines Frank utters in his sado-masochistic ritual with Dorothy is 'Daddy's coming home', with an allusion to sexual penetration. The notion of 'coming home', associated with a return to the bosom (with Dorothy, Frank alternately calls himself a baby who wants to have sex and a daddy who comes home), reinforces the sense that we are witnessing a family triad including parents and a son. Moreover, details are scattered throughout the film associating Dorothy with a maternal image. The undulating velvet cloth at the beginning will later become the material of her dressing-gown, and suggests the spacious dress one wants to nestle in. The simultaneous, double spiriting away of Jeffrey's real parents and Dorothy's real child, restoring them to each other at the end, encompasses Jeffrey's experience with Dorothy, with him replacing the kidnapped boy. And Dorothy's enigmatic words to Jeffrey, 'her secret lover' whom she keeps 'inside of her', may be understood as referring to a man's semen but also to the child a woman carries.

However, though he renounces being Dorothy's secretly incestuous lover from the day that she recovers her son, Jeffrey is not exactly home free. His new mate, Sandy, has all the traits of an idealised, unsexed woman, likening her to a mother as well. It is worth noting that the relationship between these two young persons is very chaste, without the slightest hint of sex. Later, in *Wild at Heart*, Lynch would film Laura Dern as a very sexual woman, mad about her own body. She too is shown naked. Nor is it an accident that Dern is doubly associated with motherhood, first by alluding to an abortion, then literally via her pregnancy and child. This is what shocks in Lynch: revealed nakedness, in the biblical sense, is always more or less the revealed nakedness of the mother.

6

According to Lynch, the meaning of the denouement is that Jeffrey has discovered evil but that this will not change his life, and Lumberton will go back to its normal existence. 'That is the subject of *Blue Velvet*. You apprehend things, and when you try to see what it's all about, you have to live with it.'[16] In between two frightening visions and two eerie jaunts in the night, the hero returns faithfully to his bed and to the good old house full of familiar objects. That is the only explicit comment Lynch has made, protecting the ambiguity of his work. One might, therefore, think that his initiation quest is vague and, most of all, that it reflects a fairly limited discovery of Evil if the last word is the banal notion that the world is strange and imperfect. On the other hand, do we ever learn anything more complex in tales of character formation? Does the subtlety not lie most of all in the detours used to reach these conclusions? In this respect, Lynch's strength lies in his not being afraid of literalness and of having heroes who seem like simpletons although they most certainly are not. On the symbolic level, this allows him to go much further.

There is something in the fascination generated by *Blue Velvet* which resists the usual psychological keys or, rather, which opens so easily with them that it is disconcerting. Take homosexuality, for example. Jeffrey is twice exposed to passive homosexual drives which he can no longer ignore, when Dorothy has him undress and then caresses him, and when Frank calls him his candy-coloured clown and kisses him on the mouth while simultaneously declaring his love and threatening his life (if you get involved in my affairs, I'll send you a love letter, which is to say, a bullet between the eyes). If we play the game and see these tempters as Jeffrey's symbolic parents (and Lynch does everything he can to make us think they are), is it enough to speak of a scene of parental seduction, whether real or fantasised, and to stop there? To settle for incest and an Oedipal complex served up on a film set? If we do not want to end with these clichés, we must again make our way through the film, asking ourselves whether we have seen and heard it well enough, while looking at and listening to its actual surfaces, taking them literally.

This is particularly relevant for the key scene where Frank and Dorothy make love while Jeffrey looks on. What is unusual about this scene is its theatricality. One wonders whether the characters do not enter, speak, move and behave solely to please the voyeur, knowing full well they are giving him a show. As when Isabella Rossellini dressed only in her bra and panties crawls about moaning and then gets up, with apparently no other reason than to be seen by Jeffrey and us. However, immediately afterwards, the voyeur is himself forced to exhibit himself, as on a stage, and the next time he has to hide upon Frank's arrival, things can no longer be quite as they were before. As for the ensuing fantasy scene, its unsettling quality is not simply due to the explicit violence it contains. After all, we have seen and heard many such scenes in the cinema. In this case, the scene seems to arise from an archaic acoustic impression which endows it with the kind of troubling vagueness that can inspire bizarre theories. A child who overhears the sexual intercourse of adults on the other side of a wall might imagine, for instance, that the man's voice is muffled not because he is speaking against the woman's mouth or body, but because he has stuffed a piece of cloth into his mouth. This is the kind of fantasy on display in *Blue Velvet*, reviving the surrealistic sexual theories of children. Moreover, an additional unsettling element is the scene's sense of being outside time. The sentences which Frank repeats, often word for word, at short intervals ('Don't you fucking look at me'), reverberate as happens in the memory. There is no difference between the continuous scene at which Jeffrey is present and the shots in which he remembers it. The scene is the very act of remembering, the unfolding of something which has already been inscribed. Lastly, as I have said, the scene is unsettling because it resembles a ritual played out for someone else. We assumed it was for Jeffrey, but might it not also be for Dorothy?

One could argue that Frank behaves as if he were the actor in a show designed to move the woman sexually. His way of repeating certain sentences may be the outpourings of a maniac, but might it not also be the mechanical repetition of a particular sentence designed to excite her? Previously, we heard Dorothy using the same words with Jeffrey, before asking him: 'Do you like talk like that?' as if she were trying out on someone else the very thing which excites her. This is one of the troubling aspects of *Blue Velvet*. Though common in real life, cinema, an incorrigible embellisher of existence, rarely displays characters who are unsure of their desires, who do not quite know what they want. In short, characters rather like us.

When Frank comes in asking for his bourbon, making a scene like a drunken brute of a husband, he gives the impression of being a bad actor in a realistic drama. To whom is his show and his 'Can't you fucking remember anything?' addressed? To Dorothy, perhaps, to give her pleasure? We are shown that she takes her pleasure in this scene and that she asks Jeffrey to do the same. Nevertheless, as an interpretation this is still too unsatisfactory, though it is impossible to pinpoint exactly where the resistance comes from. After repeated screenings, something that was perfectly obvious from the start begins to come to the fore. When Frank leaves Dorothy lying on the floor, and while Jeffrey watches from his hiding-place, he tells her, 'You stay alive, Baby. Do it for Van Gogh.' The reference to Van Gogh is easy: it tells us that the man who lost an ear is Dorothy's husband, but why would

Dorothy want to die? Unlike this viewer, Jeffrey heard something there, and when he tells Sandy about his experience in the flat, he shows he has understood Frank's words. We just have to follow. If Frank Booth cut off one of the kidnapped husband's ears, he says, it was to prevent Dorothy, on the verge of suicide, from letting go: 'Dorothy Vallens is married to a man named Don. They have a son. I think that the son and husband have been kidnapped by a man named Frank. Frank has done this to force Dorothy to do things for him. I think she wants to die. I think Frank cut the ear I found off her husband as a warning to her to stay alive.' It is a strange kind of logic in which Frank prevents the mother from becoming depressed and slipping into the void ('I'm falling, I'm falling,' she says as the ambulance takes her away) by beating her, kidnapping her child and husband and then cutting off the man's ear (which Jeffrey then recovers).

It takes a long time to see it, but, like Laura Palmer later in *Fire Walk with Me*, who feels herself going down faster and faster, or her prostitute mother who chain-smokes even before her daughter's death, or with the abandoned woman in *Industrial Symphony No. 1*, or with Marietta Pace in *Wild at Heart*, covering her face with lipstick in the bathroom and cracking up (this has been interpreted as a way of making her frightening to the spectator, but it is in fact a call for help), or with Mary X in *Eraserhead* ('I can't stand it. I'm going home.'), in *Blue Velvet* Dorothy is prey to a sense of terminal depression. Once we have understood this, one can find ample evidence for it. She even says as much. However, every time, we are allowed to mistake the depression as a kind of anxiety arising from the immediate situation: Marietta Pace is depressed because her daughter left with the man she desires; Mary because her baby is a monster; the broken-hearted woman because she has been abandoned; and Dorothy because her husband and child are being held hostage. However, the depression comes first in each of these cases. After all, is it reasonable to see someone as dejected because her child has been stolen? Should not this event rather galvanise her into fighting back? This seems to be what Frank is aiming to achieve through the kidnapping.

When you realise that the script's extravagant logic in fact revolves around the notion of forestalling Dorothy's suicide, by means of electroshocks and strong sensations, through blackmail (the situation is a metaphor for all of Lynch's work), *Blue Velvet* acquires a more interesting and beautiful meaning more in tune with the disturbance it provokes in us. Dorothy's hushed plea as she leans over the wash-basin after Jeffrey leaves, her touching 'Help me,' is thus not a woman's request to help her recover her son and husband. She requests nothing of the sort from Jeffrey. Nor is it a 'Help me with my sexual frustration.' It is about a woman collapsing, slipping into the void of a terminal depression.

As for the husband, our only sight of him is formless, tied up. A close-up of his ear identifies him, making him look a little like a premature child, perhaps, something which has not been completely formed and is still covered with the placenta. This insignificant husband exists for us only as the close-up of a severed ear (that is why we hear Dorothy speak to him – on the telephone). And what is shown in the last scene are his remains, a residue, even if these remains are an entire body. The line which Jeffrey overhears about Van Gogh puts the pieces back together, as it were, because the words identify the owner of the organ and relate it to the woman whose intimacy he is spying upon. It is thus related to the mother but also to the other, the father, Frank. The mention of Van Gogh, who was a wounded man but also a major figure and a great painter, is symbolic. Lynch wanted to be a painter. However, according to his own testimony, he became a film-maker instead, by way of sound, that is to say, by way of the ear.

Frank cuts off the ear and Jeffrey finds it: the ear is a message from one to the other. Another channel of communication between the two men is formed by letters. Some viewers regard the beating which Jeffrey receives from Frank as grotesque and meaningless but, along with the violence, words are also spoken. Frank declares his love to Jeffrey and tells him that if he continues to meddle in his affairs, that is to say, in what he does with Dorothy (her scream in the car, when Jeffrey interferes with Frank's brutality, can be taken as a sign of frustration), Frank will send him a 'love letter', a bullet in the head. But it is Frank who finally receives the bullet from Jeffrey in Dorothy's apartment, just after we hear a country and western song entitled *Love Letters* being played. Frank continues his declaration by repeating the words of the song which they hear in the car, like a message which he wants to bring home to Jeffrey: 'In dreams I walk with you/In dreams I talk to you/In dreams you're mine.' This can be taken, as it were, to the letter: I am the father and I will always be with you, speaking to you. It is both terrifying (you belong to me, you resemble me, we are alike) and paternal (whatever happens, I will love you and I will never leave you). This is spoken as a symbolic father and, if it is appropriate to speak of homosexuality, it is a homosexuality of a primitive sort, different from the kind that develops later. What Frank does with Dorothy is, of course, shocking, but it occurs between adults. Frank plays his role as father in forbidding the mother to the son. It is also as father that he advises him to be careful, but, at the same time, he tells Jeffrey he loves him, not with a homosexual love but the way a father loves his son, just as Jeffrey was seduced as a son by Dorothy. And it is as a son that Jeffrey will return his father's love letter in the form of a bullet between the eyes.

Blue Velvet

The ear is the gift bequeathed to Jeffrey by the father. More than the female orifice which leads to a closed interior, the ear functions here as a passageway, the symbol of communication between two worlds. The ear transmits the gift of passing through the surface, of travelling between worlds, then of recovering a normal world (at the end of the film, we exit through Jeffrey's ear). Frank thus offers Jeffrey a key to life and a gift of imagination. In short, everything in *Blue Velvet* has a dynamic sense of life, and love really is everywhere. And this too is frightening.

8

To date, *Blue Velvet* is in every respect Lynch's classic. It is neither a prototypical film like *Eraserhead* nor a more or less collective success to which the author lent his particular touch, like *The Elephant Man*. *Blue Velvet* is entirely his work, controlled and finished, something which none of his later films, more fragmented and asymmetrical, would aspire towards. It is also the film in which he establishes his universe, creates a model which may serve in all the later films (but which he will try to renew), a setting (Lynchtown), a structural scheme and a new type of romanticism. For the first time in Lynch's work, with the story of Sandy and the party, the film sets out his expression of love and consecrates it once and for all as something very beautiful (this is his truly popular dimension) midway between the Saturday night dance and the Sunday morning hymn.

This is also the film in which Lynch invents what might be called his 'forever' scene with the mad evening at Ben's. The forever scene is an evening spent by a group, steeped in endless music and during which a commonplace or stupid remark, seen through the prism of alcohol, takes on a fascinating or highly comic value. As, for instance, when Frank asks for a beer with frenetic impatience; or when an idle bystander fiercely announces his identity to all and sundry ('I'm Paul' in *Blue Velvet*); or when characters laugh at their own jokes (*The Cowboy and the Frenchman*, *Wild at Heart*). In *Blue Velvet*, there is a marvellously funny clowning scene between Frank in his role of big, bad, nervous, shouting and snarling wolf and a very collected Ben, made up like a stereotyped homosexual and acting through mimicry, delays and abrupt stops, like Coco the Clown, with a collar which is too large and accessories such as a cigarette holder totally out of proportion. In fact, the comic scenes in the *Twin Peaks* episodes Lynch produced himself are not always as successful.

Blue Velvet is the first film in which Lynch demonstrates his art of making daily life strange. The smooth, anonymous style of the shooting script provides a full measure of strangeness and terror for the simplest images, edited in a slightly unusual way, like the image of Sandy's father seen by the two young people in the recess of a doorway. The editing merely starts the shot of the father leaving his office a little earlier than would be the norm, that is to say, the setting prior to the father's emergence is held for a second longer than one would expect. This choice suffices to make what is a banal image into something terrifying (all the more so since the father's face, when he does come into the shot, is totally vacuous). There is also a disturbing shot in which Jeffrey simply opens his bedroom door one evening and walks down the stairs towards the living room on his way for a walk. This banal shot begins in total darkness before it is illuminated by the bedroom door opening, creating the impression of an opening on to another world. How is it that Lynch, unlike any other film-maker, manages to frighten us simply by showing someone going down the stairs for a walk? In my review for *Cahiers*, I attributed the visual banality of some of the scenes to the paucity of time available to Lynch to shoot the film, and I regretted that he was not able enjoy the same shooting schedule some Russian film-makers used to enjoy, shooting for months and even years, like Tarkovsky or Kurosawa when he shot *Dersu Uzala* (1975) in the USSR.[17] Even though that was a narrow view of the film, it was not completely wrong. When he embarked on the project of *Twin Peaks*, Lynch gave himself the time he needed, not in terms of the shooting schedule, but in the duration of the narrative itself.

9

The Cowboy and the Frenchman, also known as *Le Cowboy et le Frenchman*, is a short video work commissioned from Lynch under special circumstances. To celebrate its tenth birthday, the weekly *Figaro Magazine*, formerly an unacknowledged organ of the non-egalitarian New Right, which Lynch could not be expected to know, took up the suggestion of its associate Daniel Toscan du Plantier, then president of Erato Films, and decided to produce a series of short films by foreign directors on the theme *France as Seen by* .... The inspiration for this collective formula was, of course, the film *Paris vu par* ... (1964), a series of sketches which contributed to the reputation of the French New Wave. Perhaps because of the connection with the Rossellini family shared by Toscan du Plantier and Lynch, Lynch was the only American asked to participate in the series, along with Werner Herzog, Andrzej Wajda, Jean-Luc Godard and Luigi Comencini.

Lynch wrote a comic script set in a conventional Far West, in which rancher Slim (Harry Dean Stanton, making his first appearance in Lynch's universe) has been deaf ever since he was a teenager, when the firing of a large calibre bullet shattered his ear-drum. Slim goes out with his cowboy and Indian friends (among whom is Michael Horse, the future deputy sheriff Hawk of *Twin Peaks*) and captures an odd creature wearing a beret and speaking a bizarre language. Like a salesman, this individual is carrying objects as odd as a ripe, odorous Camembert cheese which Slim finds offensive, a loaf of French bread and some miniature Eiffel Towers. These tourist clichés about France are thus rehearsed and ridiculed, and the encounter between France and America ends with musical fellowship around a campfire, mixing French cancan and women singing country and western tunes, and giving rise to some noisy, dreamlike images.

The film displays Lynch's familiar obsessions: sound (with the theme of deafness) and food. He was clearly looking for an original tone, filming the actors statically in groups of two or three with fixed, frontal views, as in filmed comic sketches of the past. Despite its brevity, the film aims to create a sense of a party going on for ever. As a comic work, however, *The Cowboy and the Frenchman* has a major flaw: it does not make you laugh, but neither does it propose a personal vision. One might be able to consider this rather wearisome little work by a Tati fan as an essay in search of a new comic mode. In *Eraserhead* and *Twin Peaks*, as well as in the television series *On the Air* and in several projects which have not yet been filmed, Lynch has shown his ambitions in this respect. Indeed, this essay is entirely consistent with his procedures and his universe, especially with the humour of the everyday he deploys in the comic strip 'The Angriest Dog in the World', but there is no point in ascribing to this work a level of ambition which Lynch never sought to attain. A vaster enterprise was awaiting him.

10

'We were at DuPar's, the coffee shop at the corner of Laurel Canyon and Ventura [the corner coffee shop is important in the symbolic structure of Lynch's work] and all of a sudden, Mark Frost and I had this image of a body wrapped in plastic washing up on the shore of a lake.'[23]

According to Lynch, *Twin Peaks* was the result of compelling advice from his agent Tony Krantz, urging him to work for television. Prior to *Blue Velvet*, Krantz had introduced Lynch to television scriptwriter Mark Frost, who was already famous for his work on the innovative police series *Hill Street Blues*. Frost was to become a friend and close collaborator, and the two men would create the Lynch–Frost production company which produced *Twin Peaks* as well as the very disappointing documentary series on the American heartland called *American Chronicles* and the recent situation comedy *On the Air*.

The first contacts between Lynch and Frost dated from 1986. They worked together for a long time on a project entitled *Goddess*, which dealt with the last months in the life of Marilyn Monroe, another suicide victim. Lynch is said to own the cloth, like a holy relic, on which the star posed for her famous nude calendar photograph, and it may well be that this object was a source of inspiration for *Blue Velvet*.

'I liked the idea of a story in episodes that would go on for a long time.'[5] This is one of the primary motivations given by Lynch for his unexpected move to the small screen after seeming so thoroughly at home in the world of R-rated (Restricted) films. With nothing but the concept of a town and the need to have a series, the seed from which *Twin Peaks* would grow, Krantz brought Lynch and Frost to ABC, which ordered a script, written in eight or nine days, and a pilot episode. Before long, Lynch found himself in the region of Seattle shooting 120 minutes of film 'in twenty-one days of fast shooting and freezing weather'[5] The budget for the pilot episode was $4 million. It should be noted that 35mm film was used and the deep, warm tones of Ron Garcia's beautiful photography made fine use of the mountains and the evening light.

Advance screenings gave rise to enthusiastic articles in which the American press hailed the novelty and originality of a soap opera unlike any others. A large-scale advertising campaign was run with the slogan 'Who killed Laura Palmer?' ABC showed the first episode of *Twin Peaks* at 9pm on 8 April 1990 and the series very quickly became a worldwide phenomenon of great interest both to intellectuals and the general public. Though it had only moderate success in France, the reaction was very positive in Japan, which became the leader in *Twin Peaks* mania. In the United States, the audience for the series dropped off after Laura Palmer's murderer was revealed, but there were other reasons as well: the country's networks and hearts turned their attention to the Gulf War, and changes and irregularities occurred in the soap's time slot. When the series, the plot of which had become increasingly irrational and strange, was curtailed, the authors mobilised their fans to demand that it be continued.

The *Twin Peaks* phenomenon gave rise to major merchandising campaigns. Cherry pies stamped RR (the town coffee-shop and restaurant where the main characters often meet) and *Twin Peaks* coffee cups (FBI agent Dale Cooper's favourite drink) were put on sale. Several original works revealing the past of the two key characters were also published. Dale Cooper's memoirs, dictated into his famous dictaphone Diana just as he did more or less regularly with his progress reports, traced his life back to childhood. *The Secret Diary of Laura Palmer* revealed her baseness and early misfortunes, including the conviction that she was inhabited by an evil spirit named Bob. This *Diary* had the distinction of being written, and partly imagined, by Lynch's eldest daughter Jennifer, born of his first marriage. Jennifer Lynch subsequently wrote and directed the controversial film *Boxing Helena* (1993) about a young woman who has lost all four limbs and is kept on a glass throne by the man who loves her. The main role was eventually played by Sherilyn Fenn alias Audrey Horne, the sexiest woman in *Twin Peaks*.

Of course, Lynch did not embark on this adventure unprepared. He first produced the pilot episode of the series, then a kind of express resolution of the story for video distribution in Europe. Very short and totally unexpected, this resolution is important because it functioned as a matrix for the rest of the series and, among other things, introduced the idea of the Red Room, the eternal waiting-room outside time and space enclosed by its red drapes. Lynch also directed the first, second, eighth, ninth, fourteenth and final episodes, the latter being visually and dramatically the most unusual of all. Each episode had a budget of about $900,000. The other directors included Caleb Deschanel, Duwayne Dunham (the editor of the series), Tim Hunter, Leslie Linka Glatter, Mark Frost, Todd Holland, Tina Rathbone (Lynch's friend and the director of *Zelly and Me*), Graeme Clifford (the director of *Frances*, 1982, starring Jessica Lange) and James Foley as well as the actress and director Diane Keaton. Lynch's role was limited to supervising, along with Frost, the evolution of the script, which changed hands from one episode to the next, and to finishing touches in the mixing of words and music. For the rest, the directors were left with a certain amount of autonomy, as can be seen from the slight stylistic differences between episodes. These differences, however, do not disrupt the overall unity of the series. On the contrary, they help to renew its vigour. Episode 24, for example, directed by James Foley, uses more chiaroscuro, that is to say, a more cinematic treatment of light and shade than the others, while the episodes directed by Diane Keaton and Caleb Deschanel respectively contain bolder framing (such as extreme close-ups on faces in episode 22) and more complex camera movements which create a truly cinematographic suspense (such as Lucy walking through the police station in episode 19). It would be wrong to think that these variations are merely the expression of each director's personality. A given director may well have introduced unusual shots in order to renew the experimental spirit of the series. As for Lynch, he may have filmed anonymous, neutral angle/reverse-angle sequences in order to blend his part more fully into the overall look, but in some of the sequences he directed Lynch also managed to throw a spanner into the customary television style. His long shots were vaster and deeper than the American cinema and, *a fortiori*, television usually dares to make them, so that the characters are reduced to the size of peas (for instance, the first meeting between Cooper and Truman, and Ben Horne's address to the Norwegians in the pilot episode; the scene in the bank in the final episode). Lynch also left his visual mark with the 'disproportion shots' which use a wide-angle lens in a tilt-up on certain axes, so as to bring out the disproportions in the characters' size (see, for example, the scenes at the Great Northern with the Horne brothers) or to create an effect of spatial drunkenness which is distinctively Lynch's and is always related to the joy of walking (especially in scenes with Jerry Horne's very lively brother).

And, of course, the scenes in the Red Room are entirely Lynch's, a kind of perpetual theatre reminiscent of Robert Wilson but frozen into a psychotic duration. This is especially clear in episode 29, which contains some of the most experimental work Lynch has ever done: an interminable and fascinating series of repeated acts, sentences and appearances played by actors who are used like puppets or marionettes.

11

In the United States, Lynch is considered a European-style arty director. Many people were thus surprised when he undertook the writing, direction and production of a general-audience television series. In an interview conducted by Arnaud Viviant for *Libération* in June 1992, when *Fire Walk with Me* was released in France, Lynch elucidated his position on the supposed difference between cinema and television. When asked 'What exactly do you see as the difference?', he answered: 'Before distribution, none. After that, on television, unlike in the movies, you have a bad small image and bad small sound. But the construction processes are the same. We filmed, edited and mixed the film and the series in the same way.'[41] Indeed, he even finds certain advantages in the televised series, which are revelatory about his own desires:

Firstly, the extended duration of the narrative allowed by the series for at ('The idea of continuity on television is fantastic. Never say goodbye ...').

In *Twin Peaks* Lynch is able to evolve unusual dimensions to the story more naturally than in many of his other films because the series offers the possibility of gradually drawing the spectator into a different world. From *Dune* to *Wild at Heart* and *Fire Walk with Me*, Lynch has always suffered from the time-limits imposed on commercial features no matter how he tried to extend them. *Dune*, *The Elephant Man*, *Wild at Heart* and *Fire Walk with Me* all last more than two hours, and in each case the author clearly would have preferred a longer version still. Television is thus a room-sized medium whose limitations in screen size and sound are compensated for by a larger duration: 'Televison is all telephoto lens where cinema is wide-angle. In movies you can play a symphony whereas on television you just get a grating sound. The only advantage is that the grating can be continuous.'[41]

Secondly, and surprisingly, the episodic format represents a model of structural freedom for Lynch, the freedom to leave certain characters and take up with others, an aspect compressed into the span of a single film like *Fire Walk with Me*, resulting in a new and disconcerting kind of structure. The episodic format also offers great narrative freedom. Lynch seems to have been fascinated, for example, by the possibility that he would never have to end *Twin Peaks* if he did not reveal who murdered Laura Palmer. One recalls the open, never-needing-to-end structures of *Eraserhead* and *The Grandmother*. Narrative freedom does not mean indifference to the story, which is used as a pretext for saying something else, but rather such an intense belief in the story that, like a child, one would like to draw it out as far and as literally as possible.

Thirdly, the psychological conditions of reception: 'I appreciate television's accessibility. People are in their own homes and nobody's bothering them. They're well placed for entering into a dream.'[41] However, the impossiblity of personally controlling the whole product from start to finish was very painful for Lynch. He says that he was depressed at having to delegate some of this to others.

12

Like all television series, *Twin Peaks* started with a concept, that is to say, a preliminary definition of its genre. 'The project was to mix a police investigation with a soap opera. We had drawn a map of the city. We knew where everything was located and that helped us determine the prevailing atmosphere and what might happen there.'[5] Dana Ashbrook, who played Bobby, described *Twin Peaks* as a cross between *Peyton Place*, the well-known 60s

Blue Velvet

soap opera derived from a novel filmed by Mark Robson in 1957, and *Happy Days*, the 80s sitcom series set in the 50s, 'but with a touch of vitriol.' Understandably, Mark Frost tried to re-establish his part in the enterprise, far more important than the newspapers allowed, given their eagerness to see *Twin Peaks* as the work of Lynch alone, when he stated: 'We tried to renew evening soap operas the same way *Hill Street Blues* did with the police series ten years ago. David added a surrealistic touch.'[6] Even if it was only a touch, who is to say exactly how deep it went? Its consequences were certainly far reaching.

13

In concrete terms, *Twin Peaks* is an imaginary small town with a population of 51,201, as the sign with its drawing in the shape of an M at the town's entrance informs us. It is located in a wooded region of the north-west, several miles from the Canadian border (the first title considered was *Northwest Passage*). The town includes a sheriff's department, run by Sheriff Harry S. Truman, his deputies Andy and Hawk, and Lucy the receptionist; a high school we know through its students, like Donna, James, Bobby, Mike and the late Laura, but not through any of its teachers; the hospital where a wacky psychiatrist named Jacoby works; a large hotel, the Great Northern, owned by an ambitious, unscrupulous playboy, Ben Horne; a waterfall and a river, the hydraulic energy of which is used to operate the Packard sawmills over which the 'late' founder's sister is in conflict with his widow, whereas the grounds have become the object of Ben's appetite for land. What else? A coffee-shop and restaurant, the RR or Double R, run by Norma Jennings, is the meeting-place of most of the characters, and its cherry pie is much appreciated by agent Dale Cooper; a seamy, improbable bar and nightclub, the Roadhouse, is not very different from the Slow Club in *Blue Velvet*; and just across the Canadian border, there are the evil lights of the One-Eyed Jack, a clandestine gambling house and brothel owned by Horne. And then there is nature and the gigantic, endless forest which, instead of remaining a backdrop, never stops reminding us of its existence through its noises, animals and mysteries. Although there have been other soap operas named after a town (*Peyton Place*, *Dallas*, *Santa Barbara* and, in France, *Châteauvallon*), the setting has never been as important as in *Twin Peaks*, and some authentic sites have since been mythified. The RR and the Great Northern, both located near Seattle, have now become tourist attractions.

Twin Peaks has also been described as a kind of character haven, a harem where everyone, as Serge Daney put it in the first issue of his journal *Trafic*, 'gives you a hard on'. In short, *Twin Peaks* was first of all a setting open to everyone, a cornucopia of situations and characters. In Lynch's pilot episode, the action begins with the discovery of a floating corpse wrapped in plastic, the corpse of the high-school queen, the blond Laura Palmer. The investigation into her murder reveals that the pretty Laura, liked by everyone, took drugs, prostituted herself and had sado-masochistic sexual relations with several men. It is conducted by Truman and an FBI agent named Dale Cooper who is his own man, trusting in his dreams and intuitions and in Tibetan philosophy. The investigation introduces us to a number of the little town's inhabitants: students and parents, a mechanic and the mayor, and so on. We do not learn the name of Laura's murderer until episode 16: her father Leland Palmer, possessed by a diabolical and perhaps imaginary figure named Bob. Leland also killed Laura's look-alike cousin Madeleine Ferguson, also played by Sheryl Lee, in the same way. However, the action continues after the solution of this 'whodunit' because of the misdeeds of an ex-FBI agent Windom Earle, who has gone mad and follows Dale Cooper to *Twin Peaks*, and because of the increasingly frequent manifestations of forces stemming from a parallel universe, the Black Lodge, access to which could provide the key to power over this world. The clues which lead there are like those in all self-respecting treasure hunts: enigmatic phrases, coded maps on the cavern wall, and the like.

In episode 29, the last of the series, Dale Cooper finds the entrance to the Black Lodge and realises it is a space he has already encountered in his dreams, a room which is not black but red, where an enigmatic dwarf, a tutelary giant who appeared to him in his dreams, Laura and several other persons from the real world (unless they are their doubles) seem to dwell for all eternity. Dale enters the room to save a woman he loves, Anne Blackburne, from the forces of darkness. He manages to leave it alive but he is transformed and perhaps possessed in turn by Bob, or by his evil double. The series ended, in theory definitively, on this enigma.

For those who took the time to see the entire work, an experience facilitated by the existence of the complete series on video, there was a feeling of being introduced to a fabulous world, and almost of becoming one of the story's many characters. This world made the reputation of the series, but in spite of the many articles written about *Twin Peaks*, the last word on its characters has certainly not yet been spoken.

14

In addition to the minimal core needed for a mystery plot such as this one (the victim, the people with whom she was close, the culprit and the investigators), *Twin Peaks* also features a number of parallel plots:

– Laura's former boyfriend James and her best friend Donna fall in love, as it were, on Laura's tomb, thanks to her death; this allows their love to be founded on guilt;
– Bobby, another of Laura's ex-boyfriends, is a small-time drug dealer and the lover of waitress Shelly Johnson, who is married to a brutal lorry driver Leo Johnson; it turns out that Leo, who is also involved in drug dealing, was implicated in the last moments of Laura's life;
– Ed Hurley is an honest mechanic trapped between his mad, one-eyed wife Nadine and his attractive blonde mistress Norma, who runs the RR; Norma looks forward to and also fears her husband Hank's return from prison;
– Benjamin Horne and Katherine Martell are secret lovers scheming to acquire the sawmill from their antagonist Josie Packard, the millowner's widow; an attractive but suspect woman from Hong Kong, Josie is Sheriff Truman's mistress, but he is unaware of her past;
– Audrey Horne, Ben's daughter, investigates Laura's death for herself and so discovers her father's activities; she is hired and then held captive in a clandestine brothel, falls in love with Dale Cooper and unsuccessfully offers herself to him; in the end she meets her Prince Charming.

Clearly, there is ample opportunity here for all the identifications and projections one would wish to solicit, but what is actually new about the series? In general, the strangeness of the world of *Twin Peaks* has been explained by pointing out that each character is crazier than the next. The variety of characters is indeed somewhat mad, but, taken separately, some are more straightforward than others. Three different though overlapping categories can be distinguished:

1) The typical soap opera or police series characters who remain true to type; they may succumb to a fit of madness (like Ben Horne), but this passing condition does not affect the basic definition of the character as plotter, best friend, or whatever. In addition, none of their traits can be fetishised. Such characters include Harry S. Truman, the sheriff of *Twin Peaks*, a simple, loyal man; the paternal, understanding Dr Hayward; Deputy Hawk, the Indian; Ed Hurley, Norma, Madeleine Ferguson, Anne Blackburne and others. Among the main protagonists, the attractive Donna Hayward never ceases to be a 'good girl', even if she is possessed by Laura for a time (expressed by her sensually sucking a boy's finger). As Donna is incapable of wickedness, so her lover, the handsome James, always seems suspiciously innocent. A victim of his love relations, James is driven off and acquires a romantic dimension on account of his ever-present motorcycle, the horse on which this lonesome cowboy comes and goes.

Perhaps we should also mention the vixen Catherine and her docile husband Pete, the brutish Leo and Shelly the victim. These sado-masochistic couples remain faithful to their initial definitions and their function in the structure. None of them are double-layered and, regardless of what has been said about them, they form the basis of *Twin Peaks*'s universe and allow us to enter into it. Far from being a concession to conventional taste, they establish the story's credibility and enable identification, which is why *Twin Peaks* can operate as an evening soap opera. The episodes play out their love stories, local intrigues and games of power without any sense of derision. Quite the contrary, this is precisely why the series is beautiful, rather than because of some second-degree fooling around;

2) The second category comprises characters explicitly identified as bizarre, singled out by some physical aspect of their appearance, such as a piece of clothing or a favourite accessory which is systematically associated with them; the madness lies in the way they do not seem to surprise or disturb characters in the previous category. Through this second category, *Twin Peaks* boldly reintroduces a non-psychological logic, a system of types, costumes and poses in which the cowl makes the monk. Thus Josie Packard, an exotic beauty, is beautiful exoticism as such to the exclusion of practically everything else. She is defined by her being exotic. Although she is given a prominent place at the beginning of the pilot episode, in a fine and typically Lynchian portrait-shot which leads one to imagine that she will be

a key figure in the story, she remains in the wings for a long time. Her *femme fatale* dimension is not put to use, though actress Joan Chen's sad charm is so strong that it is enough for her to be on the screen. In the second season of *Twin Peaks*, she is put to use in a more definite way, exposed to the Martells' sadism and forced to be their servant. Another sexy character, Audrey Horne, is associated from the outset with certain teasing poses, a certain way of moving and of standing up straight in order to enchance her silhouette, dancing on the spot and strutting or walking in a sensual manner that would usually be considered extravagant or ridiculous but is not so in *Twin Peaks*. And yet, for all her provocative poses, Audrey, who is not a villain despite her unbearable behaviour in the pilot episode, is a virgin. She tries to lose her virginity and almost does so with her father, but succeeds only at the last minute when she finds her Prince Charming. Unlike Donna, who has nothing characteristic about her, Audrey is associated from the start with a kind of fetishism, signalled via an insistence on her red shoes and ankle socks. This foot fetish is later replaced by a detail which appears in the sixth episode and so marks Audrey that every newspaper article on the series inevitably mentions it as an example of exceptional sensual gifts: her ability to knot a cherry stem with her tongue.

Other characters are systematically linked to a physical weakness, an eccentricity, a phobia or sometimes all three. Harold Smith is linked to the agoraphobia which prevents him from leaving his house and to the orchids he grows; Eileen Hayward, Donna's paralysed mother, to her wheelchair; Nadine Hurley to the patch over her eye and her obsession with the silent curtain. Nadine is one of the great suicidal depressives in Lynch's universe and she survives only through temporary flights into madness during which she takes herself for a romantic high-school girl; in those fits, she is also endowed with the muscular strength of a Terminator. The list can go on: FBI agent Dennis/Denise is associated with a double sexual identity; one-armed Mike with his missing arm; Gordon Cole, Dale Cooper's half-deaf boss, played by Lynch, with the hearing-aid and wire dangling from his ear, which does not prevent him from shouting when he talks; Leland Palmer, Laura's father, with the white hair which appears shortly after her death in the course of one night; psychiatrist Lawrence Jacoby with his extravagant clothes such as sunglasses with different-coloured lenses or ear plugs. Even Dale Cooper, about whom more later, is associated with the dictaphone he calls Diana, on which he more or less regularly enters his reports, and with his black hair combed straight back and smoothed with gel. This second category of characters also includes a couple which acts as the on-duty comic duo, Lucy and Andy, who nevertheless transcend this category precisely because they unite into a couple and succeed in creating their own sphere, as Sailor and Lula will do in *Wild at Heart*. Lucy Moran is first of all a piping, shrill, prolix voice heard on the intercom and telephone lines of the switchboard at the *Twin Peaks* police station where she works. Her voice introduces the first tonal break in the series. Andy Brennan is a deputy police officer who weeps whenever he sees a corpse or hears bad news. At such moments, his expressions recall Stan Laurel, whose burlesque apparently supplied the key reference for the fine acting of Harry Goaz in the role of Andy. Requiring 29 episodes to form their lasting bond, the deputy and the receptionist make up a comic couple like the peasants in Molière and the clowns in Shakespeare. In the midst of an exorbitant plot staging the battle between good and evil, they play a role like Papagena and Papageno in *The Magic Flute*, embodying the living, modest, self-reproducing force of humanity. They are part of a hierarchy of characters, a non-psychological and non-naturalistic logic of roles which was abandoned long ago and yet proves mysteriously ravishing. It is in connection with them that the question of paternity arises when Lucy discovers that she is pregnant in the sixth episode but does not know who the child's father is. Two men claim paternity, an absurd dandy named Richard Tremayne and the stalwart Andy. After humiliating himself before Lucy, Andy will display his merits and be chosen as the only begetter. At the opening of the final episode, directed by Lynch, Andy, who in the original version was to have a voice as gentle as his physique was comic, and Lucy sing an unexpected, tender duet in which they vow their eternal love. They are the only couple en route to happiness.

3) The third category consists of characters who possess from the outset or who acquire a mythical quality. This is, of course, the case with the characters who belong to the parallel dimensions, who appear in fantasies and dreams, loom up among the gaps in the tissue of reality or communicate with other forces. Here we find Bob, of course, the strange incarnation of evil who, in the words of one surprised critic, resembles an ageing hippie; likewise, the dwarf who resides in the Red Room; the giant who dictates clues to Dale Cooper in his dreams; the senile porter at the Great Northern Hotel; the duo of the boy magician and the old lady (who reappear in *Fire Walk with Me*); and, of course, the Log Lady who never puts down the log which she carries like a child, crediting it with a visionary gift whose messages she transmits. Though it is surprising to find him here, perhaps one should also include Major Briggs, with his indeterminable mission. Briggs never removes his uniform and medals (a trait of the second category of characters), and he claims to have an obscure mission involving contact with extraterrestrial beings. A sententious bungler at the beginning, he makes us laugh just as he does his son Bobby. Later he becomes a heroic, mythical figure in the struggle with evil, especially when he has a mystical dream of family happiness in which he seeks to ensure the security of his wife and child, and when he is kidnapped and restored by a

parallel dimension, the White Lodge. Taken away then returned, tortured by the wicked Windom Earle, heroic and Christlike, Major Briggs comes to embody the father, the one-who-leaves-then-returns. Finally, there is Dale Cooper, who also begins in the second category but then moves into the third. At first he is a slightly perverse maverick, but he gradually takes on the dimensions of an Angel of Good.

15

When he arrives in *Twin Peaks*, Dale Cooper (Kyle MacLachlan, a perfect gentleman) wears a tie and has his hair plastered down. He dictates his first report to Diana as he drives along ('Never seen so many trees in my life') and it seems probable that he will offer the umpteenth version of a character dear to recent American cinema, the fish out of water. Cooper seems bound for a world where he does not fit and into which he will bring both freshness and prejudices. He is a Crocodile Dundee in reverse: a dapper FBI agent among the woodsmen. However, it does not quite turn out this way and there ensues no conflict between him and the locals. Clean-cut, courteous, full of naïve and youthful enthusiasm, Cooper in fact likes simple, unsophisticated food, possibly an ironic version of Lynch's own elementary culinary tastes such as McDonald's. Impervious to wickedness, incarnating perfection, Cooper gradually becomes a myth.

In the pilot episode, shot before ABC had committed itself to the series, Dale Cooper is potentially disquieting. He has a slightly sadistic method of questioning, aiming to destabilise people, and he extracts the letters from the victim's nails under strobe lighting, gloating like a mad scientist. Such details suggest that the authors envisaged Cooper moving in a very different direction. Instead, he becomes increasingly transparent and luminous, and this gradual decanting of the character, almost of its own accord, is the source of a specific, enormous pleasure. Similarly, the obsessive side he displays at the beginning, making notes on the exact sums spent on his mission, fades away and Cooper becomes increasingly simple and archetypal, even angelic.

The first extraterrestrial being in *Twin Peaks* may thus well be Dale Cooper. In fact, shortly before being cast in *Twin Peaks*, MacLachlan appeared in Jack Sholder's *The Hidden* (1988), playing the part of an extraterrestrial being exiled in a human body. Cooper's unreal aspect is brought out by exaggerated make-up and enigmatic behaviour. He lands at *Twin Peaks* as if he were landing on earth to discover its smells and flavours, to taste sugar as if his taste buds were working for the first time, to drink a cup of hot coffee with the wonderment of an angel fallen from the sky, like Bruno Ganz in Wim Wenders's *Der Himmel über Berlin* aka *Wings of Desire* (1987). Dale Cooper is

Lynch, a 'James Stewart from the planet Mars', but he is also Tintin, a smooth figure in a world of archetypes. As to his Diana, named after a mythological figure and to whom he addresses his dictaphone reports, she does not exist on earth because she exists only for him. None of his many FBI colleagues make even the slightest allusion to her as a real person.

16

As I suggested earlier, what is characteristic of *Twin Peaks* is not that everyone is mad, but that those who are not mad do not find the eccentric characters eccentric; the Log Lady is at home among these ordinary Eds and Donnas. *Twin Peaks* presents a non-psychological world. When someone goes mad and loses all sense of reality, and then recovers, the change is accepted without the other characters interpreting it psychologically. It is the structure of *Twin Peaks* which is mad. In joining each and every level without blending them together, and defining itself by this very act, *Twin Peaks* becomes both mythical and epic, the latter because of the insistence on everyday social comfort on a grand scale. In its very concept, *Twin Peaks* is a pleasant town. The trees smell good. There is a coffee shop where the owner is always friendly. When the police finish their investigation late at night, they find a plate of doughnuts waiting for them. Indeed, this is one of Dale Cooper's functions: he reveals *Twin Peaks* to itself as a town where everything is pleasant, the authorities affable and the police respectful of people's rights.

Twin Peaks is also the first television series where the characters interrupt the action to enjoy the smell of good, fresh air, the aroma of a good cup of coffee or of an apple pie, or even the heavenly pleasure of peeing in the woods, as in the seventeenth episode. This notion of ease, so new to the tense world of television series, in some way recalls the world of the epic poem. The *Iliad* and especially the *Odyssey* (which, according to an a neglected but fascinating theory, may have been written by a woman) attach great importance to this notion. We are told with communicative pleasure of how the diners satisfy people's appetites, how the characters bathe and afterwards smell good and put on fresh clothes, and so on. The viewers were certainly as charmed by these evocations of comfort as by the exploits of the heroes, the imaginary creatures and the appearance of phantoms. *Twin Peaks* revives the pleasure of following characters who enjoy the comforts of the place where they live, and who say so.

Of course, these comforts are simple and unsophisticated. Lynch certainly refers partly to himself here, for restaurants have an important role in his life, anecdotes and films. And the series' cult success in the United States, and perhaps elsewhere as well, seems to be closely linked to the regressive importance assigned to food. Not artful food but warming, sweet food: coffee, cherry pie, doughnuts – as if to domesticate the primitive wildness of the act of eating, and to regress by way of the uniformity of sweets. The English language, and American culture in particular, connect the words 'soft' and 'sweet', giving them a sexual connotation. The world of *Twin Peaks* begins as sugary sweet, but it is from such tender kindness, which gently leads us towards old, apparently inoffensive memories, that the horror arises. This notion of ease is first of all entirely on the surface, in this case a somewhat cracked civilisational veneer.

Twin Peaks is a world with a hole in it, a sign with a name and a population figure. Reference to a double already appears in the name. It is a kind of Bermuda triangle where everything can appear and disappear. *Twin Peaks* opens up not only to caverns and worlds of light and darkness, but also to the past, as when Ben Horne takes himself for a Civil War General and refights a battle in favour of the South, or when Major Briggs has been swallowed by a parallel dimension and then re-emerges in a 50s pilot's uniform.

The territory of *Twin Peaks* is first of all a cosy nest, a pool of nurturing nature, with water, fire, energy, space, woods and things to eat. It extends the image of a pair of endlessly nurturing breasts (the twin peaks), from which the characters, music and action flow in abundance, but it is at the same time an archaic world, with unbridled forces represented by the inserts between scenes, where we see a lonely, cyclopean traffic light in the dark, empty streets at night, dense branches tossing in a stormy wind, a mountain slope with fog ominously rolling down.

Television is an extraordinary thing. It is enough to replace the intermediate 'filler' or transitional shots of buildings or farms by images of forests, different phases of the moon, a foaming waterfall or a sky laden with clouds, and a swirl of restless, natural forces seems to be unleashed once more. However, along with this movement, night and emptiness surround the characters and their world, and are all the more frightening because *Twin Peaks* is such a tiny, pleasant place.

From the very first episode, *Twin Peaks* recreated the night in every house and apartment where the series was seen, the real night and not a night setting, the night with its persistent, deep darkness. It did so by making each television screen what it really is: a little window of light which is a little too highly coloured, shining in an ocean of night. Apparently we owe this to Lynch. His fascination with the archaic and a sense of emptiness seems to have pervaded or at least influenced even the episodes in which he least participated. Or rather, it is as though he revealed in every actor and director their own atavistic core, permitting them to fuel the collective myth which *Twin Peaks* has become. As a whole, the series transcends its authors, including Lynch. The superimposition of multiple story layers and

Blue Velvet

levels of meaning, culminates in giving the series the astonishing power of composite compilations such as epic poems or sacred books. *Twin Peaks* is both a private frenzy and a collective outbreak of madness, a myth, a nest to ease our suffering, to which everyone brings his or her little twig.

17

Too much has been made of the quotes and allusions in *Twin Peaks*. The references to Preminger's *Laura* (1944) via a mina bird named Waldo and a veterinarian named Lydecker who jointly form the name of *Laura*'s Pygmalion, and to Hitchcock's *Vertigo* (1958) via Laura's look-alike cousin Madeleine, are no more than the manifestation of a debt towards two well-known films with analogous basic situations. These situations were then incorporated and interpreted differently in each case. The only part of *Twin Peaks* which is clearly modelled on film noir is also its weakest section – James Hurley's love affair, in the second series, with a colourless 1940s *femme fatale*.

Of course the name Laura is not an accidental choice, but here, too, a superficial resemblance in plot should not lead us to overlook the more telling differences. Laura Hunt, played by Gene Tierney, was twice the victim of attempted murder by Waldo, but she escapes both times, first at the cost of another woman's life and the second time at that of the would-be murderer's. Laura Palmer is less lucky. She is killed, twice: first in person, then through her cousin Madeleine Ferguson. Laura Hunt begins as a portrait just as Laura Palmer does, but in *Twin Peaks*, the painting is replaced by a sweet photograph. The main point, which becomes clearer in *Fire Walk with Me*, is that Laura Palmer is not a sophisticated creature, but a mixed-up, small-town, high-school girl. In combining the situations of a film noir and a melodramatic television series, while adding a fantasy dimension, Frost and Lynch (and their main co-writers Harley Peyton and Robert Engels) did nothing less than to recreate romantic drama. They achieved this simply by merging tones and dimensions which it had become customary to treat separately.

Until recently, the irrational had its own cinematographic genres in which there was no time to fall in love or to cry. It was necessary to hold fast, to stand up against evil, with a hard, determined look on one's face. There are no love affairs in *The Exorcist* (1973) or in *Alien* (1979). Contemporary masters of the fantasy genre such as John Carpenter tend to be tough-minded, admirers of Hawks, who avoid sentimentality and treat the genre as incompatible with tears and lovers' vows. In contrast, neo-melodramas such as James Brooks's *Terms of Endearment* (1983) or Randa Haines's *Children of a Lesser God* (1986) have become contemporary and thoroughly bourgeois. In them, there is no room for anything other than feelings. In bringing together cosmic fantasy and emotional ardour, *Twin Peaks* brought together a time and a space which have long been deprived of one another. At one time, Romanticism was everything at the same time: the irrational with sentiment, fairies and demons along with kisses.

With its carnival of genres (including even a dash of the erotic, but an eroticism for well-behaved girls), *Twin Peaks* combines forces which multiply vertiginously upon contact. To be fair, these forces were reunited first, though in a more sterile mode, in ghost melodramas like Steven Spielberg's *Always* (1989) and Jerry Zucker's *Ghost* (1990). However, *Twin Peaks* is as it is, unique, because someone actually believed even in the most sentimental, tearful aspect of the story, thus allowing others to renew their own desire to believe, authorising them to do so. It seems to me that that someone is David Lynch. To attribute the series' success to a calculating cynicism is thus foolish. Had it not succeeded, its boldness and its mistakes would have been pointed out instead.

18

Some of the derision heaped upon the series was no doubt also prompted by the way it deploys tears, especially at the beginning of the pilot episode, where the scenes of weeping were a shock to everyone. However, tears flow in all of Lynch's films, from *Eraserhead* to *Fire Walk with Me*. Previously, only opera was permitted to make such abundant use of them. Everything about the phenomenon of weeping seems to fascinate Lynch. One might even say that he revitalises its use for the screen. In particular, he shows how the welling up of tears, like a slow constriction, alters and convulses the face without drawing the body in its wake – weeping is an on-the-spot commotion. Nor does Lynch hesitate to show what is considered to be the ugliness of a person weeping. Is this the reason why Japanese audiences were mad about *Twin Peaks*, since, as the Japanese cinema shows, they are not afraid of showing exacerbated, tense physical expressions of feeling? Weeping in the cinema normally involves an isolated teardrop rolling down the cheek, which the camera registers fairly tactfully. In Lynch's films, however, the whole face contorts and becomes ugly, without even any signs of moistness, while the rest of the body stiffens.

After causing fountains of tears to flow from the spectators' eyes with *The Elephant Man* (even though his characters contained their emotion, as was shown by the single tear rolling down the face of Anthony Hopkins), Lynch dared to make his actors sob, running the risk of stifling the symmetrical effect of tears among the spectators. Treves's wife holds back her tears before John Merrick and thus, in the grand tradition of dramatic cinema, gives the signal to unleash ours. Laura Dern's ugly grimaces like those of a sobbing child over Jeffrey's infidelity, Grace Zabriskie's shrieks at losing her child and Andy Brennan weeping at Laura Palmer's corpse can only forestall our tears, even as they arouse a bizarre, obscure emotion. This is one of the elements which has led critics to speak of ice-cold cinema. In fact, Lynch is simply aiming for another emotional dimension.

It is worth recalling Lynch's great admiration for Kubrick's *Lolita* (1961). The star of this important film is the best cinematic weeper of them all, James Mason. This no doubt inspired Lynch in certain scenes with Leland Palmer. At the same time, the way Lynch draws out the weeping scenes in the television series touches on another dimension, that of media voyeurism. I am thinking in particular of the famous scene in the pilot episode in which Sarah Palmer weeps with distress over the telephone, though her husband has already dropped the receiver. The spectator witnesses the scene with a troubled awareness of his advance knowledge. We know that Laura is dead and look on as her parents receive the news. In its length, the scene resembles the live witnessing of an event and its retransmission. By throwing the spectator back on his own voyeurism, the scene conveys the change in orientation, as exploited in 'reality shows'. An embarrassment is thus produced which in no way prevents our fascination. This becomes all the clearer since two tonal breaks in the midst of this dramatic situation have already shattered the surface of the convention: Andy's unexpected weeping at Laura's corpse and Lucy's jumbled explanations to Sheriff Truman. In the opening minutes of the series, Lynch thus walks the tightrope of tonal changes, and he succeeds. The series needed to work hard to keep up this level of audacity. Embarrassing, burlesque details were thus slipped into the most dramatic scenes, which none the less remain painful: the gag of adjusting the chairs at the bedside of poor Ronnette Pulaski who has been raped and traumatised; Leland Palmer stretching out on his daughter's coffin and going down into the grave, and so on.

However, from the moment we believe in the story and take it literally, as we must, everything becomes a source of great pleasure and everyone, including the cynics and the emotive viewers, finds something in it for them. Emotive viewers are no more bothered by the strange passages than the cynics are by the abundance of naïve, innocent scenes. Each one is allowed and allows the other, so that *Twin Peaks* becomes a bring-your-own event where we are happy to find that everything is already waiting for us, and we are grateful for the generosity of the hosts.

19

A unifying element was necessary for so strange and composite a project, a function fulfilled by the music of Angelo Badalamenti. It hardly matters whether, apart from its role within the series, the music has what is called intrinsic value. In the series the music is a stroke of genius, endowing the whole with force and continuity. First, there is the theme music played over the credits and which never fails to impress. It opens to the sickly sweet sounds of a bass with the timbre of a synthesised guitar. It is impossible not to listen to the rocking rhythm laid down by this bass. Then there is the naïve theme, the kind of music written for music primers. It opens in a fairly deep register, resounding like a whispered secret, and suggests the word of mouth transmission of high-school girls' gossip. The original idea of *Twin Peaks* seems to have involved a secret meeting of a group of well-behaved schoolgirls at night in a room or dormitory, playing at making up horror stories. The muffled, intimate tone of these notes strung together to accompany the credits provides the series with its distinctive tonality, and its presence is particularly striking at the beginning of the pilot episode directed by Lynch, setting the tone for the whole of the saga.

Twin Peaks opens in the manner of a fable: the strange and captivating shot of the beautiful Chinese woman at her make-up table, turning her head towards something we cannot make out. Perhaps she has heard something. She mumbles to herself in the same register as the music. When Pete Martell leaves his house immediately afterwards to go fishing, he too mumbles to himself, 'Another day with the land breeze blowing,' and the music is relayed by soft, muted sounds a little like foghorns. The lapping waves are subdued, rocking, just a murmur, no loud blasts disturbing the scene. It is in this padded atmosphere that Laura's corpse will be discovered, and then the high-pitched voice of Lucy the receptionist will blare like a trumpet, effecting the first tonal disruption.

When mentioning the credit sequence introducing each episode, the importance in them of silent shots associated with water and fire should also be noted. A close-up of an obsolete piece of industrial machinery throwing off sparks without us hearing the shrill noise the activity implies; a long shot of the *Twin Peaks* waterfall without the sound of its roar. However, precisely because a haunting musical theme is heard instead, we become aware of what is gentle yet implacable in the image, such as the repetitive movement of the machine turning the blade of a circular saw or what is soft yet relentless in the falling of a heavy mass of water.

Out of the confident, murmured theme which accompanies the images in the credits of the machine and the waterfall, a rising, lyrical melody unfolds like a song, ascending vertically to the high notes just as the waterfall plummets vertically into the deep. At the same time, an intermittent counter-theme, imitating the water we see, softly and steadily falls along contiguous notes. This indefatigable, steady counter-theme seems to have been inspired by one word in the lyrics which Lynch wrote for the melody: the word 'falling', removed from the expression 'falling in love' (are we beginning to fall in love?) and taken literally. It is a fundamental word for Lynch, who conjugates its various meanings in his lyrics as well as in his films. 'I'm falling,' Dorothy Vallens screams in *Blue Velvet*, and Lumberton Radio's time signal uses 'the sound of a falling tree'. Awareness of the vertical axis is fundamental for Lynch, associated as it is with ideas of collapse and bodily recovery. The music and the lyrics find a match in the images of plumes of smoke rising from the the sawmill and the mist rising from the falling water.

The second theme, Laura Palmer's, is heard later. It is always heard, not in the credit sequence but within the episodes themselves, associating it closely with the atmosphere pervading the whole series. This theme suggests a kind of dark, deep swaying within the narrow compass of thirds. As sinister as a death knell, it confirms the drama and mourning and, at the same time, gently rocks us with a sense of endless lamentation. At times, as with the credit theme but with a vaster movement and tenser harmonies, another song emerges from Laura's theme like a growing flower. This lyrical, dramatic song, which we hear especially in moments of emotion and tears, rises to the high notes with a scream. It is a surprising and innovative musical effect for television, given its exceptionally lyrical character and its broad register. Each time it rises and begins to expand, like the oblong shapes in Lynch's first short films, it creates a kind of suspense as we wonder how much further it can go.

The third main theme, called 'Audrey's Dance', is very different. Illustrating the series' humorous, sexy side, the jazzy music combines the pizazz of the double bass and snapping fingers. It is sometimes used in police scenes or in eroticised contexts, especially in relation to Audrey Horne, the most urbane character among the women of *Twin Peaks*. The theme's humour derives from its being out of place in a backwoods setting, where the conventions lead us to expect a country and western ballad. This third theme belongs to the tradition of television series. It creates a sense of urban, sophisticated and hypnotic distance, and might almost have been composed by Henry Mancini, one of Lynch's favourite cinema composers, for a Blake Edwards comedy.

The most consistant feature of this musical atmosphere, given the choice of timbre and the compositional style, is the permanence of a register suggestive of murmuring, and, as we know, the register in music (medium, medium-low and so on) is the emphasised part of the musical texture. There are also speech registers, such as murmurs, whispers, normal speech and shouting. This idea of registers, in its various senses, is fundamental for Lynch. He is one of the film-makers whose expressive resources include very wide ranges of registers, from the very deep to the overshrill, from guffaws to screams, from the everyday to the mystical.

20

Finally, we must not forget that all this is based on the memory of a dead girl, a girl who will have been everything: at first, everything wonderful and idealised, then everything dissolute and disreputable. Laura Palmer's ears must be ringing in the beyond, for in her death she is spoken about incessantly, to the point that Donna, in a beautiful graveside monologue in the 5th episode, reproaches her for being the centre of attention. Without wishing to offend her best friend, we might say that in her death Laura seems to authorise everything, generously to let it all sprout from the landscape which her body has become. One again recalls that *Sunset Boulevard* (1950), a story told by its dead hero seen floating in a swimming pool as the film opens, like Laura Palmer in the river, is one of Lynch's favourite films. It presents a dead-man-who-speaks and governs the images. A dead man who speaks, a dead girl who is spoken about. The one spoken about is also a listening corpse. And attending the dead girl who is spoken about, the dead girl who resuscitates life's effervescence, there is the live woman who is forgotten and never spoken about, the woman whom the series puts away in a secret closet, bringing her out only now and then to show that she is inconsolable: Laura's mother, the depressive, sombre, dark Sarah Palmer.

As with Dorothy Vallens, one would do anything, beating her as well as speaking to her softly, to let her know that one is there for her, to lift her with sensorial and emotional shocks, with filmic electric shocks, to prevent her from drowning. One would try anything, including the intimate physical violence of incest, that double-edged treatment which simultaneously wounds the one who uses it. In the end, in his painting as well as in his cinema, that is what Lynch seems to have devoted himself to, innocently and apparently without harm.

IV

CINE-SYMPHONIES FOR HER

(Wild at Heart, Industrial Symphony No. 1, Twin Peaks: Fire Walk with Me)

1

For several years, Lynch has been living in Los Angeles. In the same way that he established a setting for his films, he seems to have established a setting for his own working and living conditions: 'Two-thirty is Bob's time [Big Boy Bob's has been a popular restaurant chain since the 50s. Translator]. I can think there and draw on the napkins and have my shake. Sometimes I have a cup of coffee and sometimes I have a small Coke. They both go great with shakes.'[18] We know how important it is for Lynch to sit down, and not just anywhere, in order to think, his eyes wandering over the surface of a table. The setting required for the production of ideas is not at all a matter of indifference, as demonstrated by his first film painting, *Six Figures*, which presented a screen, a flat surface, on which heads appeared in relief. When he describes his favourite coffee-shops and restaurants, Lynch is also describing the world of banal comforts and familiar, easily located markers which he seems to need in order to plunge into the realms of darkness: 'I like diners. I don't like dark places. I like light places with formica and metal and nice shiny silver, metal mugs, a good Coca-Cola machine.'[18] That is the kind of revelation Lynch likes to make in press interviews, or that journalists like to highlight. In any case, such revelations form a barrier before his deeper intentions, about which he long ago adopted a particular philosophy: 'What I would be able to tell you about my intentions in my films is irrelevant. It's like digging up someone who died four hundred years ago and asking him to tell you about his book.'[16]

In contrast, he has often returned to the subject, as if it held a general lesson for everybody, of how he lets his ideas arise and take hold: 'You should always pay attention to the way you feel on a day-to-day basis';[40] ideas 'are just allowed to kind of swim. You're not subject to people judging them or anything. They just swim, and you don't really worry about what they mean. It's all feelings: it feels right and you know intuitively what it's doing, and you work from that level. It somehow turns out being an honest thing if you stay on that level, and just let those ideas swim around, down where you capture them.'[1] These ideas are neither verbal nor abstract, but concrete: 'You don't have to worry about expressing them in words. The important thing is to translate them into the language of film. Translate them by a little "plop" on the soundtrack and a little shot in a sequence. Find the feeling that corresponds to the idea you had. The script ends up killing a lot of films that could have been more abstract and different.'[12] Every idea is a small bomb or a battery, a reservoir of power: 'When an idea first comes to you, it has an intrinsic power. You have to try to remember the way you felt when the idea first came to you and to remain faithful to that.'[12]

According to Lynch, ideas do not belong to the night but to the day, to something better expressed with the notion of 'daydream': 'Waking dreams are the ones that are important, the ones that come when I'm quietly sitting in a chair, gently letting my mind wander.'[25] Starting from a number of ideas clustering around a theme, a project can begin to take shape: 'Most of my ideas are totally spontaneous. Then I roughly sort them out to see how one idea follows from another and combines with it. The same goes for scenes. How do they connect? What is their logic? Ideas combine among themselves and you begin to glimpse something which can generate lots of other ideas, but once a certain number of ideas have been linked up, the mould has been set and all the other ideas have to fit in with that.'[16] This leads to the author's conception of the cinema as a sort of sieve which remains open and available to ideas, including ideas introduced by others: 'The director is like a filter. Everything passes through me. Everybody has input and has ideas and, so, the movie has a great momentum going for it. Some things pass right through the filter and some things don't.'[3] Even during shooting, Lynch does not hesitate to incorporate ideas suggested by some prop on the set or by the situation itself: 'I use a script and storyboards like blueprints; they give me a solid structure on which to build. Nothing's fixed until the film is done.'[18]

All this helps to explain why he casts actors on the basis of their personality, intuitively, without making them do a screen test, and why he works with them repeatedly, combining them with others, like a matchmaker. He approaches his work on sound in the same manner: 'For me, film is a very strong desire to marry images and sounds. When I achieve this, I get a real thrill. In fact, I'm not sure I'm looking for anything more than just that thrill.'[40]

2

After the failure of Dune, *Blue Velvet* restored Lynch's reputation as a director and restored his confidence to return to the formal boldness of his earlier work. The result was two unusual, agitated films, *Wild at Heart* and *Fire Walk with Me*, films which can be criticised as arrogant and loud, but for those who look more carefully they are also a return to the baroque style of his beginnings. With these films, Lynch seems to extend his search for a non-psychological cinema which combines textures and themes, a cinema with a more ample, epic tone and free, unpredictable constructions. The genre he was aiming for can be called 'a cine-symphony', characterised by traits such as the use of more powerful contrasts than he previously allowed himself; the revelation rather than the concealment of the use of discontinuity in the overall structure; a broad application of Dolby sound exploiting its resources to obtain contrast, space and power in the sound; and a bolder mixture of tones and atmospheres. Of course, there was still the challenge of forming an expressive whole which is organised around elements displaying their disparateness. *Wild at Heart*, a film which divided the critics even more than did *Blue Velvet*, was the first of these efforts.

Wild at Heart

The origins of the work are straightforward and well known. Lynch's producer and director friend Monty Montgomery had purchased the rights to a number of novels, including those of Barry Gifford. In 1989, Gifford presented a new, as yet unpublished novel to Montgomery, *Wild at Heart: The Story of Sailor* and *Lula*. Montgomery read the manuscript and took an option on it. At first, he intended to direct the film himself with Lynch as producer. However, Lynch began to get involved and Montgomery accepted that, in this case, Lynch would do the directing.

As shown by his numerous productions in this period – advertising spots, video clips, painting exhibitions, a record album and a musical spectacle with Badalamenti – Lynch was in a prolific phase. He had suffered badly during his inactivity between 1984 and 1987, and jumped at the *Wild at Heart* project with a sense of urgency. At the time, he was working on a script based on a 40s detective novel for Propaganda Film, a firm run by Steve Golin and the Icelander Sigurjon Sighvatsson. They had come out of video and wished to extend their activities into features. Lynch was permitted to drop the work in progress to devote himself to *Wild at Heart*, provided he began the film at once. The production schedule was laid out, with work to begin two months after the rights had been obtained. Lynch managed to write a first version of the script in the record time of one week. Four months later, on 9 August 1989, shooting started. *Wild at Heart* is a summer film, whereas *Fire Walk with Me* is essentially autumnal. Natural locations were chosen near Los Angeles, especially in the desert half an hour's drive from the city. Another part of the film was shot in New Orleans's French Quarter and in the city's vicinity. The budget was considerably higher than for *Blue Velvet*, $9 million, but still far below that of the major American films of the day. The crew of the previous film was reunited. Fred Elmes directed the photography; Patricia Norris was in charge of production design; Duwayne Dunham was the editor and the cast once again included Isabella Rossellini and Laura Dern.

3

Gifford reacted to the adaptation of his novel by saying that Lynch had taken everything that was dark in the novel and made it much more perverse. Lynch, however, said he had contented himself with making 'everything that was bright a little brighter and everything black a little blacker', showing his familiar taste for contrast. As the novel is an interesting work in its own right, it may be useful to know something of its nuances, especially since Lynch went on to make some changes which reveal his personal vision even more than he did in *Dune*, where he was impeded by subject-matter already known to millions.

Gifford's book is a road novel, a romantic and strange tale of two young people. Sailor loves Lula and Lula loves Sailor. Sailor is not really a bad fellow but he has fits of violence. He killed a crook named Bobby Ray Lemon in self-defence. When the film opens, he is just out on parole after two years of prison. Lula and he are still in love. They reunite and make love in hotel rooms. Then Sailor breaks parole by going to another state, California. Marietta Pace, Lula's mother, is outraged to see her little girl in the hands of a 'killer' and asks her lover, detective Johnnie Farragut, to kill Sailor. Farragut refuses though he does agree to track down the couple and try to bring Lula to her senses. Marietta then considers involving a hired killer whom she knows, Santos, but does not go through with the threat. From conversations between Lula and Sailor we learn that Sailor lost his parents at an early age and that Lula's father died by pouring petrol on himself after suffering from mental problems caused by lead fumes.

On the way to California, Sailor and Lula stop in New Orleans where Johnnie picks up their trail. Having no money, the couple stop in a small Texas town with the absurd name of Big Tuna, and Sailor tries to find a job as a mechanic. They make the acquaintance of a former marine and ex-convict, Bobby Peru, who is suspected of having taken part in massacres of civilians in Vietnam. Lula becomes depressed at the thought of having to stay in this godforsaken hole, especially when she discovers that she is pregnant: as a young girl, she had been traumatised by an abortion following rape. Peru proposes that Sailor take part in a hold-up, which he guarantees will be without violence, but the hold-up goes wrong, Bobby is killed and Sailor is arrested. Marietta and Johnnie recover Lula who gives birth to a boy. Several years later, this time with a calmer Marietta's consent, Lula is reunited with Sailor when he is freed from prison. Although she still loves him, Sailor finds it best to leave Lula who can get by without him. She lets him go.

Gifford does not treat the story as a suspense plot, more like a destructured ballad where (and this may have seduced Lynch) the action is reduced to a minimum and progresses nonchalantly if at all. The film consists essentially of dialogue scenes in which Sailor and Lula, two fanatical talkers ('Talkin's good,' says Lula, 'long as you got the other. I'm a big believer in talkin''), say whatever comes into their minds as they drive along, between rounds of sex in clammy hotel rooms, or while drinking in bars. They give their immediate impressions of the places and people they meet, idiotic facts from sensationalist newspapers, personal memories, stories that happened to them or that they heard someone tell. Everything is worth communicating between them, and this is always lively, funny, unusual or refreshing.

This aspect of the novel is reflected in the book's layout, which strings together many, often short chapters which are separated from one another but not numbered. Instead, they have titles suggesting individual scenes, such as 'Girl Talk', 'Heat Wave', 'Mosquitoes'. The novel's poetic quality lies in these dialogues and in the accumulation of strange meetings and odd facts. Gifford's Sailor and Lula are unconsciously eccentric and at the same time peaceful characters. This is the meaning of Lula's sentence in the opening pages of the book and which inspires its title: 'The world is really wild at heart and weird on top.' Human beings in an abnormal, sordid world: this idea which inverts the *Bonnie and Clyde* structure pleased Lynch, and he respected it when adapting the book for the screen.

4

In other respects, however, Lynch took considerable liberties, filling out or even interpreting and overstepping what the novel had left readers free to imagine. He makes Marietta, the mother, guilty of a crime, and invents a plot around Sailor which requires the complicity of several characters who are independent of each other in the novel. This paranoid structure occurs in *Dune* as well, but here it has the advantage of fitting the concentrated form of the film. Thus Marietta killed Lula's father in a fire with the help of Santos who, in the book, is no more than a name. Lynch also imagines that Marietta calls on Santos to kill Sailor and that Santos, who is in love with her, announces his intention of eliminating his rival, Farragut, at the same time. She protests strongly and goes to warn Farragut, but when the latter has been kidnapped and murdered on Santos's orders, she pretends to believe that he has simply run off. Like a forgetful, obedient child, she allows Santos to become her new companion.

Lynch also adds a new character, Mr Reindeer, a sort of 'light opera godfather' in the words of one critic, who runs a brothel in New Orleans and unites the scattered threads of the plot by centralising the contracts for the murder of Farragut and Sailor. He steers Bobby Peru to Sailor. The hold-up is invented as a trap for Sailor.

Lastly, Lynch implies that Marietta wants to kill Sailor because he refused her advances. Lynch makes Marietta into an excessive character. Whereas in the novel she is merely rather agitated, in the film she vomits, screams and covers her face with lipstick to the sound of thundering music. In Diana Ladd's acting and Lynch's conception, this Clytemnestra crossed with Phaedra and a witch also seems a woman-child of disconcerting naïvety.

On the other hand, Lynch did not bother to rework the psychology of his two young heroes in order to bring them into line with his murder plot. When Lula learns of her father's murder, she does not become an Electra. The idea of vengeance does not even seem to occur to her. The result is a pervasive sense of impotence and absurdity. The plot is, as it were, sketched in in pencil, proceeding in fits and starts. In this respect, Pascal Pernod was right to say that 'the film's visual and sound leitmotivs and its system of alternating plots delays the emergence of something substantial so far that it never arrives'.[5] However, one may also feel that the subject of the film (and of the novel, for that matter) lies precisely in the chasm which is opened up by that very delaying mechanism.

Lynch makes his modifications at Johnnie Farragut's expense for, after Sailor and Lula, he is the novel's most important character, an unusual figure who writes screenplays and short stories. His existence in the film is limited, rather movingly, to being Marietta's lover, victim and faithful servant. His murder in a voodoo ritual with sexual undertones is Lynch's morbid invention.

The novel also includes many narratives and bizarre details which Lynch uses quite literally, centring them on Sailor and Lula, keeping or displacing the ones in which he is interested, adding others of his own making, while aiming at the same meaning as Gifford: the world's head and heart are in bad shape. For example, the harsh love scene between Perdita Durango, a beautiful Mexican who becomes the central character in the sequel Gifford later wrote, and Bobby Peru becomes, in the film, the infamous sequence of verbal rape between Peru and Lula, the latter being coerced, disgusted and aroused all at the same time.

In the book, the heroes are told of a horrible accident. In the film, they actually come upon the accident by night, but they are too late to do more than look on helplessly as a young woman dies without even knowing that she is injured. Unaware of the fact that her parents are lying at her side, she panics at having lost her handbag ('My purse is gone!'). The scene, often singled out by viewers, is both terrifying and poetic. It also summarises the spirit of the film. The film's violence leads nowhere, neither does it procure a cathartic transcendence nor is it recycled to fuel the action. Consequently, critics spoke of things being purely for effect and to shock, which was not far wrong, but that is precisely the meaning of the film and the source of its special pathos. Its rhapsodic structure resembles that of *Fire Walk with Me* and involves a rectilinear trajectory, a forward flight (Sailor and Lula's, and later Laura Palmer's) which is intersected by encounters, things that suddenly loom up, and visions.

Finally, in the constantly happy relationship between Sailor and Lula as a couple, Lynch adds a supplementary note of calm which makes their mutual understanding more harmonious and idealised. In Gifford's book, a slight sense of discord, tension and aggressiveness between the sexes remains present. For example, Lula throws a beer bottle at Sailor when she finds him dancing near a bleached blonde. This act of jealousy disappears from the film, as do some remarks on male egotism. And yet, tensions and misunderstandings within the main couple are standard fare in traditional scripts. That Lynch did not avail himself of this convention, for instance by playing on Lula's jealousy of Perdita, shows the way he thinks. Sailor and Lula are for him a dream image, merely figures of thought. In contrast, Lynch invented a scene in a nightclub where a fellow who holds Lula a bit too close is taught a lesson by the gallant Sailor, who then sings Lula a romantic song. This is a homage to the innocent films starring, for instance, Elvis Presley, which moved Lynch as a teenager. Lynch's image of the heroine conforms to 50s sentimentality. Though Lula may swear like a trooper, she remains a working girl obsessed with her body; as a woman, she stands up for her rights and her independence less vigorously than in the book.

After hesitating for a long time about keeping the book's unhappy ending, Lynch resolved to graft on a happy ending. We see Sailor taking leave of Lula and then, like a coda, Lynch adds an episode in which Sailor is beaten up by a street gang. Lying on the ground, he has a vision of a good fairy, recalling *The Wizard of Oz* (1939), who tells him to believe in Lula's love and to trust in the future. Sailor gets up, thanks the hoodlums for the lesson they have taught him, screams 'Lula' and races after her in an explosion of enthusiasm. Before their delighted son, he makes what for Lula must be the most beautiful of marriage proposals: he sings her *Love Me Tender* like Elvis Presley. This happy ending is deliberately unannounced so that it does not smooth over the rough edges or provide a sense of calm at the close of a story full of dramatic and horrible incidents. On the contrary, Lynch emphasises its unreality by stylising the attack on Sailor, which he films like a brawl in a western, and calling on a *fea ex machina*. Many spectators felt this was a derisory ending, used by Lynch to parody his hero's cheap sentimentalism, but Lynch believes so strongly, or would so like to believe, in this ending that it is necessarily unbearable. Moreover, he persisted. When he made the video version of *Industrial Symphony No. 1*, he used the same two actors for the prologue and had them play a farewell scene over the telephone. Filmed with absolute simplicity, this scene has Sailor telling a distraught Lula that he cannot stand it any more and has to move on, but that he cannot explain: 'Ain't nothing wrong with you. It's just us I can't handle.'

5

To everyone's surprise, Lynch chose to cast Laura Dern as Lula, a far more torrid role than she had played in *Blue Velvet*. 'For me,' he said, 'it was Laura all the way though a lot of people found that inconceivable. They knew and respected her work, but they couldn't see her playing Lula.'[5] The choice was indeed an original one. An American journalist who was present at the shooting of the scene in which she listens with pleasure to Sailor's account of his first sexual experience noted with amusement how, when she had to say 'That's an awful long way to go just to get some pussy,' her voice dragged and she wriggled her shoulders and arched her back like a cartoon pin-up girl. The director finally took her aside and spoke to her with paternal concern, reminding her of words like 'bubble gum' and 'cigarettes', which enabled her to retrieve the character. Lynch explained his method: 'Every character is made up of so many little subtleties, strange choices, odd little ways of saying a word. Lula is a hard character to get a handle on, and bubble gum has a lot to do with keeping her on track.'[18] The journalist who conducted this interview noted that, in *Wild at Heart*, Lynch pushed his actors to dare all sorts of novel effects without being afraid to exaggerate or stylise.

The technique proved successful for Laura Dern, who is both overwrought and adorable, without the least trace of hysteria, as she plays a woman who finds herself incredibly sexy because the person she loves thinks she is. Many scenes would border on the grotesque, as when she touches herself and stiffens on the spot (she is largely a character fixed in one spot, like an animated pin-up), were it not for her freshness. She in fact presents us with one of the least conventional young woman's characters in recent cinema.

Nicolas Cage had already played the part of a nice loser a number of times. In *Wild at Heart*, Lynch allows him to give more pathetic and comic, emotional and tender dimensions to a character with which he was thoroughly familiar. The gaudy snakeskin coat is an important clothing accessory for the role recalling Tennessee Williams's guitar-playing hero in *Orpheus Descending*, filmed by Sydney Lumet as *The Fugitive Kind* (1960). Sailor also uses it, with utter conviction, as a symbol of his individuality and belief in freedom. In fact, this famous coat is part of the definition of a character, with gestures and actions expressing a naïve identification with the stars, descending via Marlon Brando through youth cultures and, in the form of fashion accessories like belts and boots, rock music mythology.

Lynch has described how he introduced Laura Dern to Nicolas Cage in, of course, a restaurant. This one was in Los Angeles close to a cinema that happened to be on fire: 'It seemed like a sign, because fire is so important in the film.' After that first meeting, Lynch had the idea of putting them in a car and sending them off to Las Vegas for the weekend, to see 'what effect it would have on them to be a unit after having been two'. After the love affair between Laura and Kyle on as well as off the set of *Blue Velvet*, Dern and Cage also made their director's wishes come true. As many spectators have observed, the couple work very well on the screen, even if (or because) the two characters do not conform to the stereotype of a flashy, sexy couple. Instead, they are wonderfully in tune and very lively: the very image everyone would like to have of young, tender parents.

Diane Ladd, Laura Dern's real mother, energetically plays the highs and lows and the excess which Lynch requested for the role of Marietta, but something is lacking in the character and we are not always convinced. A sense of distance sets in and in the end, though the woman is supposed to be crazed and unhinged, she becomes a caricature. Ladd nevertheless expresses the 'little girl' dimension of Marietta very well. The film falters with Marietta, by not enabling us to arrive at the sum of her different images.

Harry Dean Stanton rejoined Lynch after his part in *The Cowboy and the Frenchman*. His rendition of Johnnie Farragut is successful even though the character is defined rather sketchily. It is moving to see his face express the tenderness of a 60-year-old man in love, followed by the despondency of a man undone. It is impossible to resist seeing his distant resemblance to Father X in *Eraserhead*: the role of a simple man with the thin face of an old cowboy.

To play the part of Bobby Peru, Willem Dafoe is made up as a repugnant, perverse imitation of Clark Gable, with a thin moustache and slicked hair which clash with his thick lips and bad teeth. His presence is very

Wild at Heart

intense. For Dafoe, Peru is 'a sort of rotten egg who doesn't ask himself questions. What is exciting in him is how he feels an unshakeable happiness just to be alive.'[24] Peru has the same bad man's joy at existing as Baron Harkonnen in *Dune* who shouts 'I am alive!' to express his thrill at having survived an attempt to kill him. Throughout the film, and especially in the hold-up scene when Peru has a stocking over his face, the stress is placed upon Peru's head. He is a dickhead. Until his head is blown away, it provides the bizarre image of a happy, abject penis.

The part of Perdita Durango was given, in the light of the expectations aroused by *Blue Velvet*, to Isabella Rossellini. A minor, short part even though it is fully exploited, it embodies a tremendous visionary force. In Lynch's version, Perdita Durango is the woman on the threshold who, from *Eraserhead* on, represents every temptation. In *Elle*, the actress explained how she used her experience as a model to make this apparition's part become real.[30] Her presence demonstrates Lynch's increasing taste for parts which are both episodic and strong. This frustrates the spectator since the character, having hooked the viewer, then disappears never to be seen again, which induces a sense of imbalance. However, these are neither simply picturesque secondary characters nor just utilitarian parts to make the script work, but characters endowed with as real a presence as the others for the short time they do appear on the screen.

The acting style of *Wild at Heart* is deliberately heterogeneous. Lynch differentiates and contrasts as fully as possible his actors' rhythms. For example, throughout the parallel editing of the opening section, Lynch opposes the slightly parodic acting (though with a regular rhythm) of Nicolas Cage and Laura Dern chatting in the car with the charged, exaggeratedly slow and often silent, uneven acting of Diane Ladd and J. E. Freeman. Freeman speaks slowly, with a sort of delectation as he savours his words, describing how he will kill a man, whereas Diane Ladd oscillates emphatically between speech and whispers. The strangeness of this scene is also due to the fact that it occurs in the broad, sunny daylight of a lush garden, shadows from the leaves dancing upon the actors' faces as they speak in hushed tones, though they are perfectly safe and on their own. They behave as if they were talking at night, in a darkness which is simultaneously their accomplice and a threat: they talk as if they are aware of possibly being overheard.

6

Wild at Heart changed a great deal between the beginning of production and the final version. The references to *The Wizard of Oz*, about which more later, were incorporated during the shooting, which is when the scenes and dialogues were written. It was during the editing that Lynch decided to structure the scenes between Sailor and Lula around close-ups of matchsticks: 'The matchsticks became an element which united them but which also destroyed their relationship.'[5] The rough cut of the film was very long, and editor Duwayne Dunham had to restructure it entirely. The many poetic, often very short flashbacks constantly risked dispersing the spectators' attention. According to Lynch, 'It would have been easy to remove them, but I didn't want to lose them. We worked hard to solve this problem, to go from one place to another and cross regions of strangeness without losing sight of the main direction.'[5] While editing, Dunham had the idea of beginning the film with the murder, apparently in self-defence, of Bob Ray Lemon, cast by Lynch as a black man for no immediately discernible reason. The scene creates a strange malaise. On the one hand, it clumsily presents the threat and the aggression presumably directed at Sailor (the close-up of the knife unsheathed by Lemon seems to be inserted artificially, and the lighting is too slick) while, on the other hand, the unreal manner in which Sailor despatches the more massive, stronger man leaves the spectator perplexed. The scene is closer to Popeye the Sailor teaching Brutus a lesson than to two flesh-and-blood characters. One is left with the sense of a false, cynical cartoon, which the rest of the film in no way confirms. It is an isolated case of a botched scene, poorly filmed and morally confused in its way of showing both the murder of a black man and Marietta's supposed orgasmic pleasure at the spectacle of Sailor blowing his top (with the ambiguity one finds in Lynch concerning the idea of reacting to ... about which more in the Lynch-Kit). This scene, along with several others, was responsible for the film's problems with the censors. It narrowly escaped an X rating in the USA, and to earn an R rating, Lynch was obliged to rework the sequence of Bobby Peru's death for the US version so that one would not see the head actually being severed from the body. Unlike the murder scene, the violence of seeing a head actually being torn off seems to me to be fully motivated, meaningful and in accordance with the film's overall tone, as well as with the notion of a larger-than-life character.

In the rough cut, there was also said to be a torture and rape scene involving Johnnie Farragut. This was supposed to be 'repulsive even for Lynch's entourage'[24] and thus did not appear in the version shown at the Cannes Film Festival. Plot synopses often exaggerate the disturbing nature of the situations shown by Lynch. Their troubling quality does not always lie in the explicit representation of something horrible for, on closer inspection, the images themselves often turn out to be anodyne. The discomfort relates more to a diffuse impression which one tries to localise. The violent scenes in *Wild at Heart* are, in fact, very brief, which make them harder to take in than violence spread throughout an entire film, as is common in the work of many directors. Lynch's deployment of violence is totally in line with his distinctive electric-shock poetics, often misunderstood as vicarious aggression.

In the photography, Fred Elmes uses saturated colours (especially yellow and red) to try another tack after the heady, nuanced shades of *Blue Velvet*. This time the stress is on the sun, the pitiless luminosity of the air and the deep darkness of the night. Much more than *Dune* or any other work of Lynch's, *Wild at Heart* is a film of open spaces. It may be that the gaudy photographic style and the more truculent, colourful tone, arose from a perfectly legitimate desire to reach a broader public. If so, the attempt failed, for the film quickly acquired a reputation for being sick and violent, deterring many potential viewers and masking its seductiveness and beauty. Despite receiving the Golden Palm at Cannes, the film did not receive the success it deserved even in France.

The film's video-clip style was also criticised because of its reliance on images that are highly conspicuous in themselves, as autonomous as discrete photographs. There are strong contrasts from one scene to the next, an emphatic, abrupt editing style and, lastly, the periodic recurrence of short mental visions, or rather of sound–image blocks which disappear as quickly as they arise. However, as shown earlier, discontinuity and the resulting contrasts are present in Lynch's work from the very start and they have repercussions at every level of the films' formal structures as well as on their stories. They are the basis for his poetics, which I would call romantic.

The film's sound design, this time the work of Randy Thom rather than Alan Splet, also proved controversial. It floridly calls attention to itself from the moment the title appears on the screen. The three words *Wild at Heart* are punctuated by full-strength sound effects, and it was precisely the sound's strength which caused controversy. Given that the Dolby method has made it physically possible to use sound volume as a distinct register for the new instrument which the cinema has become, why should film-makers not use it as such? To refuse *a priori* a film-maker's right to make massive use of sound whenever he or she wants (except to dubious ends) is to be guilty of 'soundism', if we can be permitted this neologism to point to the still pervasive anti-sound discrimination in film reviewing and criticism. Indeed, 60 years after its appearance, sound is still considered in some quarters as an immigrant in the clean, closed world of the cinema. In the case of *Wild at Heart*, the force of the sound relates to the good, non-destructive, vital power of love, and is an integral part of the thematic structure, stated from the outset by the very flamboyance of the credit sequence, just as a tonality is affirmed at the beginning of a symphony. Randy Thom and also Don Power produced the film's numerous sound copulas, those low, sinister, held notes which link up the different worlds edited in parallel in one section of the film as well as the explosions of sound which accompany the close-ups of cigarettes being lit and the depictions of fire. These sound effects are meaningful because they contrast with other, more muffled and subtle passages bordering on the inaudible. One forgets that Dolby stereo expands the cinema's sound field towards not only the very large but also the very small, by allowing the use of effects close to silence. Every time the parallel editing transports us to Reindeer's home, for instance, we hear rickety stage music (piano and violin) resound almost subliminally. Or in the scene when the lovers flee, driving endlessly through the night, the guitars accompanying Chris Isaak's ballad *Wicked Games*, which Lynch's film promoted anew and made into a hit, resound in a muffled, ghostly penumbra of sound which only Dolby makes possible. In fact, the piece is filtered electronically in the film so that Isaak's voice is almost entirely veiled and only a murmur remains.

Lynch uses sound cuts with special emotive force throughout the section of short, alternating scenes in which Sailor and Lula are shown driving carefree to the sound of a jazz piano, then Marietta and Santos are plotting Sailor's murder and Farragut is driving towards New Orleans, Santos is calling Reindeer, and Perdita Durango's house is seen near a rubbish dump. Each of these micro-scenes or shots receives a different sound or musical tonality. The variations in rhythm, colour and sound atmosphere among these grouped elements creates a striking impression of fatefulness, the ineluctable, because they play alternately on separation and return. We leave one sound atmosphere then recover it, lose it again and so on, as if only a fleeting relation were possible.

Angelo Badalamenti's collaboration was more limited than in *Blue Velvet* though it included a new song by him and Lynch, one of their most beautiful and imaginative, *Up in Flames*, which would be heard again in *Industrial Symphony No. 1*. Lynch generally uses a contrasting mosaic of themes from hard rock, classical music, old-fashioned jazz and crooner songs. This characteristic musical treatment for a road movie was encouraged by the novel, which was already full of allusions to the car radio and bar music which accompany the protagonists. However, the film's most striking music, as if to synthesise the incandescent strength of a love of cosmic proportions, was the orchestral introduction of Richard Strauss's song *Im Abendro*t, with its extraordinary sense of notes bursting into flower, generated essentially by a long theme in contiguous notes which, after attempting to rise, ineluctably curves downwards accompanied by a fabulous counterpoint of counterthemes growing out of it like shoots from a single branch – yet another instance of vertical symbolism. An unexpected revival of romanticism in the middle of the twentieth century, this music was written in 1947, when Lynch had barely been born. It is heard in several key passages: in the credits, with a fire in the background; during Sailor and Lula's wild kiss when they stop at sunset in an infinite landscape and during Lula's daydream when she is alone in her motel room. Lynch characteristically follows the perfect romanticism of the shot of sunset with the brutal, machine-like sound of *Slaughterhouse* by the group Powermad. This does not designate a culturally coded contrast between hard rock and classical music, but provides two expressions of the same power of love (the accent should fall on the word 'power'). Besides, Strauss is the most Nietzschean of composers, and not only because he created a symphonic poem from *Also sprach Zarathustra*.

7

Wild at Heart was previewed at the Cannes Film Festival, where Lynch had hoped to present *Eraserhead* a few years earlier. Despite many predictions to the contrary, the film received the Golden Palm (a decision that was immediately challenged) from a jury presided over by Bernardo Bertolucci. Some people took the opportunity to voice their distaste for a film-maker who had always seemed dubious to them and whose present film appeared to confirm an aesthetics of phoniness and fakery. Two years later, Godard would speak in *Libération* of 'Lynch's abject, golden-palmed laws'. Still others, who had appreciated Lynch's previous films, expressed their irritation with the new work which seemed a concession to the fashion of the day or even a cynical investment in material to which Lynch no longer sincerely adhered. With its strange humour and violent, patent contrasts between speed and slowness, violence and tenderness, *Wild at Heart* was to forge the image of Lynch as a manipulator, a cynic and a calculating, ice-cold man. This image has been proclaimed not only by his enemies but even by some of his defenders, and it has stuck. Nevertheless, it seems to me to miss the point. There is indeed a distance in Lynch, but this distance is his way of being present to the world, attentive and open. It is also a cautious distance with respect to red-hot subjects, which allows him to treat these subjects in a more personal, penetrating way than many others. Nor does Lynch concern himself with codes, since doing so would imply that things and genres have closed, determinate meanings for him. And this is not the case.

This occasion showed how Lynch's works disorient and provoke amnesia in certain critics, who seem hard-pressed to connect more than two of his films. A respectable work such as Coursodon and Tavernier's *Fifty Years of American Cinema* first praises *Eraserhead* as a 'film of surprising thematic richness beneath the apparent arbitrariness of its imagery' and then proceeds several lines later to view the sado-masochistic obsessions of *Blue Velvet* as 'gratuitious', 'grotesque' and 'taken a little too far'. This refusal to look into the work for the honesty of coherence is telling (Lynch is always a 'one-film man') and it seems to be part of the Lynch effect. On the other hand, there were also journalists and spectators who adored the film, among them the actor Jean-Hugues Anglade who defended it in the magazine *Studio*.[26] Anglade beautifully describes how *Wild at Heart* is one of those films which expands the sense of being alive by taking existence in its entirety, with its highs and lows, its give and take, as if for Lynch, from a certain perspective, nothing which exists is negative and everything is an expression of the same rage to be alive.

The reputation of *Wild at Heart* was also derived from scenes considered as particularly 'hot'. Yet the sequences with Sailor and Lula in bed are brief and stylised. Even if they are accompanied by rock or hard rock music, they serve primarily to reinforce the idea of sexual harmony between the heroes. The film's notoriety on this count is based more on the sequence with Bobby Peru, which is indeed a disturbing scene, but precisely because it stops short. The scene consists in fact of the horrible Bobby, with his thick lips and bad teeth, entering Lula's hotel room on the pretext of needing to urinate. He unnerves Lula by guessing that she is pregnant from the trace of dried vomit on the floor, and then he approaches her, pushes her around, touches her and, bringing his presumably foul-smelling mouth close to hers, leads her insidiously to plead, 'Fuck me'. When she finally pronounces the words, almost unconsciously, as in an echo, he steps back as if he had just made a good joke, saying that he would like to but has other things to do. Lynch then shows us Lula reaching out her hand with her fingers spread apart, a sign in the film of sexual pleasure; when Bobby Peru leaves, we have the disagreeable sense of having been present and nearly participated, through the projection of our desires, in a sort of mental rape which is almost worse than a physical one. One reason why the scene is so troubling is that nothing has happened. One can imagine that Bobby is impotent and flees, that his only pleasure lies in threats.

Moreover, Lula regains control of herself and the scene has no follow-up or echoes later on in the film, which reinforces its troubling quality. The actress's understanding of this scene is particularly interesting: 'It's a very weird scene, but in a way, I'm completely in control. In a way, she is thinking, oh my God, this scene is so sick, and here I am a victim all over again. And I thought, wait a minute, not only do I get sexually satisfied, but I never give myself away. There's the decision to let it turn her on, but not too far.'[18] Paradoxically, this perverse 'not too far' may be one of the keys to Lynch's cinema. Furthermore, in view of the importance Lynch attaches to the scene of parental seduction, which is in fact only a scene, an appearance masking a far older, almost foetal experience of energy exchange, this incident in *Wild at Heart* may be taken as a seduction in reverse. After all, it is Lula who exhibits her personal odours and fluids like an invitation, with the ever-present dried vomit. Lynch may have taken this detail from the novel as the starting-point of the seduction scene he invented. Perhaps on entering the room, Bobby's only need is the one he mentions, and perhaps the situation becomes meaningful for Lynch as a way of accomplishing Lula's desire, with the violence being assumed by the man who nevertheless backs off after having given pleasure but having taken none but cerebral pleasure himself. We should note that Lynch films the sequence in the same frontal way as he did the primal scene in *Blue Velvet*: something is being represented for someone.

The film is also said to have disconcerted spectators by its mixture of hard-line violence and flowery innocence. *Wild at Heart* is indeed an idyll in which the characters love each other at the beginning and the end, and are tender, touching and a bit childish, as shown by the detail of the candy necklace Sailor gives Lula. None the less, the interpretation of the film which sees the heroes as two cretins and the director as the one who is mocking them does not seem to me to get to the truth of the book or the film. Despite the humour of Nicolas Cage's acting and his Presley-like vocalising, and despite Lula's fluttering about like a groupie in heat, they are not imbeciles, but characters with their own rhythms, references and personalities, two touching live beings who are full of delicacy in their mutual relations, generally intelligent and sharp in their words. They are a pleasure to see and to listen to, as each prompts the

Wild at Heart

other in a permanent conversation dictated only by the pleasure of being together and sharing. Like Lynch's other heroes, Sailor and Lula are not desperadoes scattering hold-ups along their way. Despite Sailor's escapades, there is not a drop of defiance in them towards the law and society, much less the family. Crime, transgression, rape, incestuous seduction and the defilement of family values must be looked for among adults and parents; the children aspire to pure love blessed by a birth. *Wild at Heart* is thus an affectionate reverie about parents who would get along well together without being boring, parents who would reconcile us with the pleasure of being alive. The end of the film is seen through the eyes of the little boy to whom Lynch assigned his own favourite cap with a long peak, as if to say: I would like to be the person who is between the two of them.

8

Wild at Heart is indeed a film of childhood, a film of a child who sees everything in large, contrasting terms. The references to *The Wizard of Oz* work in the same way. Lynch had the idea of using references to this classic, which Americans have the opportunity of seeing at least once a year on television, to provide a backbone for his narrative at a time when he was hesitating about the script. Explicit quotes from Fleming's work are actually quite rare. At one point Lula has a phantasmagorical vision of her mother as a witch, inspired by the Wicked Witch of the West, the enemy of Dorothy (Judy Garland) and her friends. In the coda, the good fairy played by Sheryl Lee is another quote. In a more indirect, sexual reference, Lula is shown repeatedly clicking her heels after the scene with Bobby Peru, recalling the shot of Dorothy clicking her ruby slippers which is supposed to enable her to leave the imaginary land of Oz and return to her farm in Kansas. The allusion suggests that Lula can stamp about all she wants, but she will not be able to leave the hell which is Big Tuna. In addition, this movement on the spot has something auto-erotic about it, and is often assigned by Lynch to his female characters. The fetishistic shots of women's shoes in *Eraserhead* and *Twin Peaks* (especially Audrey Horne's) may be linked to the sexual emotion one may derive from a film which numerous Anglo-Saxon directors have echoed in their own work: Martin Scorsese at least twice, in *Boxcar Bertha* (1972) and *Alice Doesn't Live Here Anymore* (1974), John Boorman in *Zardoz* (1973), George Lucas in *Star Wars* (1977), and so on. Finally, the dialogue is littered with coded allusions to the yellow brick road, the enchanted route towards hope, colour and success, as well as to Dorothy's dog Toto.

At a deeper level than that of images or allusions which we may or may not pick up, *The Wizard of Oz* seems to symbolise for Lynch, or at any rate in the use he makes of it, two important, related themes: multiple worlds (Oz and Kansas) and the divided mother (the two witches). However, the transposition of these themes into *Wild at Heart* is not so explicit and clear. There is every reason to think that Lynch hesitated between different treatments of the character of Marietta, whom he pushes in excessive, grotesque, tragic and comic directions. Either he wished to show that Marietta was divided, ranging from an extreme childlike, touching innocence (when she weeps like Judy Garland, who also weeps buckets for half the film) to an extreme destructive cruelty. Or perhaps he wanted to situate the divide in between Lula and Marietta. Be that as it may, no clear conclusion can be drawn on this subject. Broadly speaking, Marietta does not 'work' in the film even though her character is rich and many-layered. Strangely, she is everything but a mother: a woman and a little girl, of course, playing on the seductiveness and innocence of a child-woman while, in relation to Lula, she is a rival. In all, Lula is much more of a mother than Marietta, and, moreover, an extremely sexualised mother in keeping with Lynch's imagery, which has the mother crazed about her own body, touching and exhibiting herself. And yet, as part of a couple, Marietta has some beautiful scenes, as if Lynch distinguished radically between Marietta alone, whom he does not succeed in bringing to life, and in a couple. She loves her man even though she quickly gets over his death and is not long in forming a relationship with the murderer. The scenes between Johnnie and Marietta are interesting and unusual. Lynch touchingly shows us love and tenderness in the face of a man who is not especially handsome, but who is moved. And when Marietta gets down on all fours and imitates a panther, he closes his eyes and smiles as though fascinated and frightened, enjoying his fear. He puts his head in Marietta's hands with the abandon of a child, the head which, later, he will lose to her madness.

What is it that makes the human couple and, by extension, the world hang together? This question is inscribed in the very form of the film. Formally, the linkage of the disparate, contrasting elements (grotesque, picturesque, sentimental, bloody, poetic, abrupt, gentle, and so on) which comprise the film, makes *Wild at Heart* into a film of continuity cuts and hyphens. For example, the continuity cut from Lula's feet when she is jumping up and down on the bed, as if to drive something into it, to the dancers' feet in the rock nightclub; from Sailor in bed, as he masterfully turns Lula's happily satisfied body, to the little erotic toy with which he does the same thing. There are also continuity cuts from words to images: Lula asks herself what they are doing in a hole like Big Tuna, and the next shot is of graffiti reading 'fuck you', and, more conventionally, from scenic detail to another, as when Johnnie Farragut lies dead, and a piece of metal on the roadside flaps about like his last twitch. The conspicuousness of all these effects is blatant, thus producing one more effect, violating the decorous convention that continuity cuts should be hidden and unnoticable. With Lynch, their visibility is a structural procedure, in which the continuity cut is distinct from the elements thus linked, reinforcing the impression of a faulty, poetically shaky structure. No doubt these cuts also testify to a naïve pleasure in connecting and assembling the work, like assembling pieces of wood to build a log cabin exposed to the gusting wind, but here they are also a question addressed to the world at large: why does it not fall apart?

The film's sense of tragedy and precariousness also results from the buffeting gusts which punctuate the first part: sudden apparitions of images of fire accompanied by a powerful rumbling or a diabolical laugh, mini-flashbacks (but are they really flashbacks?) to the father's death, which pierce through Sailor and Lula's world then fade out, never leading anywhere and never building up to a liberating anamnesis. The form of the gust, like a sudden flush, or the breath of a fire-eater, is obsessive, especially in the above-mentioned cases of parallel editing. Within two minutes, we see these gusts physically embodied in the flash of cars passing by the heroes, ruffling their clothes and skin; they are then repeated in Randy Thom's sound copulas which threateningly punctuate Santos and Marietta's murderous conspiracy, then again as Johnnie Farragut drives towards his tragic fate and, as if out of lassitude, heaves a short, worn-out sigh. These gusts express the way in which Sailor and Lula's present happiness and freedom are doomed, not because of the wickedness of malevolent people, since the villains fail, but because they accentuate the fragility of their bodies and spirits, a fragility fatally determined by their life stories. In effect, it is lucky for them that Marietta takes most of this fragility on to herself. These gusts may also be taken, inversely, as the chink in the door, opening on to a source of eternal, fantastic power. What is at stake in the gusts is a sense of ambiguity, and depending on the way these gusts are presented, they may express different things: a fresh charge of energy, a breath which weighs upon your fate and presses you down, or a hole which opens in despair beneath your feet.

The film also contains other quick flashbacks, more bitter and cutting in their way of appearing and disappearing, as in the evocation of Lula's rape and abortion, but no matter how sordid their subject they nevertheless function as a kind of bracing stimulus, a provocation. Finally, the idea of the fragility of the moment and of happiness is what emerges most strongly from *Wild at Heart*. Along with *The Elephant Man*, it is Lynch's most directly emotional film, especially in the night-time sequences when the heroes confide in one another. *Wild at Heart* is a romantic film, reminiscent of Victor Hugo in its mad love of contrasts. For all its shrill sound and fury, it is the most beautiful love ballad which the cinema has ever whispered into the night.

9

On 10 November 1989, Lynch presented a musical spectacle at the Brooklyn Academy of Music as part of the New Music America Festival. The spectacle, co-authored with Angelo Badalamenti and starring Julee Cruise, was *Industrial Symphony No. 1*. From a video of the spectacle, Lynch produced a version for cassette distribution. Although it is not a fiction film as such, this filmed spectacle has a special and very appealing place in Lynch's work. *Industrial Symphony No. 1* is basically a recital of songs by the partnership of lyricist Lynch and composer Badalamenti. Almost all the songs are slow ballads. The lyrics deal with love and the musical style, like that of the *Mysteries of Love* in *Blue Velvet*, is a kind of sublimation and spiritualisation of slow 50s tunes to which a religious dimension has been added by extending the melodies and rhythmic values and by providing a full, rich orchestration in the low registers (a saxophone section) and hymn-like harmonies. A note of strangeness and magic, and also of sadness, is added to the general atmosphere by the robot-like regularity of the performance and by cosmic sound effects, such as a tempest, the wind, sirens, male voice-overs as if from the tomb, and so on.

Julee Cruise's vocal style in the songs is quite specific. Composed and objective, it leaves no place for improvisation or for expressive outbursts. The aim is to let emotion arise from the overall atmosphere created by the text, music, voice, lights and so on, rather than being centred on the performer. The singer's voice is steady, with very little vibrato, deliberately moderate, slender and fine in timbre, with a little girl's diligence but without the Lolita-like nuances of seduction and sensuality. Most often, she appears suspended in mid-air, her feet hanging in the void, except when she is curled up foetus-like in the boot of a car, in a way aptly described by Colette Godard as 'disfigured by a platinum wig like a helmet, transformed into a lampshade by a strapless gown billowing above the waist, which stiffens her while revealing her legs, dangling in the void.'[34]

The subtitle of the spectacle, *The Dream of the Broken Hearted*, is explicit enough. It opens with a filmed prologue showing Sailor and Lula far away from one another, speaking on the telephone. On a blank background, shot in close-ups of Bergmanesque simplicity, Nicolas Cage announces to Laura Dern's sorrow that he must leave. Both of them seem equally disarmed, and the poignant solitude conveyed by this scene encourages us to see what follows as the dream and visions of the abandoned woman. Her solitary ego projects itself in the character of the well-behaved puppet dangling in the void and chaos by a rope, singing with a flat voice as if doped up with Valium long after the actual pain has worn away, the sound revealing only its atonal quality.

Lynch designed a spectacular set which is a blend of harbour and industrial sites swept by anti-aircraft searchlights, suggesting a derelict factory, a scrap-yard and also war. At the top of the stage, parallel horizontal pipes, like scaffolding, close off the entire width of the space and form a giant musical staff, behind which Julee Cruise is moved along like a human note. These pipes also provide a sense of high and low with which we can situate the character's spirits in keeping with Lynch's by now familiar vertical symbolism. Indeed, at one point, there is a pseudo-catastrophe as Julee Cruise falls and crashes on to the stage with a shrill sound, like an acrobat who has an accident but also like a woman committing suicide.

Among the other participants, we recognise Michael J. Anderson, the dwarf of the Red Room, steadily but unsuccessfully sawing a log placed on an X-frame and imitating the voices of the two lovers, replaying their dialogue of separation. The cast also includes a topless dancer wearing heels and black panties, moving like an animal among the jumble of pipes and car, embodying another erotic, even auto-erotic self; a troop of dancers dressed like débutantes at a ball; helmeted workers who also serve as medical attendants; and a giant, flayed man-deer on stilts, which seems straight out of a Robert Wilson piece. Lynch's video production is simple and successful in its aim of presenting and re-creating on a small screen an impression of unending spectacle. By means of numerous cross-fades, it connects and accumulates many fugitive details which are barely glimpsed in the penumbra pierced by violent lights which provide the spectacle with its dominant visual atmosphere.

Apart from its magical atmosphere of phantasmagorical lullaby, and its visual, choreographic and musical achievements, the interest of *Industrial Symphony No. 1* lies in that it shows us the basic elements of Lynch's universe removed from its cinematographic context and abstracted: bodies falling into the void; verticality as a symbolic dimension contrasting with the upright, inert bearing of the suspended woman, the horizontal pipes paradoxically accentuating the importance of the vertical; and reproduction. At the end of the spectacle, celluloid bathers rain down from hangers, materialising bodily loss, the post-partum depression of a woman who has been emptied of her life-force. It closes with a sort of cold appeasement and a rain of luminous dust.

10

When Francis Bouygues, the construction magnate and owner of French television's Channel 1 (TF1) decided to launch the film production company Ciby 2000, he instructed his American subsidiary to draw up contracts with certain independent producers and authors. Thanks to the reputation of

Twin Peaks and his Golden Palm at Cannes, Lynch was contacted and signed for four films. This time, he was offered something he had never had before, full artistic freedom on several films in a row. The only restriction, which hardly bothered him, was that he would work on reduced or moderate budgets. Lynch proposed a return to *Twin Peaks*, not to continue it but to make what was called a prequel, a return to the last days before the murder of Laura Palmer: 'I suggested it to Ciby. They very quickly gave us the green light and we raced ahead. From their agreement to the screening at Cannes, counting the writing, filming, editing, mixing and final touches, less than a year went by.'[35] Lynch seemed almost surprised by the rapidity which he himself had vaunted after *Wild at Heart*. As to why Lynch wanted to return to this story, running the risk of destroying a myth, he offered a personal explanation which there is no reason to doubt: 'At the end of the series, I felt kind of sad. I couldn't get myself to leave the world of *Twin Peaks*. I was in love with the character of Laura Palmer and her contradictions, radiant on the surface, dying inside. I wanted to see her live, move and talk.'[41] Shooting began on 4 September 1991 near Seattle, 'in the same place as the series, in the North, where the same wind blows.' After four weeks in the north-west, work transferred to a studio in Los Angeles, especially for the interiors.

The script was co-authored by Robert Engels, the producer and scriptwriter of the series. The idea of bringing Laura Palmer back to life was seductive but risky since the film would be deprived of many characters assembled or mobilised by her death, including the police (which is to say, the familiar circle of Harry, Andy and Lucy), the shapely Audrey Horne (in the pilot episode, she is presented as a stranger to Laura's group of friends) and, of course, Dale Cooper, who is reintroduced under the pretext of a prologue set a year earlier in which he plays a passing role. In short, the concept of the film was complicated. Like its heroine, *Fire Walk with Me* was in a pickle. Its ending was predetermined and could no longer be changed, and its setting and characters were already familiar. Lynch would try to surprise us and himself by the beginning of the story and by the winding path leading to it.

The film is divided into two parts: a prologue subtitled 'Teresa Banks' (an investigation concerning Bob's first victim, who is discovered dead at the beginning of the film), and a much longer second part describing the last seven days of Laura Palmer. Teresa Banks had already been mentioned in the pilot episode of *Twin Peaks*. It is her murder a year previously, implying the action of a serial killer, which justifies FBI involvement. Here, for the first time, Dale Cooper would extract a letter hidden by the killer from under Teresa's ring finger. Lynch and Engels's script establishes a direct link with Laura by making Teresa into Leland Palmer's secret mistress. The film

Wild at Heart

also includes other scenes alluded to in the series, such as Bobby killing a man while dealing drugs, the last conversation between James and Laura and the scene in which Laura entrusts her diary to the agoraphobic Harold Smith. In other words, a large part of *Fire Walk with Me* fulfils its promise by making us present at decisive moments in Laura's life which, in the series, were an object of narrative speculation, moments which, in theory, impassioned spectators would die to know about. Most of these false flashbacks are filmed in a simple, romantic and direct fashion, but the complexity of the new elements added by the scriptwriters, and the asymmetry of the overall construction, were enough to overshadow this aspect of the film, at least for certain critics hurrying to dismiss the film when it was screened at Cannes. As a result, they sketched an apocalyptic portrait of confusion and generalised whimsy.

It may be that Engels and Lynch were mistaken when they assumed that this simple pretext, to respond to the fans' curiosity about Laura's past, could provide a firm grounding on the basis of which they would then be able to develop a more complex and subtle project. And if they did make a mistake, it was their assumption that the public had a genuine interest in Laura Palmer herself. In this respect, *Fire Walk with Me* is a truly generous project because it delves into a character who, after her death, serves everyone as a prop for their own projections and fantasies, in order to say: this character existed and suffered – take an interest in this woman. Of all Lynch's feature films, *Fire Walk with Me* has the most unusual construction. Even *Eraserhead* is more linear. The connection between the prologue, the unsuccessful investigation into Teresa's death, and the main part of the film, may have a logical justification, but it willfully invites the charge of arbitrariness: as a premonition, it is overstated.

11

The prologue opens by presenting the murder of Teresa Banks through the image of a television screen imploding in a scream. Her body is found floating in the water, like Laura's a year later. FBI Inspector Gordon Cole (Lynch, doing his act of a deaf man who speaks too loudly) sends agent Chet Desmond (Chris Isaak) to investigate after transmitting coded information to him in a rather original form: the pantomime of a woman in a red dress. This information is intended to warn Desmond and his companion, coroner Sam Stanley (Kiefer Sutherland), to expect difficulties with the local police. We also learn that the case has received a special classification under the name 'Blue Rose', and this mysterious, poetic classification entrances Desmond. The only clue obtained from the inquest is that the victim, a friendless waitress, had a letter T under a fingernail. Her trailer in a dilapidated park run by a wasted old man (Harry Dean Stanton) is searched and reveals ... nothing, except that a mysterious twosome composed of a grandmother and her grandson, the Chalmonts, had recently passed through the park. Underneath the caravan they vacated Desmond finds a mysterious ring. As he picks it up, a fade-out steals him away, and from that moment on he will be declared mysteriously and definitively missing.

The action moves to Cole's office in Philadelphia for one of the film's most original scenes. Dale Cooper arrives at the office and speaks with Cole about Desmond's disappearance, then he performs an unusual series of moves to watch the recording of his own passage through the hallways on the video monitors of FBI headquarters. Then out of a lift comes – David Bowie, presented as a long-lost, phantom agent called Phillip Jeffries, who staggers into Cole's office to everyone's astonishment, as a mysterious cinematographic phenomenon occurs: the scene is parasited by another scene as both the images and the dialogues of the parasite are superimposed on to it. In a chalet, we see the dwarf Michael J. Anderson, a masked child, a monkey wearing a similar mask and the one-armed Gerard, all of them exchanging mysterious words. The dwarf speaks of a formica table, pronounces the word 'garmonbozia' ('pain and desolation') and mocks the ring as a symbol of marriage. The child calls for a victim. An indeterminable voice declares: 'We are living inside a dream.' In parallel, utter confusion reigns at the FBI. Agents call to each other and scream out as if they were lost in the dark while in broad daylight. When the parasite scene dissolves, we find that Jeffries has again disappeared.

Cooper then goes to the trailer park and finds nothing but Desmond's car and clues about the Chalmont family. He confides his hunch to Diana that the 'Blue Rose' case will see another victim. The prologue ends here, with the theme song of *Twin Peaks* and a citation of one of the series' emblematic shots, the road sign at the entrance to the town. Spectators who hoped for an exact copy of the television version may then have breathed a sigh of relief, not suspecting that further surprises awaited them. A year later, a nice high-school girl named Laura walks in the streets of *Twin Peaks*, goes to school with her friend Donna (who no longer has the lovely, proud features of Lara Flynn Boyle, but the more timid, frail features of Moira Kelly), is shown sniffing drugs in the high-school toilets, then is confronted successively by bashful, platonic James Hurley who refuses to touch her when, helpless and depressive, she offers herself, and by Bobby Briggs, jealous and in love. Then back to Donna, as Laura tells her intimate friend that she has the sensation of falling into a void.

When Laura finds that pages from her private diary have disappeared, she panics and entrusts her precious book to the fragile Harold Smith. She begins to understand that her imaginary possessor Bob is, in reality, her father. Later, as she prepares to go to deliver food to people's homes, she has a vision of grandmother and grandson Chalmont who leave her a painting depicting an open door in a wall, along with some enigmatic words. At home for dinner that evening in the distressing atmosphere of a family falling apart, her father Leland Palmer lectures her like a child because she has not washed her hands, as Sarah looks on powerless and mortified. That night, Laura dreams that by means of the passageway-painting she enters the Red Room where she finds the dwarf, who offers her a ring, and Dale Cooper who, in the role of guardian angel, begs her not to take it, as different levels of reality intertwine in a complex knot.

We next see Laura provocatively made-up and dressed as she goes to one of the places of her undoing accompanied by a Donna intent on imitating her. Despite its apocalyptic music, the lurid nightclub where she meets up with Ronnette Pulaski is, for the moment, a rather well-mannered hell because the girls are paid for the erotic favours bestowed upon them by rough but respectful men. All this is shown with the kind of humour which Lynch likes to use in his 'forever scenes', such as the lovely gag of the beer bottles which encumber and perplex Donna. Laura breaks away to save Donna and bring the lost sheep back to the fold. The next day, Laura and Leland are driving home together when they have a run-in with a mysterious one-armed man driving a pick-up van. Stopping near them in a traffic jam, the man shouts accusations and invectives in an atmosphere of extraordinary, icy panic which seems to disturb Leland most of all, making him remember his relationship with Teresa Banks and the murder he committed, thus revealing to the viewer that he is the killer. Laura then questions her father, suspecting that he is Bob. Drunk and exuberant, she accompanies Bobby Briggs one night delivering drugs, but the drop goes wrong and Bobby panics and kills the delivery-man just as the latter prepared to do away with him. Another night, when she is possessed in her own bed by her demon Bob (in the shape of a rather amusing incubus), she recognises to her horror that he is the image of her own father whom we have seen give a sleeping-pill to Sarah.

On her last night, Laura feels very dejected and accepts a meeting in the forest with James. In the face of a suitor frozen in his certainty that he loves her for ever but who is powerless to help her, she runs through a whole gamut of emotions, falls apart, screams out her love without conviction, then asks him to lose himself with her, cruelly parodies his bashful dog looks (perhaps to protect him from following her in her misfortune) and finally allows him to drive off into the night on a loud motorcycle, leaving her alone. She then proceeds to an erotic meeting with Leo and Jacques Renault where, to her surprise, she is bound by force in a scene that contradicts the series, which presents bondage as one of her pleasures. Then, along with Ronnette, she is exposed to the homicidal madness of Bob the father who takes them to an abandoned train coach where he kills Laura. Her death is at the same time a kind of complex apotheosis, for the Red Room splits into two identical places: one is a hell where infernal powers summon Bob and Leland to appear and extract a kind of fluid created by suffering from Leland's body; the other is a heaven where Laura laughs through her tears. Here, for the first time made-up and dressed like an adult woman rather than a high-school girl or a tramp, she is seemingly enthroned for all eternity with Dale Cooper standing mute and protective at her side, frozen in a tutelary pose as in a photograph. All this occurs in a rush of sound and images which can only disarm and perplex a spectator seeing the film for the first time.

12

Let us address the question of the correspondence between the film and the series, since it appears one must, if only to get it out of the way so that we are able to approach the new work in its own right. The series is part of the film, only turned inside out, as one might expect from Lynch's peculiar sense of humour and distinctive logic. Especially in the first part of the prologue, all the aspects of *Twin Peaks* are inverted. If Laura's death gives rise to a surfeit of feelings and testimonials, Teresa's does not even begin to generate an image of her. She died unknown, in total indifference, and now she is gone. Agent Desmond, too, is an anti-Cooper: bereft of any personality, totally reserved, he too disappears like a shadow. And Deer Meadow, the seat of the investigation, is another town in the north-west with a coffee-shop, a police station and a corpse – but, like a black hole somewhere in the universe, it is the absolute negation of Twin Peaks, an anti-Twin Peaks. To begin with, it is as inhospitable as its model was welcoming. Where Dale Cooper, like Homer's Ulysses, worried about finding a nice hotel and ending his first day in a comfortable bed, in Deer Meadow, Chet Desmond and Sam Stanley do not even get to sleep. In Twin Peaks, the restaurant made delicious pies, but there are no specialities at Irene's sinister establishment in Deer Meadow. Is there a big hotel in Twin Peaks with good, warm rooms? In Deer Meadow we are shown to an uncomfortable, decaying trailer park, and so on. Sheriff Truman is friendly and co-operative with the FBI, whereas in Deer Meadow the sheriff is hostile. The Twin Peaks office is open night and day, but in Deer Meadow it closes at 4.30. Indeed, the scene in which Desmond and Stanley arrive is a literal inversion of the one in *Twin Peaks*: the receptionist who sniggers and does not look up from her book is obviously the contrary of the talkative, picturesque Lucy Moran. A source of abstract comedy, these inversions are, of course, based on the

Twin Peaks: Fire Walk with Me

Lynchian oppositions of agreeable/disagreeable, cordial/grumbling, comfortable/uncomfortable. As for the obsessive references throughout the prologue to the day and the time, these create a derisive effect of precision, for we know nothing of the killer about whom there is not a single valid clue, while maintaining a dizzying sense of time passing. And what do we discover when the prologue ends? A deserted Twin Peaks without most of its population or even its emblems. The Packard sawmill, the waterfall, the Great Northern Hotel and the sheriff's department have all disappeared. There remains the RR Café, barely glimpsed, the high school and the Johnson home with Leo's lorry. Regarding Laura's house, the atmosphere from the series has changed, because it is neither lit nor filmed in the same way. Twin Peaks is no longer Twin Peaks, and not just because some of the characters are absent. It is a question of the setting, the frame. It is as if Lynch sought to reappropriate Twin Peaks, which was escaping his grasp and heading off in its own direction, by blowing it up. One cannot really blame him. The series had to end and he needed to free himself of it. Can one imagine him using a doughnut joke for the five-hundredth time, or having Dale Cooper speak to Diana for the thousandth time, or requesting yet another comic scene from Andy and Lucy?

As he blew up the planet in *Eraserhead* and burst the bubble in *Wild at Heart*, Lynch broke the toy which was *Twin Peaks*, at least from his own standpoint. What remained was a pilot episode and 29 instalments lasting a great many hours which, together, comprise one of the most stunning, troubling sagas in the history of television. Nevertheless, in the deserted Twin Peaks II of the film, one obsession from the series does remain, and that is food. Teresa Banks and Laura Palmer, the two victims, have one thing in common: both served food. The guardian angel in the primitive painting which hangs like a remnant of childhood in Laura's bedroom is of a servant angel bearing food. After the awful night during which she becomes convinced that her father raped her, Laura remains disarmed, with no wish to eat the bowl of cornflakes in front of her. And at the end of the film, in the concluding apotheosis of sound and light, is a trivial, enigmatic shot, a close-up of a fruit pie. The anorexic boy from *The Grandmother* returned.

13

Of course, a minimum number of Twin Peaks landmarks and emblems were required. Dale Cooper was certainly an indispensable part of the series' mythology, and his presence was the primary commercial argument for the film. That is why Lynch, who knew that he would be taking risks with the film, worked hard to persuade Kyle MacLachlan to play the part again though the actor feared being trapped in it for life, like Peter Falk in the part of Colombo. In Cannes, Lynch described his efforts to persuade MacLachlan, and there were other traces of them as well. To the great surprise of the international press, Kyle/Dale did not attend the world première of *Fire Walk with Me*. One may imagine that his absence from the première (though he arrived in Cannes shortly afterwards to support another film) was one of the conditions he laid down before agreeing to play agent Cooper again, to avoid a cumbersome identification which, as has been confirmed time and again, can undermine an actor's career. Thus, in the prologue, it was Dale Cooper who foresaw Laura's death in a premonition and then substituted for her departed guardian angel. With even more waxlike and plastered-down hair, he has an altogether stunning, mythical presence.

The only character played by a different actor in the film is Donna. Lara Flynn Boyle, who portrays her on television, is said to have refused to act in the film because of the nude scenes, though these are quite innocuous. Other characters and actors disappeared in the course of the editing since, as Lynch explained, 'We had to cut a lot of scenes we shot because they didn't quite fit with the rest of the story. I was sorry that I couldn't use everybody again, but you have to admit that many of the people of *Twin Peaks* didn't really have a direct connection with the death of Laura Palmer.'[42]

More than ever, Lynch took part in the construction of the soundtrack of *Fire Walk with Me*. He singlehandedly took on the film's sound design and, in addition, collaborated in the mixing, being credited as sound designer and as one of the three 're-recorders'. In the United States, unlike France, three sound engineers simultaneously mix different sound categories, words, special effects and noises, and music, having prepared effects and levels during preliminary rehearsals. In addition, Lynch inaugurated a computerised mixing system which enabled faster retakes, reverse-play, back-tracking and so on. It is clear that he made good use of this system in the film. *Fire Walk with Me* contains a whirligig of stressed sound effects, like the reverse-playback in which words are spoken back to front preceded by their end reverberations, so that the words pop up like little bubbles, low held sounds, dizzying slides and so on. This constant sound activity, the source and nature of which often remain obscure, is one of the film's most original aspects. It creates a sense of the screen as a fragile membrane with a multitude of currents pressing on it from behind.

One of the film's major sound effects is the rhythmical droning of the ceiling fan on the staircase leading up to the first floor at the Palmer house. The fan rumbles like an evil aeroplane near the door to the bedrooms. Leland Palmer turns it on as he goes to possess his daughter and we hear the sound again, detached from its source, in the final scenes in the cabin and at Laura's murder. It is one of those machine sounds with an implacable regularity which are omnipresent in Lynch's work. Their meaning is neither erotic nor sexual as such, nor can they be reduced to some primary function. They are life itself, vital power, absurd and ever-present. The music, again by Badalamenti, entirely renews the previous material. The emblematic themes of the series are used only in deformed or passing citations, again demonstrating the author's wish to distinguish the film from the series. Instead, Badalamenti composed new works in a fragmented, rhapsodic vein well suited to the project, including a low-pitched, mournful melody for the credits played by a muted trumpet, like a soft requiem for Laura. There are also a number of original songs, including some scat performed by Badalamenti himself, a beautiful mystical theme for Laura's reception in heaven and several jazzy pieces which unfold like improvisations in a deliberately casual, uncertain style. The cold, tintinnabulating sounds of vibraphone and piano play a large part in the orchestration, in keeping with the film's accent on night scenes and blue tints. Lynch also created some of the musical sequences himself. These are fairly summary in style, but they work well in the context of the film. The famous slow rock piece pitilessly hammered out in the nightclub where Donna follows her friend, and which so eclipses the dialogues that subtitles are required (the effect is created by the relation between the sound levels in the mix rather than by the volume as such) was the work of David Lynch.

Ron Garcia, the chief cameraman of the pilot episode, here produced a quality of image which was deliberately less warm and reassuring, less a 'fireside story' than in the series. With its many exterior shots and especially the sequence in the trailer park, the prologue is infused with a cold, cutting, autumn or winter light, whereas the rest of the film opposes different atmospheres suited to the different levels of reality which are presented. From a visual standpoint, however, the film's most original and striking aspect is its use of subtly upsetting shooting angles and frames, generating a sense of imbalance. The ideas of walking and standing up, and the vertigo that these can induce, are central to *Fire Walk with Me*. 'And I look down/ And my shoes are so far away from me,' go the lyrics written by Lynch for the piece we hear as Bobby rejoices over Laura's smile and takes great backward steps, drunk with the sense of space.

14

If the film was much awaited at Cannes, many critics also lay in wait for it. Lynch climbed the stairs of the Festival Palace without his main actress Sheryl Lee, detained by a theatre engagement, but with his new companion, the film's editor Mary Sweeney, who would give birth to their son Riley a few days later. With one or two exceptions, the French critics' response to *Fire Walk with Me* the day after was violently negative. Even many critics who were habitually

Lynch supporters expressed their consternation. This was the worst reception the author had received in France since *Dune*, though for quite different reasons. With *Dune*, criticism was focused on the situation of a young auteur fettered by the system and a large-scale production. With *Fire Walk with Me*, Lynch was accused of playing the spoiled auteur who thinks he can get away with anything, even with showing contempt for the public.

The question of the film's relation to the series was raised: was it better to have seen the series already, though one then risked being disappointed by not finding on the large screen the very things one liked about the series, or to be a newcomer and thus to miss all the film's allusions to the series? In my view, the best position is that of a spectator who knows and enjoyed the series, but who is ready to find it distorted and deformed, anamorphosed, on the screen; who is ready to play a new game with familiar pieces. This game is not impossible and, contrary to Gérard Lefort's prediction in *Libération* the day after the screening, the film did gain its admirers, including myself, among those who had been fans of the series. Admittedly, the game I am advocating is not an easy one. If one wishes to criticise the film's relation to its public without entering into what Lynch's intentions might have been, a simple fact can be observed: the film does not totally fulfil the contract with the public which is suggested by its title. The beautiful title remains inert on the screen, and even on a symbolic level, the role of fire in the film is minimal. Was Lynch afraid of repeating *Wild at Heart*, where flames had so great a role? This is the most likely explanation, but in that case, we should not have been promised walking fire. One must likewise admit that, formally, the film does not succeed in joining together all its disparate elements. The inserts of nature and the forest, which are so beautiful and terrifying in the series, here seem paradoxically like a foreign body, a remnant, perhaps because they point to an idea of depth (the depth of nature) whereas the truth of the film lies in its relation to the surface. Nor can one deny that there are some awkward moments, such as the excessive number of shots showing Leland Palmer in place of Bob and vice versa. Lastly, the resolution, that is to say, the expected murder, leaves one with the impression that the promised ritual has not been carried out. The immolation is no more morbid than the representations of Christian martyrs which were long the delight of Western painting. The ritual is to some extent tucked out of sight by the editing, as if a little shamefaced. As a result, the unsuspecting, literal viewer (and I persist in holding to this position) leaves with the feeling of an opera without a finale, which unbalances the film as a whole.

Yet the film also contains some of Lynch's, and contemporary cinema's, strongest scenes, especially those which depict with freshness and violence some of life's elementary sensations: the impression of urban confusion and panic in the middle of a street (the encounter at the intersection with the one-armed man) or the sense of having wings when the girl you love smiles at you. In the title *Fire Walk with Me*, at least one word especially inspired Lynch: walk. Our first sight of Laura after the prologue shows her walking in a lane, young and touching. She is accompanied by a camera 'walking with her'. The idea of the film is indeed to walk with Laura to the very end, something none of the characters can do, to the end of her night. The scene after school in which Laura faces Bobby is one of the most surprising walking scenes in all cinema, and for good reason: if Lynch is fond of characters who are fixed on the spot or represented like tree trunks rooted in the ground, it is because the act which consists of placing one foot in front of the other is not self-evident. Even if it is the best way of walking, this act engenders a euphoria tinged with panic. The occurrence of walking, as such, in his work is thus naturally spectacular. Laura has just told her jealous, gloomy lover to smile, and she provides an example, prompting the boy to smile radiantly (again, action/reaction). He walks backwards towards the entrance to the high school as we see a number of other shots of young people walking. It is no more complicated than that, but in the angles and rhythms of the shots (to shoot this scene, Lynch had music played to harmonise the extras' pace) Lynch makes us feel the situation the way a child might when it walks for the first time, as something grandiose, a slightly scary appropriation of space.

In the pilot episode of the series Dana Ashbrook, who plays Bobby Briggs, had performed his role as a kind of agitated clown, walking with large gestures. In the film, he is decked out in a shirt which comes down to his knees like a dress, accentuating his long silhouette and his gesticulating gait, a wonderful contrast when compared with the stiff, awkward gait of the Fremen in their stillsuits. The other important walking scene providing a somewhat similar impression occurs earlier with the reappearance of the FBI agent Phillip Jeffries, and there David Bowie walks with determination while at the same time vacillating as he moves towards the camera. Just before, we saw Dale Cooper stride towards the seated Gordon Cole, then towards a surveillance camera. Walking towards the camera: this occurs at other times in the same setting, especially in the first scene when a secretary who has just received Cole's orders twice exits via the foreground of the image field. At the same time, there is a wall decoration behind Cole, a large two-dimensional photo of a forest. As the secretary advances against the backdrop of this flat decoration, we may wonder if the idea of looming up from a surface has not returned, an idea that was very important to Lynch's entry into the cinema (see *Six Figures*). Cooper's and then Jeffries's appearance, walking in the office or the hall, seem to represent something which stirs and goes into motion in a perpetual new beginning, as if to recover an old sensation, that of advancing in space and thereby driving a hole in it, adding another dimension.

Twin Peaks: Fire Walk with Me

Particularly with the walking motif, *Fire Walk with Me* is very close to our sensations, making it a very physical film, at least in certain scenes, for it does not always succeed in threading along the paths laid out by the script. Yet, at the same time, where more experienced and, in theory, greater directors than Lynch, such as Kurosawa in *Dreams* (1990) and Fellini in his fabulous chronicles, have renounced introducing their wealth of impressions into a narrative, it is a pleasure to see that Lynch continues to attach such moments to the story of Laura Palmer, as if this story permitted everything and as if indeed everything could be related to it. He failed, many viewers losing interest in Laura's drama, but it was a glorious failure in which, by way of numerous successfully realised and original scenes, Lynch expanded and extended the cinema from within through its daring narrative structure.

15

In part, this achievement is due to Lynch's return to his own origins, especially *The Grandmother*, in two ways. Firstly, by resorting to a series of shots encompassing the totality of a space or a place, aligning the image-frame with the frame of living space, as in Hap's café run by Irene, the RR, the Red Room and Leo and Shelly's seedy house, all of which are shown like tableaux within which the characters are enclosed. Secondly, by mixing his techniques and image textures, which gives a two-dimensional effect. This two-dimensionality is unlike that of comic strips, at least in so far as the latter are identified with a joke world and light entertainment, though it is true that comics can also be an important medium for the transmission of myths, which is the level on which Lynch's commitment to archaic idioms actually operates. This is also why it is beside the point to criticise the lack of psychological complexity of the characters surrounding Laura, particularly her father. The different and varied characters certainly convey a dominant emotion reflecting the main character's condition: solitude and distress. *Fire Walk with Me* is a film of defeated, undone, lost faces, like Laura's, her mother's, Harry Dean Stanton's in the caravan park. Sarah Palmer, Leland, Donna, James and Bobby are all alone and thrown back upon their solitude, trapped in their two-dimensional world. In this world of character types, the one figure which ordinarily would be treated like an image-object is Laura Palmer, and yet it is her character which Lynch wished to present in three dimensions.

Laura is not treated like the conventional lost girl: she is not a mythified, diaphanous creature, nor a frozen image. Nor is she a Lulu or a creature fit for a poster. She is a pretty girl but not stunningly so, rather well endowed, so that when she prepares for a night of debauchery she has trouble getting into her sexy gear. Laura Palmer is, however, anything but a vixen. She tries to protect her lovers and her best girlfriend from everything that happens. Her moments of perversity (when she laughs at Bobby in difficulty) occur at times when she is clearly under the influence of alcohol or drugs. Perhaps there is a touch of directorial timidity here. Only once does Lynch show Laura, rather unconvincingly, when she is possessed by Bob, in the scene at Harold Smith's when she bares her teeth. Even then, there is no doubling. Laura is not the two-faced woman, the angel–demon, portrayed in so many famous films. Lynch does not know how or did not want to treat Laura in this way. His Laura Palmer is a coherent person, she is real.

This apparent incapacity to mythify a woman is rather bizarre. She is all the film's beauty or, for those who rejected the work, its failure. Some critics were ironic about this hussy in ankle socks who was obviously not a Marilyn Monroe or a Gene Tierney, but on what grounds did they assume that Lynch wanted a *femme fatale*, a vamp, when the film makes clear that he did not. An endearing, disoriented young girl, Laura Palmer is fatal only for herself. She is the only one who dies. She is also a mothering, compassionate girl, a big sister who kisses fragile youngsters on the forehead and cares about their safety. It is no accident that when Dale Cooper has a premonitory vision of the future victim, he imagines her 'preparing a great abundance of food', for she delivers meals. Laura Palmer is a protective, nurturing mother. Sheryl Lee's part is an overwhelming one, for it combines all women in the one image: a normal woman but also a woman-child, a young high-school girl, a whore and a good friend, a mother, a girl who makes a perfect partner for a gentle slow dance, a teasing or scolding sister, a teacher for small children, a shapely girl and an idealised figure. There are many moments when Sheryl Lee's performance is remarkable: Laura Palmer with her jaw hanging down, disoriented and upset by her father's maniacal madness; Laura drunk and talking nonsense over the body of the man whom Bobby just shot, with a youthful laugh; Laura being gruff, demanding and imperious, then going to piueces the next day and throwing herself at James when she is depressed and seems prematurely worn out, shivering in her sweater. If only for the actress's outstanding performance, the film deserves to be seen again.

Like Tarkovsky's *Zerkalo* aka *The Mirror* (1974) or Ridley Scott's *Thelma and Louise* (1991), *Fire Walk with Me* is a film about the image of the mother in motion if we accept that, when a film-maker condenses all possible aspects of a character or of a temporal period into a single, all-encompassing image, he is in fact dealing with a maternal image, asking questions such as: What is ailing her? Isn't she better now? What is worrying her? In other respects, Laura also combines Dorothy and Sandy from *Blue Velvet* in a single person, but here, for the first time in Lynch's work, the mother is one single person, undivided. In *Fire Walk with Me*, it is no longer the case that a man is offered two women to define himself, as happened in *The Grandmother* as far as the boy was concerned, or when Henry Spencer has two women in his bed in *Eraserhead*, or when John Merrick has two bedside portraits in *The Elephant Man*, or when Jeffrey alternates between mistresses in *Blue Velvet*, nor is there a good and a bad witch as in *Wild at Heart*. Now, there is just the one woman. Donna does not count, except when she is paired with Laura in the eyes of the lusting, voyeuristic Leland Palmer.

Twin Peaks: Fire Walk with Me is an impossible film. Not only is it a film presenting an image of all women rolled into one, an image of Woman as a compilation figure with all its maternal overtones, it is simultaneously an essay on schizophrenia and a visit to parallel worlds. There is also something monstrous as well as naïve about the ambition to make, all at once, Kubrick's *The Shining* (1980), Fellini's *Giulietta degli spiriti* (1965), Bergman's *Vargtimmen* (1967) and Richard Brooks's *Looking for Mr Goodbar* (1977) with 40 characters rather than with just two or three, as the original directors did. It is hardly an accident that this film of all-women-in-one is at the same time a film in which the coexistence of worlds ceases to be pacific and relatively feasible. Instead, Lynch's worlds tend to fuse, oscillating dangerously from one to the other, each preying parasitically on the other. In *Fire Walk with Me*, the interval between these worlds, usually marked by a strobe effect localised in one specific scene in Lynch's films, spins out of control and goes mad, but in a systematic way. The worlds overlap, interpenetrate and merge, as in the scene of Jeffries's reappearance; they grind against and crush each other on two parallel planes. This process starts from the very beginning in the film's prologue, with its clues leading nowhere and the images of the deserted trailer park. We see the surface, but nothing appears. It is seamless; there is no way in. Another surface is the snow-white television screen which provides the visual matter for the credits and which crops up again fleetingly at different times throughout the film. Towards the end, when a distressed Laura walks through the streets of the town, she raises her eyes towards the clouds unravelling in the sky. For her at that moment, the sky is a mere depthless surface, a two-dimensional plane on to which the outlines of clouds have been traced. At many different times, and especially through the eyes of the investigators, *Fire Walk with Me* operates on an impenetrable, unreadable surface, like that of a portrait, a setting, an impression or a surveillance screen. Then we hear a bell, and the elevator in an office building ejects a man as if he came from another world. In those moments, a third dimension exultantly opens like a vertiginous, intoxicating hole. A figure advances, is alive, walks and then, suddenly, the third dimension closes up again. On another occasion, the opening up of a third dimension produces a superimposition and makes everything go blurry, leaving nothing but confusion.

The film operates in such an impossible dimension, related to the all-women-in-one theme, which attains its full value only at the end, reaching its climax when Laura is killed and goes to heaven. Then it becomes as impossible for the film to distinguish one world from the other or to signify their separation, as it is for the spectator to locate himself or herself in the interval between them. The Red Room represents this impossibility, with its striped floor motif, recalling the hallway of Henry's building in *Eraserhead*. Striped or, to be more precise, in alternating black and white zigzags, that visual motif calls to mind the old zebra joke: is the floor white with black stripes or black with white stripes? We cannot say because the Red Room is the double setting of this interval. It is a hell or a heaven, depending on the moment, and we cannot identify the moment.

16

It was into this very abstract dimension that Lynch drove his film, pursuing his exploration of Möbius strip worlds, trying to find out whether he could not break out of the strip's pitiless trajectory by piercing a hole in it or holding it up to the light. It is astonishing that this experimentation did not prevent him from also making a very human, emotional and direct film, as the beautiful, pure scene between James and Laura shows.

Neither does Lynch's cine-symphony, or rather his electro-symphony, shy from bringing into play the maximum number of registers and dimensions, making them resound together, literally fulfilling the programme announced by the musical term itself: *sumphonia* (Greek for 'with sound'). This is what I meant when I labelled his style romantic, in the full, multiple senses of the term. Lynch clearly is *the* romantic film-maker of our times, down to his way of seeking to eliminate the barriers between genres as well as between audiences, maintaining contact both with average television viewers the world over and the more limited audiences keyed in to certain experiments, without despising either side. Who else could we imagine producing the pilot of *Twin Peaks* and then *Twin Peaks: Fire Walk with Me*, two lines of research in which he places equal faith? He is a film-maker without any *a priori* judgment of what cinema is, whether it be an *a priori* he wishes to respect or one he wishes to contest. He is a one-film-at-a-time director who tries to renew himself on each occasion and to rediscover what he is doing while every time extending his field and his experiments, like a child constantly jumping to try to snatch a fruit from ever-higher branches. Or, in musical terms, Lynch attempts to play in every scale, whereas other film-makers narrow their work down to two or three keys. Whether he runs through the notes infallibly is another matter: the important point is that in the history of cinema, Lynch is one of those figures who enlarges its scale of expression and brings the cinema back to its variegated wealth.

He is a film-maker who enables us to breathe the night air and feel the force of the wind, who touches directly on the mythic and the archaic. He celebrates the beauty and immenseness of the world in all its disparity, its tonal breaks, its sublime as well as its derisory aspects. He speaks to us about ourselves in our totality, including the utter dereliction of human experience, and as the world we live in tends ever towards greater abstraction and repetition, he renews man's connection with both his or her deepest emotions and the infinite universe.

For someone engaged in all those projects, there is no better word than 'romantic' in the sense given to the word by artists of the past: E. T. A. Hoffman, Achim von Arnim and Edgar Allan Poe, artists who combine the grotesque and the terrifying, the supernatural and the familiar; or Liszt and Berlioz, who sought new forms, new techniques and another space; romantic, too, in the sense of Victor Hugo, who mixed popular themes and genres while adding to them the darkest elixirs, structuring the whole through contrasts and antitheses. However, this Hugo is not the venerable bearded figure of schoolbooks, but Hugo as he was seen in his heyday, especially during the period of his theatrical successes: morbid and tearful, fond of the trivial and the shockingly strange.

And, of course, romantic in the most clichéd sense: a lover of amorous effusions who makes the vast world and nature the theatre of his sentiment, populating them with infinitely colourful and contrasting figures.

Lynch, moreover, is a romantic film-maker in a period of film history where cinema itself is romantic, that is to say, impure, hybrid and reinvigorated, renewing its alliance with its popular base. Lynch's sense of curiosity makes him discover cinema with every step he takes, but he externalises this discovery, that is, he places cinema in the service of a narrative while seeking to renovate its forms. In other words, his films do not mistake themselves for their subject.

Through Lynch and a few others cinema is advancing and renewing itself, not only on the margins and by extremes, but both on the margins and from inside, thus surprising and refuting the prophecies of current cinecrophiles, that is to say, those who maintain that cinema is no longer what it used to be and must therefore be dying.

That the cinema is no longer what it used to be is in fact proof of the contrary, that it is alive.

V

LYNCH-KIT

From Alphabet to Word

As I was sorting out the many episodes of *Twin Peaks* I had recorded as they were shown on France's Channel 5, one of the tapes jammed. I had to open the VHS cassette to try to unjam it and so, for the first time, I saw the inside of one of these objects millions of which are proliferating throughout the world. I saw the zillion little pieces needed to regulate its flow and I realised that I did not know how to put the thing back together again. That experience was a little like this Lynch-Kit: an attempt to reconstitute an impossible whole. This kit* (* marks the terms which reappear as entries later in the kit) is inspired by Lynch's themes, but it is neither an inventory nor an index, nor even a repertory of all the insects*, flows*, scissors* and logs* in Lynch's films. A certain number of scenes and major signifiers were simply chosen from the film-maker's work and connected to one another. The challenge consisted in organising them in a double order, at once alphabetical and analytical. A box of elements for a verbal kit, the alphabet is a closed, reassuring list whose enumeration can never fill the gulf separating it from the simplest word* formed by drawing on and combining its elements. There were good reasons why the alphabet was the subject of Lynch's first film.

Translator's note: For this English edition, the alphabetical succession of the Lynch-Kit's ingredients has been rearranged in accordance with the English terms even though such an arrangement infringes the sequential logic of the kit's organisation in the original. The French terms have been indicated in brackets with every entry.

ALPHABET (*alphabet*)
The Alphabet is the title and the subject of Lynch's first short film, a dramatic inventory of all the letters from A to Z. The letters do the rounds and emerge from all over the place, but they are never able to break away from the implacable linearity of the list.

The images of isolated letters move through space and are associated with women's bodies* as violated and disjointed as puppets. In *The Alphabet*, the gesture of the pointing index finger or of the arm which comes loose is associated with a fragmenting letter. The letters of the alphabet gone mad suggest bodily fragmentation. The gesture is itself fragmenting, cutting the body into pieces. In the beginning, then, was the word? And only afterwards the letter, a shred of the dismembered word?

In *Twin Peaks* and *Fire Walk with Me*, Dale Cooper extracts tiny pieces of paper from the bodies of the female victims. These pieces of paper contain individual letters of the alphabet, *R* and *T*, hidden under the victims' nails. The killer Bob (*R*ober*T*) thus sows the letters of his own name. Given Lynch's description of *The Alphabet* as a film about pedagogical force-feeding, one may be tempted to see Bob as a teacher who is rather over-zealous in bringing his young female students to assimilate the alphabet, to the point of having them literally incorporate it.

Or did Lynch, one of whose art school projects was about women turning into typewriters, see a woman's hands on the keys of a typewriter when he was a child and believe that the letters they pressed remained stuck to their fingers?

The word 'letter' is equivocal in English, as it is in French: a letter can be an item in an alphabet, a postal letter or the letter in the sense of something being literal. One may say, therefore, that in Lynch's world the letter kills, taking the Apostle Paul's words literally. Why else would Frank in *Blue Velvet* tell Jeffrey that if he continues to meddle in what he does with Dorothy, he will send him a 'love letter', a bullet between the eyes?

A letter is also that abstract, neutral part of a whole which no longer has anything to do with the part, and which is called a word. For a child who has learned the letters separately, the written word is the very symbol of an object having mysterious, incomprehensible, arbitrary and incommensurable relations with the detachable, universal parts which comprise it.

Traces of such an alphabetical system remain in Lynch's films, especially in *Dune* and in *Fire Walk with Me*, when he literally repeats brief shots of single objects, containing a discrete piece of information like a hand, a rose, a flame, and so on, and uses these shots like letters capable of forming various configurations when edited to others.

BODY (*corps*)

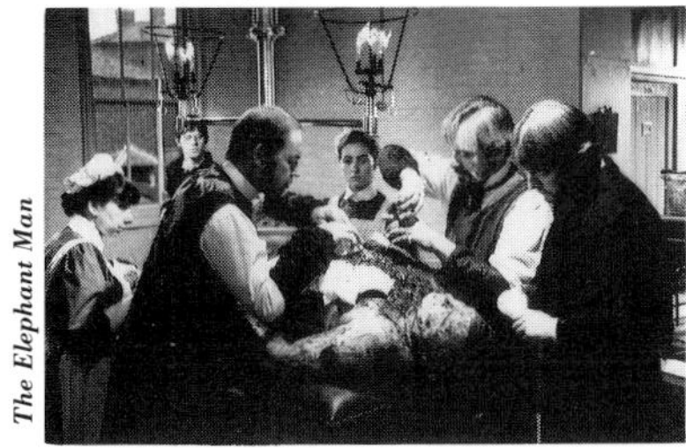
The Elephant Man

In Lynch's work, the human body tends to be presented in the form of a primary mass, the lower limbs attached to the trunk as a single, oblong, stiff and slightly shaky column, with head and arms as exposed, severable extremities, detachable or rather subtractable from the whole. This characteristic type of body, in which the base is undivided, can be seen in the animated sequences of *The Grandmother* and also in some of Lynch's paintings.

The dramatic and at times (as in *Fire Walk with Me*) intoxicating, joyous sense of walking in large steps seems to be linked to the splitting which walking imposes on the lower part of the body and to the way two legs can act as scissors*. Up to this point, the characters in Lynch's films frequently walk without overly separating their legs, or else they remain stiff as if to preserve the phallic unity of the body. For example, in *Eraserhead*, Henry Spencer walks with a measured gait as if he wished to gather in the whole of his body so as not to expose any single part. Even his head is retracted as if he wished to enclose it within his own body, though this does not prevent him from losing it in a dream. At such moments, it seems that the trunk does not know what is happening to the head. The decapitated body remains standing* and straight for a moment, while the hand extremities alone express panic by nervously twirling a metal bar. When the man in yellow is mortally wounded in *Blue Velvet*, his body remains standing and collected, bleeding, and another pistol shot is needed before he falls, all at once, like a bowling pin.

When part of a body becomes individualised and removed from the trunk, emphasis is given to its being only a part, an excrescence. Thus, a rigid, isolated arm stretches out (Sailor's in his eccentric gestures) or a hand stiffens (Lula). Arms which culminate in widespread fingers often belong to women who are falling apart or reaching their feelers towards a child. Raised, pointing arms belong to women, whereas arms providing support and authority belong to men. In *Eraserhead*, Father X's reaching to detain Mother X on the threshold of the kitchen is important even if it does not prevent her from entering. It is the only physical contact between them (he is paralysed). In the apotheosis of the finale in *Fire Walk with Me*, Dale Cooper stands* near Laura who is seated on a chair*, and he extends a protective arm towards her.

Lynch made two films with titles referring to parts of the body (taken symbolically): *Eraserhead* and *Wild at Heart*, and a severed ear is the starting-point of *Blue Velvet*. In *The Elephant Man*, where other directors would have highlighted Merrick's gait or his eyes, Lynch depicts his monstrousness by using frames and cuts to accentuate the hypertrophy of his head. We should recall that a normal infant has an enlarged head, and the disproportion between the head and the rest of the body constantly diminishes as the child grows.

When the human body is assembled and welded into a totemic mass extended by feelers, it does not react to internal pressures or external aggressions as would a supple whole with flexible, co-ordinated limbs extended in space. When there is an emotion in Lynch's films, one part of the body, and only one part, will frequently display this emotion with great expressiveness, while the rest of the body does not follow. For example, the face contracts and grows convulsive while the body remains frozen. The head's solitude is especially clear in scenes of weeping.

The inside* of the body sometimes seems to be made of a single substance, a sort of mush or fluid which would escape if the body were pierced. Just as the grandmother seems to die like a deflating balloon, so the victims of the monstrous, obese, floating Baron Harkonnen are killed the way an air-bed or a plastic duck is deflated, by undoing a small valve at breast-level which releases the vital stuff. It is only fair that the monster dies in the same way: stabbed by little Alia, he flies off and gyrates on himself like a burst balloon.

CHAIR (*siège*)

In the interiors of *The Grandmother*, the sitting position is the whole family's favourite posture. And in the Red Room of *Twin Peaks* and *Fire Walk with Me*, a dwarf, a giant, Dale Cooper and Laura Palmer are all seated like divinities. In *Blue Velvet*, Jeffrey's mother and aunt are almost always seen sitting silently in front of the television.

When Lynch's characters are seated, they look like colossal Egyptian statues. His cinema is a device for filming their immobility and the micro-movements which occur when everything seems still. Perhaps, after all, these people are just waiting.

'Travelling without moving,' Paul says to himself in an inner voice as he and his parents leave for the planet *Dune* in a spaceship which works mysteriously. There is no movement; space is 'folded up'. The voyage of the Atreides family in hyperspace is worth seeing: Daddy in his uniform, Mom, the big boy and the little dog are all seated, mute, immobile, frozen like statues in a tomb. This is not a still photograph, nor merely an evocation of a painting by Lynch's favourite painters, Bacon or Hopper. It is cinema, chronographic cinema, which fixes time in the most striking way possible, through immobility. In the scene from the pilot episode of *Twin Peaks* where the high-school principal makes a long-winded speech over the loudspeakers to announce Laura Palmer's death, a dramatic high point, all the characters are seated. One can also be seated in front of the surface* of a table.

CLOSE (*près*)
Two bodies drawing near to one another, or a mouth exhaling its foul breath into another mouth, are enough to create a scene. Proximity is not a given for Lynch. It is dramatic, troubling, theatrical and sexualised. Irrational phobias arise from it at will: contamination, oral rape, murder (Duke Leto uses his mouth to kill someone who comes too close to him), vampirisation (Mary's mother closing in on her son-in-law with a nosebleed) and, of course, the real or fantasised seduction of children by their parents (in *The Grandmother*, the mother's ambiguous way of touching her little boy, to whom she makes a disquieting gesture with her index finger, as if to say 'now you come here'). Physical proximity is incandescent and also suggests a risk of electrical contact, of bursting into flames.

CORD and SCISSORS (*cordon et ciseaux*)

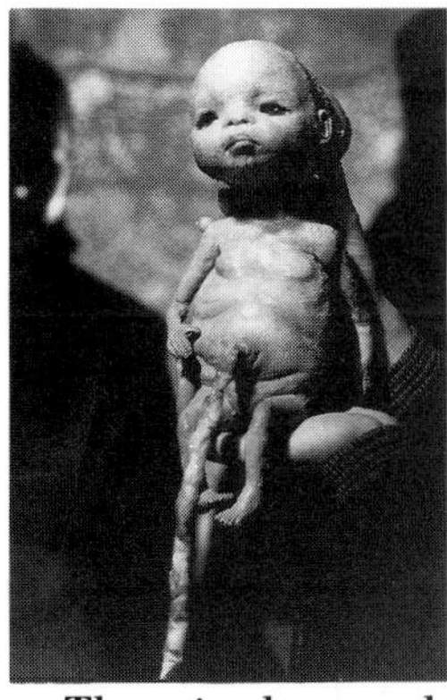
Eraserhead

God said to the serpent: 'And I will put enmity between thee and the woman, and between thy seed and her seed; it shall bruise thy head, and thou shalt bruise his heel.' Is there a reference to this verse of Genesis, occurring just after the original sin, in *Eraserhead* when the little Lady in the Radiator uses her heel to crush the strange serpents which fall on to the stage? These serpents were in fact real umbilical cords obtained from a hospital, like that expelled by his wife which Henry produces from under the sheets of the marriage bed and throws against the wall.

There is always a bit of umbilical cord somewhere in Lynch, even down to the derisive and horrible thing at the top of Bobby Peru's head when he is shot at point-blank range and his head is severed from his body*, flies into the air and smashes against the wall before tumbling to the ground. This time, in fact, it was a pair of woman's tights which Peru put on his head for the dud hold-up. Barry Gifford's novel had already made mention of it: 'Panty hose. Work better'n stockings. Pull one of the legs down over your face and let the other leg trail behind your head.'

Or again, in the form of a shapeless piece of blue velvet cut from Dorothy's nightgown, her large fragrant blue velvet night* dress, which Frank uses to join her mouth to his and which he keeps on his person like a transitional object, a token, when he goes to hear her sing at the Slow Club before stuffing it into her dead husband's mouth (the cord is coiled and twisted like a plant) and which he at last retrieves from the husband's corpse and is holding when he is shot.

This is also the electric cord of the radio which Sailor toys with as he lies in a hotel bed, in a complex electrical assembly involving his feet, the radio, the sound, the bed and Lula. Lastly, of course, there is the telephone cord in *Twin Peaks* when Sarah Palmer learns of her daughter's death over the telephone. The father, to whom she phoned for news, already understood when he saw Sheriff Truman come his way. Unconcerned about his wife, he drops the phone. Stretched by the receiver, the cord hangs there, swinging, transmitting Sarah's weeping for the father who is no longer listening. He clutches at Truman's coat, standing* upright, swaying.

This whole ramshackle assembly may seem utterly twisted or perhaps poetic if, for example, we associate it with images of climbing plants, branches, leaves. At the same time, the cord is a remnant, the inert dangling remnant of what communicated the flow of life. Its presence suggests that the separation of birth is not yet completed, and that the body* has not yet closed up again.

At the end of *Eraserhead*, the father takes a pair of scissors to cut the bandages on the lower part of his baby's body. Is this infanticide or midwifery (answering to the gesture of the man in the planet who works a lever, after which the foetus oozes)? Henry's act is monstrous, but it is at the same time an image of deliverance. Even as he pierces it, Henry brings on a premature birth (the mother has gone) and frees something in his body* which was not growing*. In the same way, the horrible Frank plays with scissors and also performs the symbolic role of the father by keeping Dorothy apart from her little son. No doubt Henry remembers his meal at the X home when the father assigned him the task of carving the chicken, releasing what it contained: a bloody fluid which could also throw the mother into a trance.

CURTAIN (*rideau*)
A blue velvet cloth undulating like a curtain in the credits of *Blue Velvet*; pleated red curtains around the Red Room of the Black Lodge; a theatre curtain in the radiator in *Eraserhead*; a painted curtain in front of the cabin where the elephant man is on show; the hood over his head like a theatre curtain which, for 30 minutes, we wait in a state of delicious apprehension to see raised; the brief, magnificent shot in the pilot episode of *Twin Peaks* where we see a woman at sunset alternately drawing and reopening the curtains of the picture window in her living room. This woman is Nadine Hurley, the mad woman with a patch over one eye who tests the silent curtain rail, obsessively insisting that she wants the installation 'up by nightfall'. This shot precedes the meeting of the townspeople of Twin Peaks at which Dale Cooper announces to the community that caution will be necessary and that to protect their children, parents will have to prevent them from going out, because the murders which the FBI is investigating all took place at night. Then the night commences as in an opera, full of music and mystery, secrets, enchantment and shivers. Through the magic of an edit, Nadine's curtains are the ones which rise on this theatre of the night*.

DARK (*noir*)
Lynch made a comment about shooting the evening at Ben's house in *Blue Velvet* which attests to an unusual sense of synaesthesia between light and sound: 'Strangely enough, the darker Dean Stockwell's apartment in *Blue Velvet* became, the less I heard [the song]. As soon as it got a little brighter, the sound was perfect.'[21] In this hilarious scene, Stockwell mimes to the playback of *In Dreams* with a torch which he uses as a microphone, illuminating his face from below.

'Now it's dark,' Frank grunts at Ben's after downing his drink. He is also the one who shouts at Dorothy in the course of their sexual rite: 'Don't you fucking look at me.' The shout may be evidence of a character beset by anxiety and who finds the shadows reassuring and protective. Perhaps it is a way of saying, like the abandoned woman chanting her loneliness in *Industrial Symphony No. 1*, 'Now we can begin.'

DOG (*chien*)
The French word for 'setting', *cadre*, is literally a frame, as, for instance, a frame in a comic strip such as the one which Lynch published for some years in the *Los Angeles Reader*, 'The Angriest Dog in the World'. The dog's world fits entirely into a frame; it is given once and for all, unchanging. It consists more or less of a house, a garden, a picket fence*, a tree and, beyond the gate, chimneys from which trails of smoke rise at a slant, and a sky in which night and day follow each other. And there are also the words which the dog hears, words which seem to make him angry.

However, we cannot be sure of this, and it would be too much to assert that there is a causal (action/reaction*) relationship between his stiffness and the words in the bubbles. The introductory text, which does not change either, says only: 'The dog is so angry he cannot move. He cannot eat. He cannot sleep. He can just barely growl. Bound so tightly by tension and anger, he approaches the state of rigor mortis.' This is an allusion to the violent fits of anger which Lynch said he experienced against people close to him. He said he cured himself by meditation.

The dog is black and resembles a fish. He is clearly oblong and his limbs are barely differentiated. His anger locks him into a permanent stiffness which binds and strangles him on his leash. Is he bound so tight because he must suffer the banality of the words he overhears from the house? One thinks of Lynch's description of how, as a boy, he was distressed at never hearing his parents argue. The important word is 'hearing'. The dog hears and is thus maintained both outside and inside by an acoustic scene. When the dog tugs at his leash in the direction of the tree in the foreground, is he seeking to yoke the house to the tree? Or, more trivially, to do like all dogs do: to go and release a flow* of urine?

The strangling leash, like Lynch with his buttoned collars, prevents him from reaching it. He cannot pee anywhere: not there nor on the spot, rigid as he is with anger. One thinks of Françoise Dolto's remark about the cruel discovery which awaits every little boy between 18 and 24 months. Until then, he could urinate with an erection, but then, one day, with the development of an organ called the *veru montanum*, he cannot any more. Henceforth, there will be an incompatibility between an erection and the happy release of a long spurt of urine.

In the miniature Lynch-Kit which is 'The Angriest Dog in the World', one observes that many things are presented on a slant: the dog, the leash, the branches of the tree, the housetop, and also, more enigmatically, the trails of smoke leaving the factory smokestacks. Materialising the flow* of energy, is the slant in these trails of smoke perhaps due to the cosmic force of the wind*? In a rigid structure, the slant implies a trajectory, thus an intention or an attraction which breaks with rigidity. This could also be the *clinamen* which Lucretius made the principle for the meeting of atoms.

DREAM (*rève*)

The Elephant Man

'When you sleep, you don't control your dream. I like to dive into a dream world that I've made, a world I chose and that I have complete control over.'[16] Is a dream which you cannot control the dream of the Other, a dream in which you risk being ensnared?

At the beginning of the pilot episode of *Twin Peaks*, the philandering Bobby Briggs teasingly tells Norma before going off for a good time with Shelly: 'I'll see you in my dreams.' And Norma answers him in the same breath: 'Not if I see you first.' The exchange recalls the song heard in *Blue Velvet* which Frank spells out to Jeffrey to make sure he gets the message: 'In dreams you walk with me/In dreams you are mine.'

So, whose dream am I in? This is the question which the Lynchean hero must avoid asking himself too clearly. In *Dune*, Paul's actions are guided by the sentence left by his father ('The sleeper must awake') and, in fact, all he does is make the dream of the two women at his bedside come true. His awakening drives him deeper and deeper into this dream. At the end of *Blue Velvet*, Jeffrey actually falls into the paradisiacal world dreamed of by Sandy and which she rapturously described to him, a girlish dream hatched in her wonderfully corny bedroom, a happy snare. However, in the final scene, where everything corresponds to the dream, the only detail which Sandy did not relate and which tarnishes the harmony of the moment is the maybug writhing in the bird's beak. Sandy overlooked the fact that robins are predators. The inhuman world of insects provides no escape from a world clotted by politeness. Is this not a way of falling from the frying pan into the fire, like Laura Palmer who fell into a hell because she wished to flee the cloying sweetness of the world of *Twin Peaks*, a world too much like a sickening dream?

EAR (*oreille*)

What Sandy, whose room is above her father's office, tells Jeffrey could be said by a great many characters in Lynch's films: 'I hear things.' Lynch remarked: 'People call me a director, but I really think of myself as a sound-man.'[3]

It is difficult not to notice that the ear and hearing are at the core of Lynch's cinema. Dale Cooper confiding in a dictaphone named Diana which records him even when he is close to death, the severed ear in *Blue Velvet*, the angry dog which hears things and, of course, the highly personal sound atmosphere of all of Lynch's films, with Lynch himself wearing a headset during shooting to listen directly to the actors' voices – how could one fail to notice such things?

Nevertheless, all this would be merely anecdotal if Lynch had simply added on a 'high-quality' or 'original' (horrible terms) 'soundtrack' (more horrible yet, for the term has never in fact corresponded to what sound cinema really is) to a cinema conceived like everyone else's. Instead, it is from the inside of the narrative and even of the image that Lynch's cinema is transformed by the central role allotted to the ear, to the passage through the ear. Even if he made silent films, his films would still be auditory.

For Lynch, sound is the very origin of certain images. A character hears someone or something and this brings on visions. The shots often occur like images summoned by a narrative, even when the latter is not explicitly present, or as the visual equivalent of a particular word (Lynch's word-shots). At other times, the bizarre and seemingly blurred, deformed aspect of the shot suggests the confused representations formed in the imagination by the verbal or acoustic evocation of things which have never really been seen.

There is no doubt that hearing is related to the primal scene, that is to say, the scene mostly heard, or guessed at, of a child perceiving the parents having sex. Françoise Dolto redefined it as the scene of the subject's own conception in which he or she actively participates as a third party and desires to be embodied. Whereas the eye acquires the role of an organ that distinguishes (we do not see until after birth), the ear remains in contact with the foetal stage and preserves a close relation with the umbilical cord*.

Jeffrey is hidden in the closet and seems to spy on a primal scene between Frank and Dorothy, but the scene in fact resembles a construction based on things overheard. Lynch dreamed of creating a character who would see what he (Lynch) had only overheard, but because Lynch remains faithful to the truth of his impressions, he presents us with a scene which, from a visual standpoint, does not say much more than what hearing alone would allow us to imagine. The scene is told from the viewpoint of someone who, on the basis of things heard, reconstitutes an incomplete fantasy. What is seen does not answer the questions raised by the sound. The sexual act remains vague, we do not see which, if any, genital organs are involved and how. This enabled the author to fantasise that the act concerned the mouth, for the voices we hear are alternately muffled and clear. This is perhaps the source of the idea of stuffing a rope in somebody's mouth, which would explain the impeded voices.

The vagueness of the sexual shots in *Wild at Heart* does not bespeak some desire to be arty nor is it hypocritical prudery, but a desire to stay close to a strong, indelible primary impression created by the ear.

Listen again to Lynch's films. Listen with your eyes, tuning in to what happens in the image, its rhythmic modulations and vibrations, and you will notice variations, waves and movements perceptible only by not looking. There are, to begin with, certain changes in the timbre of the voice, highs and lows in the intonations and nuances in the sound presence which can be perceived and which have force only in an 'acousmatic' situation (when we hear without seeing). We need to recognise how the outbursts of voices in Lynch's films, and the effects of a suddenly muffled timbre, convey the force of an impression received by the ear, an impression which is so powerful that it invades and reconstructs reality in its own terms.

The ear conveys what is whispered, threatening or shrill, levels in-between speaking and shouting or almost-a-breath, the levels which endow certain scenes of *Dune* with their legend-like tone. There is also the sweet softness of intimate exchanges, the delicacy and subtlety of impalpable communication. Despite all the talk of Lynch's violence and abruptness, there are many soft-spoken scenes in his work: Paul's dialogue with his father by the seaside in *Dune*, the amorous talk between James and Donna or between Andy and Lucy deep in the night in *Twin Peaks*.

Besides, why should the force of an acoustic impression not be able to modify what one sees, rather like the way sound interference can deform a picture on a television monitor. Are not certain visual deformations and convulsions in Lynch's work of this type? It is amazing how a voice issuing from a throat can change so much. The face conjured up by the voice is constantly changing, much more than the one we actually see. Imagine that faces were as flexible, deformable and unpredictable as the voices which issue from them.

Cartoons sometimes present distortion structured by hearing, but this is done within the conventions of comedy. When Lynch resorts to such distortions, however, it is not to get a laugh, but because he tries to remain true to his sense of things.

ECLIPSE (*éclipse*)

As Lynch fans know, whenever he mentions his perennial *Ronnie Rocket* project, he never fails to mention that the main character is a red-headed three-foot dwarf who works on sixty-cycle alternating current. Electric current is also called power*. That he should specify the type of current may seem odd, but is not. In Lynch's work, reality is alternating, subject to eclipses and returns. Such eclipses may be blinding when a sensation's excessive intensity blanks out everything else, as in *Eraserhead*, or fades to yellow, as in *Wild at Heart*.

However, there are also eclipses of characters, disappearances which may be prolonged and mysterious, as in *Twin Peaks* and *Fire Walk with Me*, or just a matter of one or two seconds, a simple visual effect whereby the character simply vanishes, leaving an empty field. At the end of the evening at Ben's in *Blue Velvet*, a close shot of Frank shows him shouting, with the enthusiasm of a boy scout leader, 'Let's fuck,' then he totally and magically disappears from sight, leaving the setting empty for two seconds (film spectators rarely register such brief but visible effects consciously). Frank is back again in the next sequence. Perhaps he was simply swallowed up for two seconds by another dimension, like the two FBI agents in *Fire Walk with Me*.

Likewise, in the long scene in the Red Room in episode 29 of *Twin Peaks*, Dale Cooper vanishes for several seconds from the background in which he appeared previously. Like the child observed by Freud who rejoiced in the power to make an object disappear and reappear, and to master this disappearance through language, to cease to be its victim, Lynch plays with the characters' presence. Absence is no longer an interruption or a cut. He masters the leaps from one world to another.

The eclipse is also the father, the discontinuous parent, the one who leaves and comes back, like Major Briggs in *Twin Peaks*. 'Daddy's coming home' is one of the lines which Frank belches out during his sexual therapy with Dorothy. In her apartment, he is the one who constantly passes through, leaving and coming back.

In the same way, intermittent lighting plays an important role. The crackling discontinuity of electric lighting, lamps which crackle and blink irregularly before blowing, often at crucial moments, seem to express too strong a tension leading to a short circuit (or as an alarm, when separate worlds come into contact). Discontinuous, short circuiting, stroboscopic electricity is the visual emblem not only of the production company which Lynch founded with Mark Frost, it also figures in the climactic scenes of three of his films: the death and transfiguration of the baby in *Eraserhead*, Dale Cooper's arrival in the Red Room in episode 29 of *Twin Peaks* and the murder of Laura Palmer in *Fire Walk with Me*. In the apotheosis at the end of this last film, the intervals of light seem at last to be regulated and harmonised, forming a stable rhythm, a new continuity.

END (*bout*)

Barely into this Lynch-Kit, I was already wondering how to connect Alphabet to End [the second entry in the French edition] when it occurred to me that connecting is precisely a matter of ends, in the sense of connecting extremities, putting things end to end. Extremities are important for Lynch in two ways. Firstly as traces of a cut in a continuum, the whole* from which they have been removed; and as poles of contact, in the sense that we say 'extremes meet'. Contact in Lynch's work produces energy, whence the dramatic, intense nature of being close*, in proximity, when the ends are about to meet. An implicit question remains: which end lights up the other?

As we know, the visual leitmotiv of *Wild at Heart* is an extreme close-up of a matchhead lighting up the end of a cigarette, an image punctuating each of the intimate scenes between the two heroes. And when the dreaming Henry touches the tip of the Lady in the Radiator's hand, the result is nothing less than the image bursting into flame, and everything disappears. Fire seems to exist in itself and for all eternity. What burns and propagates the fire is merely a conduit.

The human body* is a kit* the parts of which are especially singled out and accentuated in Lynch's films. The head as a phallic substitute, the hand, the arm, the feet, the nose and the ears, all seem to be viewed specifically as ends, extremities. See, for instance, the visual leitmotiv of the hand in *Dune*, *Wild at Heart* and *Fire Walk with Me*. Lula's sexual pleasure, for example, is signified by a stiffening of her hand to the very fingertips, turning them also into claws. What protrudes from the body makes it vulnerable. In *Fire Walk with Me*, the rude deputy sheriff of Deer Meadow is seized and overcome by the end of his nose.

Eraserhead in particular is the story of an extremity. Henry's head is truly the end of his body, and it is expressly shown as capable of being severed. It finally pops like a cork under the effect of internal pressure and a boy recovers and takes it to a factory, where a substance is derived from it with which to make erasers for the ends of pencils. As the demonstration in the factory scene shows, the pencil is sharpened at one end and has an eraser at the other, so that what is written with one end can be erased* with the other, achieving an apparently perfect closure.

However, at the outset, a pencil is not an object closed in upon itself. In *Eraserhead*, the machine used to reproduce scores of pencils aligned as though on parade reminds us that, in the beginning, each pencil is cut out of a continuous whole and its two ends are as yet interchangeable. It is only after it has been sharpened and an eraser has been attached to it that it is circumscribed as an object.

In the beginning, this object was a log* cut from the continuum of nature and its two ends are made non-interchangeable, capable of relating like positive and negative, as with the poles which generate a flow* of electric current, although without effacing its log* aspect. However, if the sharpened point is still part of the pencil itself and thus derives from the continuum of nature, the eraser is added extraneously. In the same scene, the factory worker erases with one end of the pencil what he has traced with the other, then says 'OK', but the disappearance is not absolute. Something remains on the paper, a bit of powder which he brushes away with the back of his hand, a worn part of the eraser and pencil which is scattered into the void*, but which also resembles seed or pollen thrown to the wind*.

ERASURE (*effacement*)

In an interview in 1992 by Michel Denisot on the French cable station Canal+ for the release of *Fire Walk with Me*, Lynch was asked about his taste for textures and materials, including things which are considered repulsive, like the series of dead flies he used in compositions. He answered that it is the name we give, the associated word* ('dead flies'), which prevents our seeing them as beautiful, and that all we have to do to see differently is to erase the word.

So, to all those who had difficulties understanding a title such as *Eraserhead* and why the pencil scene occurs at all, Lynch provided a key with his characteristic kind of extraordinary logic. Anyone would say that what prevents our seeing the dissected organs of a cat as something beautiful is our recollection that this is or was a cat, but for Lynch the problem lies in the fact that it is called a cat, that a word* comes with it.

Everyone has tried to some extent to determine what the erasure in *Eraserhead* actually was, this mark written with one end of the pencil and effaced with the other. Derrida too was invoked but, as usual, the core of the mystery remained. What is left behind when a mark is made and then erased? Not a blank or a void*, but a surface*, something like a skin, a texture. Words are written on the skin of the world, like maps bear the inscription of names written on the earth's surface. A word cannot be erased, not even by Lynch, but unlike everyone else, he is dangerously aware of the surface.

He is that singular being who thinks of the indefinite continuum of the surface of paper.

FENCE (*clôture*)

The tree which the dog seems to crave is located in the garden*, inside the fence. A recurring image from Lynch's earliest memories, the fence is represented in his two short films by a setting* drawn into the frame. It is physically present in the first images of *Blue Velvet*. As a voyeur and adventurer, Jeffrey needs the fence. At the beginning of the film, just after the coroner tells us that the human ear which Jeffrey found was severed from someone's head by a pair of scissors*, we see and hear another pair of scissors cutting a piece of tape, a protective cord* around the site of the discovery, running along its perimeter to form an enclosed setting*, the very setting of the work.

FLOATING (*flotter*)

Floating is the state which precedes birth and the acquisition of weight: at the beginning of *Eraserhead*, Henry floats horizontally, lying* down. It also follows death, as with Laura in her plastic bag on the surface of the water, but here the body* is stretched out and elongated rather than coiled in on itself in a foetal position. When Donna and Laura stretch out on couches in *Fire Walk with Me*, they are viewed from above, like fish floating in an aquarium. And they speak of the feeling of falling into a void*.

Lynch describes how his ideas come to him and the way he builds them into films in terms of fish which he allows to float freely. At some point, they cannot be left to float any longer, they must be brought into the open air and set in a rigid frame. So there is necessarily something, like the placenta after birth, which must be rejected, swallowed by a drain under the force of its own weight.

FLOW (*flux*)

Spurting urine is far from a negligible factor in *Blue Velvet*. It even offers a parallel between Jeffrey and his real father, which is all the more significant since the film has marginalised his father. After his heart attack while watering the garden with a hose which became tangled and blocked (a possible metaphor for the heart attack), Jeffrey's father is stretched on the ground with the hose at groin level, seeming to piss a steady, straight stream of water. When Jeffrey breaks into Dorothy's apartment at night, he has to stop to relieve himself because he drank too much of his favourite beer ('Heineken? Fuck that shit!' according to Frank). It is precisely because he needed to stop and because the noise of the flushing toilet drowns out Sandy's warning that he cannot 'eclipse'* himself in time and that events follow their course.

It is under the same pretext of satisfying a natural need that Bobby Peru enters Lula's hotel room. He even makes a bad joke about the noise: 'You are about to hear the deep sound of Bobby Peru.' This is both troubling and beautiful, since Lynch cannot prevent himself from enhancing everything he touches.

Time is linked, as it were, to the outpouring of a spurt of urine. They have the same modalities, problems, pains ... and pleasures. Perhaps one ought to talk of urethral time in Lynch. Often, as in *The Grandmother*, time is full of jolts and discontinuities, an intermittent, spasmodic crackling. Even more often, it is interrupted, mastered and regulated by frequent cuts. However, time in *Twin Peaks* flows gently, continuously and harmoniously, like the current in the river shown in each episode's credits, because in the television series Lynch had all the time he needed, a huge expanse of time measured in hours stretched out before him.

In Lynch's work, time does not flow by itself. Either it seems an eternity, is if it were set on 'pause', or it flows by in abrupt spurts. Lynch has a kind of incapacity to stylise time, to make use of the standard, average duration which cinema invented and which allows an alternation between action and dialogue. Time either drags on and on and seems frozen or it races by.

The temporal harmony of *The Elephant Man* is all the more poignant for having been won by great pains rather than built from a conventional, homogenised cinematographic time-span. In *Dune*, certain parts of the action are dealt with at high speed, such as the idyll between Chanee and Paul, while others are frozen, as if things could only drag on forever or happen very fast.

In Lynch's works, the flow of time or other things is often all or nothing, scanty or unending; the same goes for the outpouring of emotion. Characters are frozen, then weep endlessly. The elephant man at first withholds speech, then, touched by grace, a paean gushes from him.

To regulate the flow, Lynch uses his scissors* to fragment and stop it when he wishes, to master it. This may be the reason why it can course through us without necessarily sweeping us away. In *The Grandmother*, we see it pouring into numerous corridors and tubes. Indeed, a flow is one of the forms of the natural continuum, the whole* maintaining itself within a circle and flowing through everything. The kits* which the artist makes are comprised more or less of cuts in the flow, cuts which constantly reaffirm the flow as crossing the bounds assigned to it by human art.

The work is both an exercise of mastery and of cutting, as well as a reaffirmation of the whole which lies beyond the bounds of the setting* created by the artist.

FOR EVER (*éternel*)

Eternity is lying in wait for you everywhere. Even in a dull moment of the day, while you are waiting for the lift in a sordid building, if you wait a couple seconds too many, whether you are seated or standing, the sense of eternity is there. This is one of Lynch's marks of genius: his way of creating a sense of for ever as soon as someone waits, even for the shortest time. Of course, he had to make the Red Room of *Twin Peaks* into a waiting-room. In the Deer Meadow police station (*Fire Walk with Me*), when Chris Isaak and Kiefer Sutherland are waiting, Lynch needs exactly one second to give us the feeling that the wait has been endless.

You hear someone singing 'I'll love you for ever' as you slow dance with your girlfriend. You start to whisper it to her and you do not know what you have just got yourself into. One hears 'For ever' a great deal in love songs, but it can also resound in the vaults of a church. This assimilation of religion's promise of an eternal paradise (or hell) to the for ever of sentimental love songs is manifest in *Blue Velvet*. The same melody is heard as a kind of hymn when Sandy and Jeffrey are parked in front of the Williams's house, which looks like a temple, pervading Sandy's account of her ecstatic dream, and then in the slow dance music which brings them together. There is a party in Lumberton. Jeffrey and Sandy take to the floor and dance to Sandy's dream music. She says, 'I love you, Jeffrey,' and he answers, 'I love you too.' In the slow tune which they hear, Julee Cruise sings, 'I kissed you for ever,' and they kiss, and then it is over. The dance which brought them together for eternity did not last very long.

Nadine and Ed in *Twin Peaks* seem to represent the diabolical, infernal side of the couple bound together for all eternity in the church. Despite all their cheating and their various other shortcomings, Ed cannot manage to break out of their relationship. According to the dwarf in *Fire Walk with Me*, the fatal ring which makes agent Desmond disappear and binds Laura Palmer to Bob is a wedding ring. It is like the word 'heaven': it derives from religion and is used a great deal in sickly sweet slow tunes.

From slow tunes to the next life: the word hurtles you into the unknown. *Eraserhead*'s happy end is, of course, the arrival in heaven. The Lady in the Radiator alludes to heaven in a song whose derisive character should not hide its gravity: 'In heaven everything is fine. You've got your good things and I've got mine.' This is a heavenly promise for couples, though in this case they are not united and merged but united and separated, separated and linked.

If this promise is later turned into an infernal parody, violated, sullied and ruined, as in the waltz during which Madeleine is murdered in *Twin Peaks*, this does not mean that it is no longer believed in; on the contrary. The incurable nostalgia for a promise of heaven, something one used to believe implicitly once upon a time, provides Lynch's films with their absolute authenticity of feeling, and places them beyond ironic detachment.

The only peaceful eternity in Lynch is the admirable ending of *The Elephant Man*. We watch as John Merrick slips towards a death he has consciously accepted. Everything about his life is in order. He has thanked his benefactor, received the latter's request for pardon, and twice bid him good night* (the first time as Treves leaves and the second time, softly, for himself when he is alone). He is surprised to realise that his model cathedral is finished and he affixes his name to it. He has put away his things, expressed his gratitude and lies down without regrets. He looks at the engraving which he put on the wall, a simple engraving of a woman in bed. With calm gestures, he removes the pillows from his bed which serve to keep his torso upright when he sleeps. He prepares his deathbed, smoothing the sheet which he has just uncovered. He turns to us before getting into bed. Slowly he leans back and lies* down with a slight moan. The curtains of his partly open window wave in the soft night wind. The camera ranges in close-up over the miniature cathedral in front of the curtains. The elephant man's head is heavy. The portrait of Miss Kendall is nearby. The tiny portrait of his mother. The curtain swaying in the wind*. The stars are fixed points at first, then one has the feeling of softly entering into the firmament. A woman's voice speaks of the eternity of things: 'Nothing will die, never.' The woman's face which we see and which does not move is the same as at the start of the film, this time looking slightly worried. The wind blows, conveying the eternity of things and forces. The face disappears in a wisp of smoke and then reappears, still worried (eclipse*, but with the happiness of finding her again, and the feeling that she will always be there). 'Nothing will die.' Fade to white, very softly.

To a diffused music score, the end credits float in the sound of a cosmic current.

GARDEN (*jardin*)

If Lynch did not have the storyteller's virus, he would be increasingly tempted to make his films into gardens of characters.

A gardener of characters does not necessarily always try to cultivate the same flowers. He likes a variety of species, every species in its own right, even if bad guys tend to produce more colourful plants.

In particular, the prologue to *Blue Velvet* situates the film within the symbolism of flower-beds, and it is explicitly plantlike in the range of colours used: mauves, yellows and the deadly tones of poisonous plants. This also applies to its characters: Dorothy Vallens is a kind of fragrant orchid and the 'yellow man', named after his bright-yellow suit, remains standing like a wounded tree when he is shot.

The various girls in *Twin Peaks* form clumps as though in flower-beds. As Gordon Cole (that is to say, Lynch himself, who plays the part) would say, you do not know which one to pick. The men from the sheriff's office and the FBI are lined up as in group photos, but also like rows of plants.

Differentiation and individuation, proliferation of the garden: Lynch has deliberately taken the risk, especially in *Fire Walk with Me*, of making his films splinter into fragments.

GROUP (*groupe*)

They were all sitting on chairs* and there they are now, all standing* up. In Lynch's films, groups frequently behave with a sluggish solidarity, follow-the-leader fashion. Whether a gang of villains (the evening at Ben's house in *Blue Velvet*), high-school students, revellers at an orgy in a clandestine bar

(*Fire Walk with Me*) or an evening's guests (*Wild at Heart*), Lynch's groups are inert, viscous entities, clumps of individuals who are differentiated but also welded together by a mimetic relationship.

Often, and even in the most ill-famed places, the gang seems a continuation of a school class or a scout camp, with its collective behaviour and regressive atmosphere tying them all together. Some rowdy group situations in Lynch's films are already familiar from teenage comedies, but he is one of the few directors who presents them truthfully, not via the conventional image of frenetic activity (hysteria, exaggerated dormitory excitement and chain reactions providing some of cinema's purple passages), but via viscous, gregarious non-activity, fixed in place.

Among these scenes of men and women in gangs, we may mention the uneventful festivities on the prairie in *The Cowboy and the Frenchman*, the evening at Ben's in *Blue Velvet*, the idle carousing which drags on and on in the motel in Big Tuna (*Wild at Heart*), the vague parties given in the Grand Hall of the Great Northern Hotel in *Twin Peaks* and even Dale Cooper's endless wait in the Red Room. Nobody ever moves. The characters sit still, quietly, or else they stand and sway, shuffling about on the spot, drinking and accumulating liquid they will eventually need to piss away, accumulating time as well, to the sound of clammy, slow-paced music.

Recalling Lynch's fondness for *I vitelloni*, it is worth noting that Fellini, too, has sung of dreary orgies, evenings that never end and aimless outings in streets emptied by the night. Lynch shows more specifically the solitude felt by discrete individuals within the homogeneous mass, and also the vertical relation between the group and the site where it provisionally settles down: Ben's vast living-room, the large dining-room of the Great Northern and even the useless throne room in *Dune*, which thus become veritable gardens* of characters.

However, people in groups do speak. Naturally, the discussions are dull and absurd sentences launched into the void, islands of sentences removed from the flow* of an ordered conversation, enigmatic aphorisms repeated or laughed at for unknown reasons, but people do speak and words* stand out, isolated words whose impact we have the time to feel, words we can give free rein to in our minds, even when people simply introduce and define themselves with 'I am the Fart' and 'I am the Muffin', as in the nightclub of *Fire Walk with Me*, without expecting an answer.

GROWING (*grandir*)

Nothing is as immobile as a house-plant, unless a draught happens to stir it, but nothing is as dramatically and horribly agitated and gesticulating as the growth of a climbing plant, filmed in stop motion over a long period. 'It's premature, but it's a baby,' asserts the grandmother of the ignoble fruit of

Mary and Henry's bed. Now that the child has come, will it finally develop? Even though it is fed and left lying on the table, it does not grow. Instead, the plant on Henry's bedside table does grow, although we never see it being fed or watered, unlike the seed which the boy in *The Grandmother* uses to try and make a friendly, loving parent. Either the plant feels a kind of solidarity with the baby, which makes the plant the baby's double, or it grows energised simply by the flow* of time itself, that flow which Lynch regulates and organises with such care.

Time is like an outpouring which ripens things. On the scale* of the plant world, time is identified with growth. One might even think that time is what actually makes things grow.

HUT (*cabane*)

'Between *Eraserhead* and *The Elephant Man*, I spent years building huts. I delivered the *Wall Street Journal* and very often I would find pieces of wood on my way. That's how I built a lot of very elaborate huts. Some had electricity, plastered walls, a glass roof, little windows, everything you need. Nothing makes me happier than to build something or to cut wood.'[12]

Lynch is a very constructive film-maker. Even if he lets his ideas arise freely, his films are highly structured. They are solid. You can live in them.

INSECT (*insecte*)

A rather gregarious animal, the insect had an important role (perhaps because of Kafka's influence) in a project which Lynch worked on before *Eraserhead*, but never finished. An insect there represented what circulates between the girl you are looking at and yourself.

Insects later returned to play an important part in *Blue Velvet*. At the beginning of the film, a hellish swarming fills the screen as beetles pullulate on the lawn of a smart, well-kept garden, while Jeffrey's father is lying on the ground, with his ear at ground level. Shortly afterwards, Jeffrey, having visited his father in hospital, returns to find a severed human ear* lying in the grass. Ants have begun to gnaw at it. Jeffrey has the idea of disguising himself as a 'bugman' in order to enter Dorothy Vallens's apartment, though Lynch does not provide a close-up of the extermination he is supposed to carry out. The insect which Lynch shows insolently ranging over a piece of ear belonging to a much larger species, is also the direct prey (in the predatory cycle) of the species situated immediately above it on the evolutionary scale*: the bird. Thus, at the end, we see a maybug struggle in the beak of the charming robin foreseen in Sandy's dream*. Jeffrey is imprisoned in a paradisiacal dream, but he does not struggle.

The insect incarnates the brutal, anonymous, swarming animality of the species, an animal horror in its most alien, incomprehensible form, contradicting our existential notions of life. For insects, living is reduced to mechanical reproduction and pullulation.

INSIDE (*dedans*)

Dune

In the early years, when David Lynch was not yet familiar to the public, every journalist or interviewer who met him invariably professed surprise at the fact that the man's physical appearance did not match his films. The author of the sick nightmare called *Eraserhead*, with the most repugnant baby-monster in all cinema, this fellow who was said to dissect cats for pleasure, was a proper, courteous and clean young man remarkable only for a trace of dandyism. By not resembling his films, Lynch was their living illustration: the outside does not reflect the inside, any more than the surface* it covers.

Lynch is often described as a private man. This privacy, which prompts the question of what is inside, has a literal equivalent in the way he dresses. Lynch often wears his shirts buttoned at the collar without a tie. We might also mention his caps with very long peaks, covering his eyes. Lynch inverted this image to make *The Elephant Man*. The outward appearance of the elephant man is repulsive and clumsy, but his soul is pure and innocent. However, if there were no difference between outward appearance and the world inside, we would not know what it means to go inside, to enter into something.

'All my movies', said Lynch, who claims to have starting making films to enter into his paintings, 'are about strange worlds that you can't go into unless you build them and film them. That's what's so important about film to me. I just like going into strange worlds.'[18] And yet his first attempt, *Six Figures*, did just the opposite: from a surface (the screen), heads and arms in relief emerge towards the spectator.

Women, for Lynch, are the very image of the container. They incarnate the mystery of what is inside. 'I still have you inside of me,' Dorothy says to Jeffrey after their first meeting. He had been in her cupboard, but was not the cupboard an extension of her self?

When Henry Spencer pierces his baby with a pair of scissors, he is like a child who wants to see what is inside. And when the baby's insides pour out in an unending stream, a spatial turnabout occurs. There is a paradox in the scale of things. The inside is bigger than the outside. The basic elements of Lynch's cinema, the edits, the lighting, the framing and especially the all-engulfing sound seek to create and maintain a constant sense that, on the inside, a scene is always something bigger, and that it contains parts which are smaller than itself ... or perhaps bigger.

Take *The Elephant Man*: breathing sounds, noises and smoke constantly situate us, physically rather than abstractly, in a world which we see as being inside a vaster world. And the elephant man himself, with his cape and the sack with holes which cover his head, is the tantalising incarnation of a container. More than once, the camera cannot resist entering the window in his hood.

Lynch's question is how to master the relationship between different scales* so that the proportions do not acquire a life of their own and engulf what has been made. In order to avoid falling into the dream* of the Other, one must arrange the overlapping of different scales, organise passageways and locate corridors and vestibules between worlds which are, in any event, plural.

KIT (*kit*)
As we know, Lynch had the bizarre habit of dissecting animals in order to piece them back together again afterwards, to put them in bottles, to stretch the skin and organs on planks and then name them 'mouse kit' or 'cat kit'. This suggests that, for him, a dismantled cat no longer has the Platonic form of that animal, but none the less remains a cat kit. At the same time, it is what he discovers in the parts that impassions him: details and, as he says, textures which are normally invisible unless one plays at erasing their names.

It was in an entirely different context, in the living hell of Philadelphia (but this also applies to his animal kits), that Lynch exclaimed: 'Very often, when you only see a part, it's even worse than seeing the whole. The whole may have a logic, but out of its context, the fragment takes on a tremendous value of abstraction. It can become an obsession.'[5]

Whether willingly or not, an artist is always trying to create a unity. Even slightly ambitious creations speak to us of the One, if only by its opposite, disparity. Lynch's works invite us to do this in their own way, by actively and boldly reflecting on the relationship between the part and the whole, especially when the parts question the unity of a work at different levels, in the action, the dramatic line and even in the technique (see, for instance, the heterogeneous alternation between animated and filmed sequences in *The Grandmother*) and in their special attention to disproportion. Even as he seeks to recreate a unity, Lynch seems to aim for the part as such to subsist, the part which is incommensurable with the whole (that is, which operates on another level), the part which stands out from the whole and thereby completes it.

There is an animal which fascinates Lynch on account of the disproportionate but also harmonious relation between its parts and the whole: the duck. Lynch has spoken about ducks on many occasions, and especially in the film devoted to him by Guy Girard for the French television programme *Cinéastes de notre temps* in 1988.

For Lynch, the duck's eye, that little shiny part of a head which is unbalanced by an oblong beak, strikes us like a 'jewel'; starting from disproportion and asymmetry, the eye gives meaning to the whole and completes it. According to Lynch, what one needs to find in making a work of art is just that: the duck's eye. The duck also appears in a statement which Lynch made to a journalist during the last stages of work on *Dune*: '*Dune* is made up of an infinite number of distinct elements and I'm not sure, even today, that some of them don't stand out like the ugly duckling in the middle of the brood.'[12]

Creation, for Lynch, thus consists of building kits which do not exist in nature but which derive their parts from it, and which, ideally, would obey the law of the incommensurability of the part and the whole, whereby the part confers a specific, authentic weight to the whole and at the same time runs the risk of breaking free from it. 'I like to have one little thing in a scene which on its own would be nothing, but in the context and the balance of things around it, pops out and just gleams, and it makes everything else work.'[2]

An example of this kind of detail is mentioned by Godwin in his essay on the making of *Eraserhead*. When Henry rummages in his drawer for Mary's torn-up picture, there is also, and for no apparent reason, a pot full of water in it. Henry throws a little object into the pot which goes 'plop', like an echo of all the film's different instances of falling into water, and the flooding, fecundating irrigation of *The Grandmother*. When Godwin spoke to Lynch about the particular impact of this detail, he replied: 'I don't even know why I put that there. I can't even take credit for these things. It's not like I sat down and said, "I'm going to make something that's mathematically right." You get an idea, and you go with it, and later you find that the proportions were correct.'[2]

Perhaps Lynch's later works are related to each other in the same way. The relationship between a fragment from *Wild at Heart* and the film as a whole may be the same as between *Wild at Heart* and the totality of his films, assuming that the totality does exist. The question of the kit, a composition which allows the part to subsist in its opaque, enigmatic presence, seems to be closely tied to the question of scale*. In so far as Lynch's works display each thing as belonging within the larger ensemble of the next higher scale, and also as containing something smaller from the scale below, the small is not seen as simply a reflection of something bigger, nor as one of its neutral ingredients.

The part and the whole, the container and the contained, are incommensurable, which may be a way of affirming that a little being is not the duplicate of its progenitors, just as the monster baby of *Eraserhead* could not be predicted from the laws of heredity. This is one facet of the stimulating enigma of life.

LINK (*lien*)

It does not take much to notice that Lynch's universe swarms with long, sometimes rigid and sometimes flexible shapes. The most visible and at the same time the most hidden example is the CinemaScope screen itself, used systematically from *The Elephant Man* to *Wild at Heart*, which enables Lynch to create more space, a greater void around his characters.

His comic strip dog deformed by anger is an image of the deformation, the anamorphosis, of erection. The minimal comic strip centred on the dog is full of elongated shapes: smokestacks and the straight smoke plumes which rise from them, branches, trees, the leash and the picket fence. In *The Alphabet* and *The Grandmother*, a great many tubular shapes are drawn and animated or are integrated into the set. In *Eraserhead*, there is first of all the baby, who is all length. Mary's father was a plumber and speaks with vehemence about the many pipes he installed in his day and which, as he says, don't 'grow in their holes' (possibly alluding to the male procreative function). Living-room standard lamps, an inevitable accessory in Lynch's sets, are already present at the X's.

Umbilical cords are also omnipresent, such as the little animated worm performing cartwheels on its mini-stage and, in the matrix-sequence of the entire film, pencils; in *Dune*, there are the giant worms (of course, inspired by the novel) and the mutant Guild Navigators, those oblong, wrinkled, speaking things. And the stillsuit costumes conceived according to Lynch's wishes, which accentuate the length and the almost obscene nudity of the body's oblong outline; in *Blue Velvet*, there is the watering hose, the jet, the protective cord; the blind black man's cane; the lamps and the thin, straight plants in Dorothy Vallens's apartment; the logs carried by the lorries; in *Wild at Heart*, the close-ups of matches and cigarettes; the cord already mentioned; Laura Dern's silhouette, even; in *Twin Peaks*, the trails of factory smoke, the Log Lady's log and the telephone cord when Laura's death is communicated; in *Fire Walk with Me*, the saw at the Deer Meadow police station, the corpses, the telephone lines and the antennas.

In all these films, the acting and clothes styles accentuate the length and the phallic stiffness of the body. Many of these elongated shapes, links and cords have a common trait: they have been carved from a continuity which they recall and of which they are finally a sample from. The umbilical cords in *Eraserhead* are removed from the continuum of mother and child; the plumber father's pipes and Jeffrey's father's garden hose are cut and isolated from indeterminate lengths of material; father Beaumont's urethral-looking jet is part of a flow of liquid; the Log Lady's log is a fragment of a tree, and the strip of dressing-gown in *Blue Velvet*, which is used in so many ways, is a piece taken from the dress of nature, the mantle of night.

Even the phallus is cut out of nature! Thus it does not completely reach the symbolic stage, but remains a part of the world's body and signifies something like a wound, a violence done to nature.

The second trait of the elongated entity is very prominent in the cartoons of *The Grandmother*, where its shapes pullulate: being hollow and tubular allows it to conduct a cosmic energy originating elsewhere, an energy it is satisfied simply to convey.

Thirdly, what might be called the tubule is affirmed in its function of copula or hyphen in the sense given by Jacques Lacan in his *Ecrits* when he says that the signifier-phallus was 'chosen because it is the most tangible element in the real sexual copulation, and also the most symbolic in the literal (typographical) sense of the term, since it is equivalent there to the (logical) copula. It might also be said that, by virtue of its turgidity, it is the image of the vital flow as it is transmitted in generation' (London: Tavistock, 1977, p. 287, translated by Alan Sheridan).

The tubule is a link.

Other copulas may be noted in Lynch's films and, intangible though they are, they are no less important since they extend and generalise tubular, elongated, worm-like shapes. The sustained sounds in *Eraserhead*, *The Elephant Man* and *Wild at Heart* are both elongated and sectioned, functioning as sound copulas.

Some camera movements function as forward penetrations into a setting, into the interior of a world. Then there is the continuity cut itself, especially Lynch's beloved rhyming effect between the end of one shot and the beginning of another, as in *Wild at Heart*. The shot as such, as an intermediate fragment linking two other shots, is also the fragment of a continuum to which it refers, effecting a copula between them.

The continuity of generations, the flow of time, the spurt, the energy current, the leash: there is always something which links and carries over, connecting the universe of microscopic animals and the cosmos, connecting spaces and worlds. Something always links and separates the inside and the outside of the body, and is individuated only by being separated from the continuum of 'natural' energy and matter, of which, by virtue of its substance, it is none the less a part. The copula is and remains a part of nature.

The copula is also the child in so far as it sustains the parental unit, remaining between father and mother, linking and separating them, like the dog between the tree and the house.

Once the copula is individuated and attains to the symbolic order, it aspires to annul and erase, even itself, as it withdraws from the blind proliferation of life.

LOG (*bûche*)
A log is two ends which display where they were cut and separated from the continuum. The fragment which has been cut is shown by the two extremities which lay bare the inside of the wood, the heart.

In *Blue Velvet*, the passing trucks loaded with logs remind us that the little town of Lumberton makes its living by cutting nature into pieces. The local radio station's amusing jingle ('at the sound of the falling tree') is another reminder. Time is cut up like tree trunks. Much cutting goes on in Lumberton, and it is not surprising that ears too are cut. This cutting may well be what language does to the continuum and the body*.

The Log Lady in *Twin Peaks* owes her name to the log she carries at all times, cradling it like a baby. In fact, her log has the same oblong shape as the baby in *Eraserhead.* The 'log' has heard things, she maintains. In the family, the infant is the privileged listener. Often it cannot do anything else since it can hardly see, but its ear* already functions perfectly well.

LYING (*couché*)
At the beginning of *Eraserhead*, Henry Spencer, of whom we see only half a head, seems to be stretched out in mid-air, weightless, as if he had been carried off by a gust of wind. He floats horizontally, reclining in a void*. It is only when the seated man with the burnt face works a lever which 'frees' the cord that we see Henry standing*. Birth, weight and verticality are closely linked, as is only appropriate, but Henry, and Lynch's later heroes as well, often return to a reclining position, not only to sleep or make love, but also to think, dream and talk, as in the long hotel room conversations between Sailor and Lula, or the exchanges between girlfriends Donna and Laura, or when Henry lies across his metal bed on his stomach and stares at the radiator from which the consoling vision of the Lady emerges.

Beginning with *The Alphabet*, Lynch's first short feature film, there is a bed, and in this bed with white sheets there is a woman. Her body is visible, emerging from the surface of the bed and swelling it with her shape, as if she were literally being born from it (compare the rippling screen made of bodily shapes in *Six Figures*).

Already central in Lynch's two short features, the double bed is the most important place in *Eraserhead.* Infernal nights are spent in it, listening to machine noises from an equivocal environment, hearing a baby crying and also seeing one's other half transformed by sleep into a strange, agitated creature tossing and turning horribly. The husband and wife sleeping in this bed are totally estranged, separated by miles of distance in terms of physical intimacy.

Fortunately, the bedside table is a place of hope, a kind of altar lit by a special light, like a divine, fecundating beam from some unidentified source. On Henry Spencer's bedside table, for example, a plant grows mysteriously from a little mound of earth. On Lula's, in a sordid motel room, there is a radio decorated with a horse, and Lynch has a beam of light fall on it in the pregnant heroine's darkest hour.

NIGHT (*nuit*)

Eraserhead was shot almost entirely at night and most of the story occurs by night. It is common knowledge that since then, the night is the heartland of Lynch's realm, the place where everything converges, joins and fragments. In *The Elephant Man*, night is, from the very outset, central to the film. Surprisingly, even *Dune* takes place mostly at night: Paul and Jessica's arrival, the night of Paul's ordeal and, especially, the night of the revelations concerning his fate.

During the crucial night in *Blue Velvet* which Jeffrey survives bruised and humiliated although no crime has been committed, nothing really happens except that time passes, emotions are unleashed and a lesson is taught. Night is when a person can take his or her time, the duration itself providing the opportunity for something to happen. On the other hand, there is also the night of secrets told on a pillow and words spoken in shadows, as in the deep, dark nights of *Wild at Heart*, with characters driving along an endless road through a total void*, killing time in a remote motel, menaced by unspeakable horrors.

The night is made theatrical, staged by putting out the lights or shutting the curtain, as in the sunset at the hospital in *The Elephant Man* or by Nadine Hurley's curtains* in *Twin Peaks*. The night as a black hole, the day's negative: the day/night dissolves in *Fire Walk with Me* are sometimes so sudden that each seems to be already present in the other.

The night is feminine. Dorothy Vallens is essentially a woman of the night. Even by day, when Jeffrey sees her for the first time, the landing outside her flat is plunged in darkness because of an electricity failure.

Why should night acquire such meanings? Perhaps because its mantle of darkness erases the distinct contours of objects and reconstitutes a lost whole*. Darkness unifies and fuses what light separates. Night rejoins what day disjoins. And also because the night sets the stage for the primal theatre, the theatre of sound.

OPEN MOUTH (*ouverte [bouche]*)

The sight of a woman's mouth opening, without knowing whether it opens to emit or to swallow something, is the sign of her orgasmic pleasure (*jouissance*). In Lynch's films, sometimes wild animal noises, roars and possessed gurglings are heard at such times (*The Elephant Man*, *Fire Walk with Me*). Parted lips delineate the female mouth, but the mouth is also an orifice that emits things, an ejaculating phallic mouth, spitting something out, like Bobby Peru's obscene mouth or the baby's in *Eraserhead*, phallic but at the same time penetrable. The baby in *Eraserhead* has a mouth and throat in the form of a meatus, without lips.

The phallus is often symbolised as drilling, hard and long. In Lynch's work, on the other hand, the phallus is clearly presented as permeable, especially if you remember how in his films everything elongated has a tubular nature. Henry puts his hand on his monster-baby's mouth, as it cries endlessly. In *Blue Velvet*, Jeffrey's father loses his voice and he forbids his aunt to raise hers. Frank uses the blue velvet cord to obstruct words. And Johnnie Farragut in *Wild at Heart* dies gagged.

In Lynch's cinema, there is something which does not have the right to speech*.

POOL (*flaque*)

The Elephant Man

The pool is a space that lights up in a dark void, an area for spatial or temporal apparitions which isolates and closely frames a character, a detail or an object; at the same time, it makes present the surrounding primal night, the infinite, the continuum of the void*. In visual terms, the pool is created by the very unusual, unrealistic lighting used in certain scenes of *The Grandmother* and especially in *Eraserhead.* Pools of light fall from we know not where and detach part of a wall or the space of the bed from the darkness, or Henry's head or the baby at its place on the table. There are also pools of light surrounding the light bulb in the living room, as if the bulb could wrest only a limited portion of space from the night*.

This lighting isolates a part of the image and accentuates the surrounding shadows. It is also reminiscent of the circle of light created on the stage or at the circus by a long-range spotlight.

The lighting in Lynch's later films is less aggressively unreal but the pools remain. They become more discreet visually and always have some source in the setting itself, such as the dimly lit landing outside Dorothy Vallens's apartment. At the same time, such pools are displaced on to the temporal level, systematically becoming pools of time, brief moments in which an image or sound appears.

The temporal contours of these moments are blurred, that is to say, they are not delineated by a cut but by a fast fade, and they vanish the same way. In *Wild at Heart*, for instance, these images and sounds (flames, visions, recollections) rise to the surface and loom up abruptly, like flames from a fire-eater's mouth.

The pool's effect is to make the surrounding emptiness palpable, and also to inscribe within the same space a content and a container, an inside (what is in the pool) and an outside, interdependent and mutually conditioned. The pool is also a kind of nest, willfully dirtied and organic, keeping a character, a detail or a situation warm.

POWER (*puissance*)
In Lynch, power is not only a means of action, of obtaining effects. It aims at expressing one of life's dimensions, and Lynch places it where we have lost the habit of seeing it. For example, as much or even more than pleasure, sex is power. Lynch's films express the idea of a gigantic force being released when two people who are attracted to each other finally make physical contact. The hard rock music in *Wild at Heart* by a group revealingly called Powermad is an expression of this energy. Power is also a kind of shock which, hopefully, will rattle a depressive mother and prevent her from sinking. Though it may be dangerous, power is also good when it aims to provoke a reaction.

REACTION (*réaction*)
A number of times in Lynch's films, a character physically recoils or throws back his or her head in response to a brutal sight or word, as Merrick does at the theatre, or Cooper before Earle in the Black Lodge. This is a direct, physical way of showing an internal reaction, all the more so in that the reaction is conveyed by way of a specific type of shot, appropriately called a reaction shot, linked to the previous one in such a way that the cut both affirms and deepens their connection as well as their separation, the cause and the effect, the action and the reaction, with a typically Lynchian sense of a 'loose link', evoking a loose connection between electric cords* or wires.

What I mean here is that the reaction shot is so individuated and detached from the cause that it acquires a kind of autonomy and ambiguity. It often concerns a woman who has been struck, literally or figuratively, by a man and who derives such pleasure that she exposes her teeth (see, for example, the Reverend Mother defeated by Paul at the end of *Dune* or Dorothy being struck by Jeffrey at her own request, Marietta exulting when Sailor savagely kills an aggressor). The woman may also sob, as Sandy does at the sight of the naked woman who wants to steal away her boyfriend. And in this scene from *Blue Velvet*, the two shots of her reaction are odd and may even arouse laughter from spectators who are at the same time shocked, not only because Laura Dern's face is unpleasantly deformed but also because the continuity-cut linking the two shots to what Sandy sees is abrupt and harsh. The strangeness of this effect on the screen is also due to a contradiction between the explicitness of the technical procedure (the continuity cut is clearly signalled as such) and the ambiguity of the relationship which it establishes (what is he trying to say?).

If there is something perverse, something like a cinema-for-effect, in Lynch's cinema, particularly since *Blue Velvet*, it is because he has recourse to very blatant and aggressive procedures (which is why he is often accused of being manipulative) to signify things which are, on the contrary, ambiguous and vague.

Reaction is thus not simply a return-action. In Lynch, the very idea of action/reaction, which he chooses to express through editing, renovating it in the process by rubbing our noses in the fact that an edit has the power to create meaning, remains a mystery and a source of wonder. Reaction shots disclose cause/effect relationships as tottering, unstable and disjointed. The driving belt and gear shift connecting cause and effect no longer function smoothly, allowing us to overlook them. Many examples can be cited of this insistence on a notion of action/reaction which renders the most simple situations enigmatic: the absurdity of the dinner at the X's in *Eraserhead* derives from bizarre relationships of cause/effect and action/consequence through the disconnection between questions and answers in the dialogue, the illogicality of their relationship and the exaggeratedly long interval between them; the elephant man is afraid of the fear he arouses and this fear amplifies his own which in turn, as if by contamination, re-stimulates the other's emotion.

By means of shots which are highly dissociated from one another, the spectator witnesses this mechanism like a third party who does not quite know where he or she stands, which is disturbing and has even given rise, in some critics as well as among spectators, to a vague sense of revolt against the film. In *Blue Velvet*, Dorothy Vallens begins by bullying Jeffrey with words while brandishing a large knife. Then, to our surprise, she asks about the effect this produces in him. The relationship between the operation of the lever and the expulsion of the foetus from Henry's mouth in *Eraserhead* is obtained through editing, but the cause/effect relationship between the two remains enigmatic: it is expressed, but also left unexplained, by the continuity cut. In another passage from *Eraserhead*, Henry carves a tiny chicken at Mary's father's request. Even as it wriggles about, the chicken releases a kind of bloody fluid, and the hostess falls into a trance.

These last examples may lead us to wonder whether the paradigm of all cause/effect questions is not simply this fundamental question: what is the father for? What is the relationship between what men do with women and the children women bear? Or, from another angle, is a woman's sexual pleasure caused by the man or not?

The loose link of action/reaction is perhaps also meant to impress the woman who is to be saved, thus avoiding a bodily interaction which is felt to be too dangerous.

SCALE (*échelle*)

During the shooting of *Dune* someone asked Lynch if he was a vegetarian. 'I eat fish and chicken,' he answered, 'little animals.'[3] According to the journalist who related the anecdote, no one knew whether he was joking. Lynch's 'joke' seems to refer to the traditional depiction of the predatory cycle (which is in fact inaccurate): the big eat the small at every level of the scale – as if there were a relation in Lynch between variations in scale and predation.

The passage from one world to another sometimes occurs through a change of scale (entering into the microscopic, as in *Alice in Wonderland*). Lynch shows that the universe is unified but at the same time that the microcosm does not exactly reproduce the macrocosm, and vice versa.

An aeroplane passes, humming in the immensity of the sky. Little ants crawling in the grass. In Lynch's way of describing his childhood impressions, those of a man-child caught between sky and earth, there is the dizziness of the extreme scales between which we live. Hence his taste for contrast, particularly strong in *Wild at Heart*, between vast wide-angle shots and extreme, microscopic close-ups. *Wild at Heart* is the film in which we see the cosmic stretch of the horizon with the last beams of the setting sun glowing at its edge, the kiss of earth and sky, and the macro-photography of match flames.

Lynch's way of affirming contrasts, like Victor Hugo, in every aspect of his work – in the characters, tones, scales, rhythms, worlds and sizes, from dwarf to giant – makes him a world-separator. He introduces separations into the natural continuum, which is perceived symbolically as being undifferentiated because everything is a matter of intermediate stages, or, in the words of Leibniz, *natura non fecit saltus*. His is the work of creation.

SCISSORS *See* CORD and SCISSORS

SETTING (*cadre*)

'Each film is different. Whatever genre it's in, as soon as you start a film, you're inside a setting and you have to stay in it.'[9] Lynch might almost be speaking of the Black Lodge, a world created for *Twin Peaks*. Anyone who ventures into it seems destined to remain there for ever.

The hero in each of Lynch's films inhabits a setting, a totality, a world which is his or her bubble and earliest habitat, depicted as containing and enclosing, imprisoning him or her. This world is presented at the start of the film. In *The Grandmother*, the setting is composed of drawings created around the characters. In *Eraserhead*, it is a planet and on that planet, an industrial area. Henry's room, to which the action is confined after a certain point, is constantly situated, with respect to the machine noises which surround it, as being on the inside* of this world, like in a pulsating, working body*. *The Elephant Man* multiplies visual and sound allusions to an organic environment, machines and smoke, which envelop the action as well. In the opening seconds of *Dune*, the four planets where the action will occur are visually presented in a single shot, but the film fails to make us feel the cosmos in which these planets float. *Blue Velvet* and *Twin Peaks* invent Lynchtown, a town where you find everything you might need, be it energy, food or anything else. As a road movie, *Wild at Heart* would seem to break free of this system. Of all Lynch's films, it is the one most in love with open spaces, and it presents the unforgettable image, to the music of Richard Strauss, of the horizon at sunset, a horizon just large enough to contain all of Sailor and Lula's love. At the same time, however, Lynch uses a lens for this shot which emphasises the curve in the horizon, reminding us that the totality is closed in upon itself and that it refers back to the setting which the characters move in: the crystal ball of the witch who observes them, Lula's mother. Sailor and Lula's love is enough to enclose them in a bubble, which is the relationship they have together, a relationship of respect and tenderness in the middle of a hostile world.

'People differ according to place,'[37] Lynch enigmatically commented when Paul Grave asked him about his parents. His father was brought up in the wide, open spaces, his mother was a girl from Brooklyn. What did he mean? That their original setting shaped and conditioned each of them, making them definitively different beings? That people change by moving from one setting to another? In any case, the remark confirms something which can be felt in Lynch's films, an element of mysterious, non-psychological, non-social solidarity between the individual and his or her setting.

'It's a strange world,' Jeffrey says to Sandy in *Blue Velvet*. Why does he speak of this world? Is there another? Actually, there are a number of worlds and since we cannot maintain ourselves constantly in the same one, we have to manage with this plurality.

This is the only constant in all of Lynch's cinema: his postulate that more than one world exists, starting with *The Grandmother*, where the boy leads a double life on two different storeys, connected by a staircase which he alone uses. The divide between these world settings seems to be linked to the divided mother. Where there are two women (in the form of two sides of the same woman), there are two worlds. The proof is that *Fire Walk with Me*, a film about one woman, is also a film in which different worlds are so closely knit that they are but one, though unstable and flickering.

Lynch described *Blue Velvet* as a story 'about a guy who lives in two worlds at the same time, one of which is pleasant and the other dark and terrifying'. This is the same scheme as in *Twin Peaks*. And the word 'pleasant' should be noted, for Lynch might have said 'good' as opposed to bad, 'bright' rather than dark, 'human' rather than inhuman. The world of pleasant things as such which is insistently presented seems to condition the terrifying world.

The problem is that the characters can never stay in just one of the two. They have to pass from one to the other, at their own risk.

SMOKE (*fumée*)

Wild at Heart

The pulsing smoke of *Eraserhead*, the powerful, enveloping smoke of *The Elephant Man*, the decorative and unfortunately too intermittent smoke of the planet Giedi Prime in *Dune*; the straight columns of smoke like those of the sawmill in the credits of *Twin Peaks*, or the small atomic mushroom punctuating John Merrick's birth and then his return to the Great Whole in *The Elephant Man*. Smoke, obscure and diffuse, is life. When Merrick watches a pantomime of Puss in Boots, what we see through his eyes are images of a milky, whitish, bright texture which forms over and over into round, white puffs of smoke.

'I was raised on very ecological principles. To me factories are symbols of creation, with the same organic processes as in nature. I like soot, smoke and dust.'[10] Factory smoke is like a phallic symbol for production. Far from being simply infernal, the pulsing smoke of *Eraserhead* is the index of productive machine activity. Factories are good, and it is perhaps because the decision is taken to shut down the machines and close the sawmill at the beginning of *Twin Peaks* that other forces are awakened and things begin to go wrong.

SPEECH (*parole*)

Lynch reputedly has the habit of muttering to himself, and he sometimes bestows this behaviour on his characters: the inner voices in *Dune* are one case of such a transposition, at the same time renewing cinematic conventions. On several occasions in *The Elephant Man*, Merrick and Treves are shown talking to themselves. An element of primal theatre is thus restored to cinematic speech, as words no longer have to form part of a psychological dialogue (words addressed to another character), but can exist in themselves, communicated directly to the spectator. This is one of the many ways in which Lynch reinvigorates rather than renovates cinematic language.

In *Eraserhead*, the dialogues may be scanty, but they exist all the same. Resonating in a kind of void, intermittent and separated by blank expanses, these words influence and reduce to silence all that surrounds them. Time and silence grow between these words like grass between paving stones. In *Eraserhead*, speech has the ring it did in some of the first sound films, where noises still had their place and where gaps could be felt between sentences. In addition, the constant industrial noise in the film recalls the background noise of the first spoken films, a kind of raw material substance from which sounds would emerge. The sentences spoken are surrounded by emptiness: they too are like pools*. Lynch never lost this taste for monologues and soliloquies, rejoinders detached from one another, each character speaking in turn. Speech is never trivialised.

The registers of speech are far more open and varied in Lynch's work than in that of most other film-makers. The range of variations and nuances between the thinnest voice and a howling scream is far greater. Beginning with *The Elephant Man*, and especially in *Dune*, his films contain vocal modulations, changes of colour (whispers on the verge of speech and speech bordering on a cry) which convey the feeling of living in a dream. It is amazing how different speech registers combined into a continuum and made to work in a flexible, open manner, including half-screams and three-quarter-whispers, reminding us that there are no discontinuous levels of the voice, contrary to what habitual forms of cinema try to suggest, can amplify space and charge it with a sense of wonder as well as menace. This is especially the case when a character speaks with the tone of someone who risks being overheard, justifiably so for the women at Paul's bedside in *Dune*, and a little less so when the head nurse speaks to Treves, criticising the way his protégé is being exhibited, since nothing suggests that the elephant man himself is close by; and it is altogether bizarre when Santos and Marietta, in broad daylight in a vast garden, discuss how to kill Sailor in muffled tones, as if they were standing by a baby's cot at night.

The mythic tone Lynch aims for springs from such elements. They are enough to mark speech, and the film as a whole, as perpetually spied upon by a primal witness whose ear takes in bits of something and who imagines being the centre of things. Such speech creates a huge space around it, hanging on its every word.

STAGE (*scène*)

If life puts you in the disquieting situation of having to travel between different worlds (and if possible, to survive by mastering these passages), for Lynch, the theatre is one of these worlds. It is a world which, although placed under the enchanted auspices of the night, can be controlled.

Henry's private theatre with the singer in the radiator, the unlikely, old-fashioned club where Dorothy Vallens sings before a large 30s microphone, the Roadhouse at *Twin Peaks* where Julee Cruise sings, these are the kinds of shows which Lynch wants for himself and us: a place where one can sit in ecstasy before a woman on a stage as she sings in a thin, fragile voice. However, we cannot content ourselves with remaining spectators. Soon or later, we have to go up there ourselves.

When he enters Dorothy Vallens's apartment by night, Jeffrey does not yet know that he has just climbed up on the stage and is about to become an actor in the play. Her apartment is conceived as a stage set, filmed frontally. It is easy to imagine the stage description: to the right, the door to the landing; in the background, we can just glimpse the bathroom; a sofa against the wall; plants and a large lamp stand. The curtain rises. The woman enters, undresses, remains in her panties and bra for a moment, then puts on a dressing gown. The telephone rings; a pathetic conversation in which we do not hear the voice at the other end. A little later, Jeffrey is discovered and forced to show himself in a fantasy scene; suddenly: boom, boom! Open up, goddamit! Heavens, it's Frank. Quick, hide in the closet, and so on. With entrances, exits and voices in the wings, we are indeed in the theatre. And Lynch's set for these interior scenes absolutely requires the presence of armchairs and sofas.

STANDING (*debout*)

Lynch likes to depict a verticality which is ambiguous, either too stiff and slightly unsettling, archaic, mythic (Dale Cooper strapped into his raincoat, as upright as justice itself) or else trembling and faltering, as with old people or the crippled (the man who uses the pedestrian crossing in *Fire Walk with Me*, leaning on a walking frame).

Such verticality often requires a stake (to use a botanical term): one remains standing by leaning on a vertical prop. Thus Leland Palmer clings to a button on Truman's coat, and Dorothy Vallens, naked, covered with bruises, her arms dangling, hangs on to Jeffrey like a climbing plant before Sandy's stunned gaze.

When we see a woman standing up, leaning against a door, the door too serves as a vertical prop. Such images of women and doors traverse all of Lynch's films, beginning with *Eraserhead* and the bizarre shot of Mary X behind a pane of glass. We imagine she is at a window in her house but when she opens it for Henry, we see that the window is in fact the door as well. In *Wild at Heart*, there is the shot of Perdita Durango leaning against the door to her house which lasts longer than necessary and thus sticks in the memory. In the finale of *Twin Peaks*, Audrey Horne chains herself to the gigantic door of a bank vault to demonstrate her commitment to ecology. This is also an image of woman as passageway, like the old woman and the Log Lady in *Fire Walk with Me*, both of whom remain near the door which Laura must pass through on her stations of the cross.

In Lynch's world, standing, especially in a group*, is often a standing-still. The characters remain fixed on the spot, as though taking root, often swaying slightly, or else they dance on the spot, like Audrey in *Twin Peaks*. Standing in a group, with each person leaning at a different angle, human beings form tableaux vivants (though in this case one could hardly call it living) which seem timeless, outside of time.

There are also licentious tableaux vivants and sometimes gardens* of girl-flowers, naïve brothel imagery. In *Wild at Heart*, a rich, distinguished old man orders killings over the telephone from his chair while behind him two topless servants remain standing and chat.

SURFACE (*surface*)

A typical anecdote from the shooting of *Eraserhead* was related by Frederick Elmes, one of the film's two chief cameramen: 'We were doing a close-up of the baby, and David had looked through the camera and lined it up, and it was all ready to go. And I went over to the table, and I moved this little prop over so that it was not hidden so much by something else. And Catherine [Coulson] turned to me and said, "Fred, we don't move things on that table." And I said, "Well, it's just that it was blocked, and I wanted to see it more clearly." And she said, "Well, David has never moved anything on the table." So I put it back and said with a laugh, "Heaven forbid David should see!"'[2]

There are two tables in *Eraserhead*: one for the meal at the X's where the horrible little chickens which wriggle about as they are carved finally do not get eaten; and the other at Henry's, on which the repulsive monster-baby is set once and for all and where Mary tries in vain to feed it. The baby, of course, challenges the others to eat it, to be treated as food.

Restaurant and coffee-shop tables are the principal surface for day-dreams in Lynch's creative activity, the surfaces where ideas and shapes appear among the crumbs and the saucers. And out of the table-tops, ideas emerge. This film-maker who speaks of entering a surface invents forms which emerge from it. Lynch's first film was made for screening on a surface comprised of shapes in relief. His second film, *The Alphabet*, presents a bed like a white surface on to which a woman's body wrapped in the sheets is profiled. However, to enter into and animate a surface, there is nothing like sound. It is sound which provides the third dimension, of whatever kind.

Nevertheless, even when animated by sound, the surface is always there, questioning and presiding through its texture*.

TEXTURE (*texture*)

After once shaving the fur from a mouse, Lynch dissected a cat in the hope of using the result in *Eraserhead*: 'I examined all its parts, the membranes, the hair, the skin, and there are so many textures which may be pretty gross on one side but when you isolate them and consider them more abstractly, they are totally beautiful.'[2]

For Lynch, the notion of texture has a very personal meaning, although it appears almost universal judging by the countless different contexts in which he refers to it. Texture, as he tries to present it in his films, involves superimposing different layers and levels of multiple meanings. In a broader sense, texture denotes the aspect of a surface* or a skin, its patterns, its grain, micro-reliefs which appear whenever one erases* words. In this case, texture refers to the idea of a fragment from the natural continuum, a close-up on the dress of nature.

Very early on, Lynch acquired the habit of opening his films, in the credits or just afterwards, with moving textures which associate the film with a certain material or substance. *The Elephant Man* presents mushrooming white smoke, and the film is set in an atmosphere of smoke, both theatrical and organic, pouring out either in dense streams or dispersing, hiding and revealing at the same time. In the credits of *Dune*, there are, of course, sand dunes and the wind raising curtains of sand, but curiously, this texture does not play a significant part in the rest of the film. There, Lynch is interested most of all in the wood, metal and leather of the interior sets. A blue velvet curtain slowly undulates in the credits of *Blue Velvet*, but we do not yet know that we will see it again, fashioned into a dressing gown on the body of Dorothy Vallens, the mother figure. With pomp and circumstance, this curtain announces the dominance in the film of night and sensuality, shivering leaves in dark lanes, the odours and folds of the body*.

If we see a texture in the 29 sets of credits of *Twin Peaks* on television, it is that of water: first falling in a cascade, then forming a gently wrinkled surface and flowing away with insidious softness, concealing a thousand dangers. Water provides the series with its tone and rhythm. The spiralling flames in the credits of *Wild at Heart*, accompanied by the orchestral music of Richard Strauss, are grandiose and theatricalised. They announce the film's leitmotiv, fire, associated with the power of sex. Finally, the credits of *Fire Walk with Me* present corpuscular movement in blue tones. It will turn out, at the end of a long zoom out, that we are looking at the snowy texture of a television screen after the programmes have ended, announcing straight away the abstract and solitary dimension of the film, the sufferings of a solitary person who feels herself slipping into emptiness*.

Smoke, velvet, water, fire and snow are animated by undulating, shimmering, shivering, flashing and tentacular movements which largely overflow the visual field. They bring us face to face with the overwhelming immensity of nature, which is not only a benevolent, sustaining divinity, but also something inhuman in which man must make a place for himself. The whole*.

VOID (*vide*)
The emptiness traversed by wind is also, for someone in a depression, the space of a perpetual fall. This is the space of *Industrial Symphony No. 1*, in which the broken-hearted woman's voice, like a lullaby addressed to itself, resounds, fragile but clear as a line drawn with a ruler. Sound and music are what remain in the emptiness of the night. With its trembling and scintillating notes, the song is a thin strain which we can hum, allowing us to survive – like the murmured presence of Chris Isaak's song in *Wild at Heart* as the two lovers in flight drive miles and miles through the night, with the road like a ribbon lit up by their headlights between two immense gulfs of jet-black emptiness.

Here, and in *Twin Peaks*, Lynch shows himself one of the few film-makers (perhaps the only one) who allows us to feel the territory of the United States the way it really is, and the way cinema never shows it: a few human encampments, pitched rather too recently, scattered in the horror of the desert.

Nevertheless, the desert, void of human beings, can be a luxuriant, primal forest as well as empty nature. In this void, an echo chamber for the solitude of a little wormlike being, the loudest cries of distress are lost.

However, by virtue of the exacerbated contrasts it permits, this void separates and isolates, its plenitude, its fusion effect offering protection against dissolution.

Such a void enables us to go on living.

WHOLE (*tout*)
One is reminded of old films which presented their titles on a prop, a piece of some material like parchment or velvet, like the waves in the sea which undulate in the credits at the end of *Dune*. The whole is when the surface wrinkles and undulates. It is water, a dress, undulation itself. The credits of *Blue Velvet* show us an image of the whole: cloth moving in soft contact, into which we would like to plunge and find a nook. Or the dress scintillating with stars worn by Koko Taylor, the blues singer in *Wild at Heart*. The solid red dress worn by Lil the dancer at the beginning of *Fire Walk with Me*, except that this dress has been darned with a different coloured thread.

In any case, the whole pre-exists us, independently, without us, but we make cuts in it and tear away pieces.

WIND (*vent*)
A cosmic force of divine nature, the wind is not to be identified with the whole. It is what works and moves it, as in *Fire Walk with Me*, which is sustained by a sort of permanent whirlwind of audible forces: storms, gusts, breaths, the swirling wind of the fan above the stairs. The wind is that current between

worlds that we hear in Lynch's films, beginning with *Eraserhead*. The wind crosses every passageway, waking energies and perhaps bringing together those who should love one another: 'Sometimes a wind blows/And you and I/Float/In love/And kiss/Forever/In a darkness/And the mysteries/Of love/Come clear.' The hymnlike, slow tune *Sweet Mysteries of Love* contains these words for Jeffrey and Sandy. And indeed for Lynch, music, that breath which travels through space, is related to wind. 'Every note of music', he says, 'has enough breath to carry you away and as a director, all you have to do is let the right wind blow at the right time.'[44]

WORD (*mot*)

The word is a physical entity which issues from the mouth and can hit home: 'My name is a word that kills,' Paul marvels in *Dune*. Jack Nance confronts Lula with something like an enigma: 'My dog barks sometimes.' A little later he belches out the word 'but' as if he had barked and Lula reacts*, totters, under the impact of the word.

The only word we hear in *The Grandmother*, a sound film, is a kind of brief barking aggressively unleashed by the boy's parents when they call and reprimand him. We seem to hear the name 'Mike.' *Blue Velvet* marks the solemn entrance into Lynch's cinema of obscene language via the character of Frank Booth who speaks in bursts of 'fucks' and 'shits', his trademark. These obscenities are so many tiny spasms, discharges, word-rockets, word-blows, looking for a reaction.

VI

LYNCH-DOC

I. Filmography

Six Figures
USA 1967. Made by David Lynch. One-minute animation loop for a screen-sculpture in collaboration with Jack Fisk.

The Alphabet
USA 1968 4'(138 ft) 16mm col/b&w (part animation)
Direction, script, cinematography, sound and *editing* by David Lynch; *Prod.*: H. Barton Wasserman; *Music*: opening song by David Lynch, sung by Bob Chadwick; 'Alphabet Song' sung by Peggy Lynch.
Cast: Peggy Lynch.

The Grandmother
USA 1970 34'(1215 ft) 16mm col (part animation)
Direction, production, script, animation and *cinematography* (and probably *editing*): David Lynch; *Prod.*: American Film Institute (& David Lynch); *Music* and *music effects*: Tractor; *Assistants*: Margaret Lynch, C. K. Williams; *Still photography*: Doug Randall; *Sound recording, editing* and *mixing*: Alan R. Splet; *Sound effects*: David Lynch, Margaret Lynch, Robert Chadwick, Alan R. Splet.
Cast: Richard White (*Boy*), Dorothy McGinnis (*Grandmother*), Virginia Maitland (*Mother*), Robert Chadwick (*Father*).

Eraserhead
USA 1976 89'(7977 ft) 35mm b&w
Direction, production, script, sets, special effects, editing: David Lynch; *Prod. company*: American Film Institute for Advanced Studies; *Song*: 'Lady in the Radiator' composed and sung by Peter Ivers; *Organ*: Fats Waller; *Cinematography*: Frederick Elmes, Herbert Cardwell; *Special effects cinematography*: Frederick Elmes; *Special sound effects*: Alan R. Splet, David Lynch; *Sound recording, sound editing, mixing*: Alan R. Splet. Location: the American Film Institute in Beverly Hills.
Cast: John Nance (*Henry Spencer*), Charlotte Stewart (*Mary X*), Allen Joseph (*Bill X*), Jeanne Bates (*Mary's mother*), Judith Anna Roberts (*Beautiful girl across the hall*), Jack Fisk (*Man in the planet*), Laurel Near (*Lady in the Radiator*), Jean Lange (*Grandmother*), Thomas Coulson (*Boy*), John Monez (*Vagrant*), Neil Moran (*Boss*), Darwin Joston (*Paul*), Hal Landon Jr (*Pencil ma-*

chine operator), Jennifer Lynch* (*Little girl*), Brad Keller* (*Little boy*), V. Phipps-Wilson* (*Landlady*), Peggy Lynch* and Doddie Keller* (*Women digging in alley*), Gil Dennis* (*Man with cigar*), Toby Keller* (*Brawler*), Raymond Walsh* (*Mr Roundheels*).
*: credited, but when cutting the version currently in film and video distribution, Lynch eliminated these parts. After the success of *The Elephant Man*, the film was re-released in France under the title *Labyrinth Man*.

David Lynch acted the role of a painter (providing his own paintings) in John Byrum's *Heart Beat* (USA 1979)

The Elephant Man
USA 1980 124'(11,143 ft) 35mm b&w
Panavision Dolby Stereo
Director: David Lynch; *Prod. company*: Brooksfilms; *Exec. Prod.*: Stuart Cornfeld; *Prod.*: Jonathan Sanger; *Script*: David Lynch, Christopher de Vore, Eric Bergren, based on *The Elephant Man and Other Reminiscences* by Frederick Treves and *The Elephant Man: A Study in Human Dignity* by Ashley Montagu; *Cinematography*: Freddie Francis; *Editor*: Anne V. Coates; *Prod. design*: Stuart Craig; *Art direction*: Bob Cartwright; *Special effects*: Graham Longhurst; *Music* and *music direction*: John Morris; *Orchestration*: Jack Hayes; *Music extract*: *Adagio* for strings by Samuel Barber; *Costumes*: Patricia Norris; *Elephant Man make-up*: Christopher Tucker, applied by Wally Schneiderman; *Sound recording*: Robin Gregory; *Sound design*: Alan R. Splet; *Special sound effects*: David Lynch. Shot at Lee International Studios, Wembley (UK).
Cast: Anthony Hopkins (*Frederick Treves*), John Hurt (*John Merrick*), Anne Bancroft (*Mrs Madge Kendal*), John Gielgud (*Carr Gomm*), Wendy Hiller (*Mothershead*), Freddie Jones (*Bytes*), Michael Elphick (*Night porter*), Hannah Gordon (*Mrs Treves*), Helen Ryan (*Princess Alex*), John Standing (*Fox*), Dexter Fletcher (*Bytes's boy*), Lesley Dunlop (*Nora*), Phoebe Nicholls (*Merrick's mother*), Pat Gorman (*Fairground bobby*), Claire Davenport (*Fat lady*), Orla Pederson (*Skeleton woman*), Frederick Treves (*Alderman*), Stromboli (*Fire-eater*), Patsy Smart (*Distraught woman*), Richard Hunter (*Hodges*), James Cormack (*Pierce*), Kathleen Byron (*Lady Waddington*), Carole Harrison (*Tart*), Marcus Powell and Gilda Cohen (*Midgets*).

Paintings exhibition at Puerta Vallarta (Mexico) while shooting *Dune* in 1983.

Dune
USA 1984 137'(15,232 ft) 70mm
Technicolor Todd-AO Dolby Stereo
Director: David Lynch; *Prod. company*: Dino de Laurentiis Productions/Universal; *Prod.*: Raffaella de Laurentiis; *Assoc. Prod.*: José Lopez Rodero; *Script*: David Lynch from Frank Herbert's novel; *Cinematography*: Freddie Francis; *Addit. ph.*: James Devis, Frederick Elmes; *Special effects*: Barry Nolan, Universal City Studios Matte Dept, Albert J. Whitlock, John Hatt, John Stirber, Kit West; *Editor*: Antony Gibbs; *Prod. design*: Anthony Masters; *Art direction*: Pierluigi Basile, Benjamin Fernandez; *Music*: Toto, Brian Eno, Daniel Lanois, Roger Eno, Marty Paich; *Costume design:* Rob Ringwood; *Make-up*: Giannetto De Rossi, Luigi Rochetti, Mario Scutti; *Sound recording*: Nelson Stoll, Shep Lonsdale, Tom Knox; *Sound editing*: Les Wiggins, Leslie Shatz, Teresa Eckton; *Mixing:* Bill Varney, Steve Maslow, Kevin O'Connell; *Sound design*: Alan R. Splet; *Mechanical creatures*: Carlo Rambaldi. Shot at Churubusco Azteca Studios, Mexico.
Cast: Francesca Annis (*Lady Jessica*), Kyle MacLachlan (*Paul Atreides*), Sting (*Feyd Rautha*), Dean Stockwell (*Dr Wellington Yueh*), Max Von Sydow (*Dr Kynes*), Jurgen Prochnow (*Duke Leto Atreides*), Silvana Mangano (*Revd Mother Ramallo*); Brad Dourif (*Peter De Vries*), José Ferrer (*Padisha Emperor Shaddam IV*), Freddie Jones (*Thufir Hawat*), Linda Hunt (*Shadout Mapes*), Sean Young (*Chani*), Alicia Roanne Witt (*Alia*), Leonardo Cimino (*Baron's doctor*), Richard Jordan (*Duncan Idaho*), Virginia Madsen (*Princess Irulan*), Everett

McGill (*Stilgar*), Kenneth McMillan (*Baron Vladimir Harkonnen*), Jack Nance (*Nefud*), Sian Phillips (*Revd Mother Gaius Helen Mohiam*), Paul Smith (*Beast Rabban*), Patrick Stewart (*Gurney Halleck*).

Blue Velvet
USA 1986 120'(10,814 ft) 35mm
Technicolor CinemaScope Dolby Stereo
Director, *script*: David Lynch; *Prod. company*: De Laurentiis Entertainment Group; *Exec. Prod.*: Richard Roth; *Cinematography*: Frederick Elmes; *Editor*: Duwayne Dunham; *Prod. design*: Patricia Norris; *Special effects*: Greg Hull, George Hill; *Music*: Angelo Badalamenti; *Make-up*: Jeff Goodwin; *Sound design*: Alan R. Splet; *Sound recording*: Ann Kroeber. Locations: Wilmington and North Carolina.
Cast: Kyle MacLachlan (*Jeffrey Beaumont*), Isabella Rossellini (*Dorothy Vallens*), Dennis Hopper (*Frank Booth*), Laura Dern (*Sandy Williams*), Hope Lange (*Mrs Williams*), Dean Stockwell (*Ben*), George Dickerson (*Detective Williams*), Priscilla Pointer (*Mrs Beaumont*), Frances Bay (*Aunt Barbara*), Jack Harvey (*Tom Beaumont*), Ken Stovitz (*Mike*), Brad Dourif (*Raymond*), Jack Nance (*Paul*), J. Michael Hunter (*Hunter*), Dick Green (*Don Vallens*), Fred Pickler (*Yellow Man*), Philip Markert (*Dr Gynde*), Leonard Watkins and Moses Gibson (*Double Ed*), Selden Smith (*Nurse Cindy*), Peter Carew (*Coroner*), Jon Jon Snipes (*Little Donny*), Andy Badale (*Piano player*), Jean-Pierre Viale (*Master of ceremonies*), Donald Moore (*Desk sergeant*).

Paintings exhibition at the James Corcoran Gallery, Santa Monica (1987)

Le Cowboy et le Frenchman
France 1988 22' Video colour (Series: Les Français vu par ...)
Director and *script*: David Lynch; *Prod. company*: Erato Films, Socpress, Figaro; *Exec. Prod.*: Paul Cameron, Pierre Olivier Bardet; *Assoc. Prod.*: David Warfield; *Prod.*: Daniel Toscan du Plantier; *Music*: Offenbach, Radio Ranch Straight Shooters, Eddie Dixon, Jean-Jacques Perrey; *Cinematography*: Frederick Elmes; *Prod. design* and *costumes*: Patricia Norris, Nancy Martinelli; *Choreography*: Sarah Elgart; *Sound engineer*: John Huck; *Editor*: Scott Chesnut.
Cast: Harry Dean Stanton (*Slim*), Frederic Golchan (*Frenchman*), Tracey Walters, Jack Nance, Michael Horse, Rick Guillory, Marie Lauren, Patrick Hauser, Eddi Dixon, Magali Alvarado, Ann Sophie, Robin Summers, Kathy Dean, Leslie Cook, Manette Lachance, Kelly Redusch, Michelle Rudy, Debra Seitz, Dominique Rojas, Audrey Tom, Amanda Hull, Talisa Soto, Jackie Old Coyote.

David Lynch acted the lead role in Tina Rathbone's *Zelly and Me* (USA 1988) opposite Isabella Rossellini

Paintings Exhibition at the Lou Castelli Gallery in New York (1989)

Twin Peaks
USA 1989 TV Serial in 29 parts Video colour
1st TX (pilot of 120'): 8 April 1990 at 21.00 on ABC (UK: 23 October 1990 at 21.00 on BBC2); Episode 1: TX 30 September 1990 at 21.00 on ABC (120').
Directors: David Lynch (pilot and eps. 1, 2, 8, 9, 14 and 29), Tina Rathbone (eps. 3 and 17), Tim Hunter (eps. 4, 16 and 28), Lesli Linka Glatter (eps. 5, 10, 13 and 23), Caleb Deschanel (eps. 6, 15 and 19), Mark Frost (ep. 7), Todd Holland (eps. 11 and 20), Graeme Clifford (ep. 12), Duwayne Dunham (eps. 18 and 25), Diane Keaton (ep. 22), James Foley (ep. 24), Uli Edel (ep. 21), Jonathan Sanger (ep. 26), Stephen Gyllenhaal (ep. 27); *Script*: David Lynch, Mark Frost; *Co-writers*: Harley Peyton (eps. 3, 6, 9, 11, 13, 16, 19, 20, 22, 25, 26, 27 and 29), Robert Engels (eps. 4, 10, 11, 13, 16, 19, 22, 25, 27 and 29), Jerry Stahl (ep. 11), Barry Pullman (eps. 12, 18, 24 and 28), Scott Frost (eps. 15 and 21), Tricia Brock (eps. 17 and 23); *Exec. Prod.*: Mark Frost, David Lynch; *Supervising Prod.*: Gregg Fienberg; *Prod.*: David J. Latt, Harley Peyton, Robert

Engels, Robert D. Simon, Monty Montgomery, Philip Neel; *Cinematographers*: Ron Garcia (pilot), Frank Byers; *Art Direction*: Patricia Norris (pilot), Richard Hoover; Locations near Seattle, Washington State and in Los Angeles.

Cast (grouped according to families and narrative clusters): **FBI cluster:** Kyle Maclachlan (*Agent Dale Cooper*), David Duchovny (*Denis/Denise Bryson*), Miguel Ferrer (*Albert Rosenfeld*), David Lynch (*Gordon Cole*), Kenneth Welsh (*Windom Earle*), Brenda E. Mathers (*Caroline Earle*); **the Sheriff's Department cluster:** Michael Ontkean (*Sheriff Harry S. Truman*), Harry Goaz (*Deputy Andy Brennan*), Michael Horse (*Deputy Tommy Hill 'Hawk'*), Kimmy Robertson (*Lucy Morgan*), Ian Buchanan (*Richard Tremayne*), Joshua Harris (*Little Nicky*); **the Packard Mill cluster:** Joan Chen (*Jocelyn Packard*), Piper Laurie (*Katherine Martell*), Jack Nance (*Pete Martell*), Dan O'Herlihy (*Andrew Packard*), David Warner (*Thomas Eckardt*), Brenda Strong (*Jones*); **the Diner cluster**: Peggy Lipton (*Norma Jennings*), Chris Mulkey (*Hank Jennings*), Andrea Hays (*Heidi*), Mädchen Amick (*Shelly Johnson*), Eric DaRae (*Leo Johnson*), Jane Greer (*Vivian Smythe*), James Booth (*Ernie Niles*), Heather Graham (*Annie Blackburn*); **the Horne and Great Northern cluster:** Richard Beymer (*Ben Horne*), Jan D'Arcy (*Sylvia Horne*), Sherilyn Fenn (*Audrey Horne*), Robert Davenport (pilot)/Robert Bauer (*Johnny Horne*), David Patrick Kelly (*Jerry Horne*), Hank Worden (*Bellboy*), Diane Caldwell (*Hotel employee*), John Charles Sheenan (*Bellboy*), Jill Rogoseske-Engels (*Trudy*), Arnie Stenseth (*Sven Jorgenson*), Billy Zane (*John Justice Wheeler*), Catherine E. Coulson (*Log Lady*), Carel L. Struycken (*Giant*); **the One-Eyed Jack cluster:** Victoria Catlin (*Blackie O'Reilly*), Walter Olkewicz (*Jacques Renault*), Michael Parks (*Jean Renault*), Clay Wilcox (*Bernard Renault*), Mike Vendrell, Bob Apissa (*Bodyguards*), Gaylin Görg (*Nancy O'Reilly*); **the Palmer cluster**: Sheryl Lee (*Laura Palmer and Madeleine Ferguson*), Ray Wise (*Leland Palmer*), Grace Zabriskie (*Sarah Palmer*), Frank Silva (*Bob*); **the Briggs cluster:** Don Davis (*Major Briggs*), Charlotte Stewart (*Betty Briggs*), Dana Ashbrook (*Bobby Briggs*); **the Hayward cluster:** Jessica Wallenfels (*Harriet Hayward*), Lara Flynn Boyle (*Donna Hayward*), Warren Frost (*Dr Hayward*), Mary Jo Deschanel (*Eileen Hayward*), Alicia Witt (*Gerstern Hayward*); **the Hurley cluster:** Wendy Robie (*Nadine Hurley*), Everett McGill (*Ed Hurley*), James Marshall (*James Hurley*), Gary Hershberger (*Mike Nelson*); **the Pulaski cluster:** Phoebe Augustine (*Ronnette Pulaski*), Rick Tutor (pilot)/Alan Ogle (*Janek Pulaski*), Michelle Milantoni (*Suburbis Pulaski*); **others:** Russ Tamblyn (*Lawrence Jacobi*), Troy Evans (*George Wolchezk*), John Boylan (*Dwayne Milford*), Yony Jay (*Doug Milford*), Robin Lively (*Lana Budding-Milford*), Rodney Harvey (*Biker Scotty*), Brett Vadset (*Joey*), David Wasman (*Gilman White*), Jane Jones (*Margaret Honeycutt*), Tawnya Pettiford-Waites (*Dr Shelvy*), Shelly Henning (*Alice Brady*), Dorothy Roberts (*Mrs Jackson*), Julee Cruise (*Singer*), Marjorie Nelson (*Janice Hogan*), Michael J. Anderson (*Man from another place*), Ben DiGregorio (*Max Hartman*), Al Strobel (*Mike/Gerard, One-armed man*), James V. Scott (*Black Lodge singer*), Ed Wright (*Dell Mibler*), Arvo A. Katajisto (*Bank guard*), Mark Takano (*Asian man*), Nick Love (*Malcolm Stone*), Annette McCarthy (*Evelyn Marsh*), John Apicella (*Jeffrey Marsh*).

Twin Peaks

USA 1989 112' Video colour (Pilot of the television series, with scenes from other episodes, released as a feature).

Director: David Lynch; *Prod. company*: Lynch–Frost Productions in association with Propaganda Films and Spelling Entertainment; *Exec. Prod.*: Mark Frost, David Lynch; *Prod.*: David J. Latt; *Assoc. Prod.*: Monty Montgomery; *Script*: David Lynch, Mark Frost; *Cinematography*: Ron Garcia; *Editor*: Duwayne Dunham; *Prod. design* and *costume design*: Patricia Norris; *Special effects*: Greg McMickle; *Music*: Angelo Badalamenti; *Songs*: 'The Nightingale' and 'Falling' by David Lynch and Angelo Badalamenti performed by Julee Cruise;

Make-up: Lizbeth Williamson; *Sound design*: Douglas Murray; *Sound recording*: John Wentworth. Locations near Seattle in Washington State and in Los Angeles.
Cast: Kyle Maclachlan (*Agent Dale Cooper*), Michael Ontkean (*Sheriff Harry S. Truman*), Sheryl Lee (*Laura Palmer and Madeleine Ferguson*), Peggy Lipton (*Norma Jennings*), Jack Nance (*Pete Martell*), Russ Tamblyn (*Lawrence Jacobi*), Joan Chen (*Jocelyn Packard*), Piper Laurie (*Katherine Martell*), Troy Evans (*George Wolchezk*), John Boylan (*Dwayne Milford*), Rodney Harvey (*Biker Scotty*), Robert Davenport (*Johnny Horne*), Jan D'Arcy (*Sylvia Horne*), Kimmy Robertson (*Lucy Morgan*), Jessica Wallenfels (*Harriet Hayward*), Wendy Robie (*Nadine Hurley*), Don Davis (*Major Briggs*), Charlotte Stewart (*Betty Briggs*), Phoebe Augustine (*Ronnette Pulaski*), Brett Vadset (*Joey*), Frank Silva (*Bob*), David Wasman (*Gilman White*), Jane Jones (*Margaret Honeycutt*), Tawnya Pettiford-Waites (*Dr Shelvy*), Shelly Henning (*Alice Brady*), Dorothy Roberts (*Mrs Jackson*), Julee Cruise (*Singer*), Arnie Stenseth (*Sven Jorgenson*), Andrea Hays (*Heidi*), Rick Tutor (*Janek Pulaski*), Marjorie Nelson (*Janice Hogan*), Michael J. Anderson (*Man from another place*), Ben DiGregorio (*Max Hartman*), Diane Caldwell (*Hotel employee*), Catherine E. Coulson (*Log Lady*), Al Strobel (*Philip Gerard, One-armed man*), Mädchen Amick (*Shelly Johnson*), Dana Ashbrook (*Bobby Briggs*), Richard Beymer (*Benjamin Horne*), Lara Flynn Boyle (*Donna Hayward*), Sherilyn Fenn (*Audrey Horne*), Warren Frost (*Dr Hayward*), James Marshall (*James Hurley*), Everett McGill (*Ed Hurley*), Eric DaRae (*Leo Johnson*), Mary Jo Deschanel (*Eileen Hayward*), Grace Zabriskie (*Sarah Palmer*), Harry Goaz (*Deputy Andy Brennan*), Gary Hershberger (*Mike Nelson*), Michael Horse (*Deputy Tommy Hill 'Hawk'*).

Wild at Heart
USA 1990 124'(11,182 ft) 35mm
Technicolor CinemaScope Dolby Stereo
Director: David Lynch; *Prod. company*: Propaganda Films for Polygram; *Exec. Prod.*: Michael Kuhn; *Prod.*: Monty Montgomery, Steve Golin, Sigurjon Sighvatsson; *Script*: David Lynch from Barry Gifford's novel; *Cinematography*: Frederick Elmes; *Editor*: Duwayne Dunham; *Prod. design:* Patricia Norris; *Special effects*: Don Power, David Domeyer; *Music*: Angelo Badalamenti; *Make-up*: Michelle Buhler; *Sound design*: Randy Thom; *Sound recording*: John Huck, John Wentworth; *Mixing:* Randy Thom, David Parker. Locations in and around Los Angeles and New Orleans.
Cast: Laura Dern (*Lula Pace Fortune*), Nicholas Cage (*Sailor Ripley*), Diane Ladd (*Marietta Pace*), Willem Dafoe (*Bobby Peru*), Isabella Rossellini (*Perdita Durango*), Harry Dean Stanton (*Johnny Farragut*), Crispin Glover (*Dell*), Grace Zabriskie (*Juana*), Freddie Jones (*George Kovich*), Sally Boyle (*Aunt Roonie*), Michele Seipp (*Girl in Zanzibar*), J. E. Freeman (*Marcello Santos*), Eddie Dixon (*Rex*), Belina Logan (*Beany Thorn*), W. Morgan Shepherd (*Mr Reindeer*), Glenn Walker Harris Jr (*Pace Roscoe*), Charlie Spradling (*Irma*), Calvin Lockhart (*Reginald Sula*), Gregg Dandridge (*Rob Ray Lemon*), Bob Terhune (*Earl Kovich*), Tracey Walter (*Roach*), John Lurie (*Sparky*), Jack Nance (*O. O. Spool*), Sheryl Lee (*Good Witch*), Sherilynn Fenn (*Girl in accident*), Peter Brownlow (*Hotel manager*), Lisa Ann Cabasa (*Reindeer dancer*), Billy Swan (*Himself*), Brent Fraser (*Idiot punk*), Shawn Rowe (*Waitress*), Jack Jozefson (*Chet*), David Patrick Kelly (*Dropshadow*), Marvin Kaplan (*Uncle Pooch*), Scott Coffey (*Billy*), Frank Collison (*Tommy Thompson*).

Industrial Symphony No. 1
USA 1990 49' video col
Director: David Lynch; *Prod.*: Steve Golin, Monty Montgomery, Sigurjon Sighvatsson; *Exec. Prod*: David Lynch, Angelo Badalamenti; *Music*: Angelo Badalamenti; *Cinematography*: John Schwartzmann; *Editing*: Bob Jenkins; *Sets*: Franne Lee; *Choreography*: Martha Clark
Cast: Laura Dern (*Heartbroken Woman*), Nicolas Cage (*Heartbreaker*), Julee Cruise

(*Dreamself of the Heartbroken Woman*), Lisa Giobbi (*Solo dancer*), Felix Blaska (*Solo dancer*), Michael J. Anderson (*Lumberjack/Twin A*), Andre Badalamenti (*Clarinet player/Twin B*), John Bell (*Deer*).

American Chronicles
USA 1990–91: television documentaries produced by Lynch–Frost Productions with David Lynch as one of the executive producers. Lynch and Frost co-directed one contribution to the series: **Champions** (UK TX 21 June 1992 at 17.00 on Channel 4 Television). Other items in the series include: *Farewell to the Flesh, Manhattan After Dark, High School Reunion, Miss Texas, Autos, Biker Convention, Semper Fi, Eye of the Beholder, Defenders of the Faith, After a Fashion/An American Camelot, Here Today Gone Tomorrow/Truck Stop, Once Upon a Time, Diamonds Are Forever/The Future That Never Was, Class of '65. Directors* included Robin Sestero, Ruben Norte, Gregg Pratt, Marlo Bendau and Mark Frost.

David Lynch acted as Executive Producer for Peter Sellars's feature, *The Cabinet of Dr Ramirez* (US 1991)

Wicked Games
Video promo for Chris Isaak, directed by David Lynch and released in 1991.

Dangerous
Video promo for Michael Jackson's tour. Produced by Joseph Wilcots for MJJ Ventures. Robert Arthur directed the section 'A History of Michael Jackson', John Landis directed the 'Black or White' section and David Lynch made the 'teaser' for the promo. The 30-min. programme was first broadcast on 17 November 1991 at 19.30 by Fox Broadcasting Company.

Twin Peaks: Fire Walk with Me
USA 1992 134'(12,099 ft) 35mm
Technicolor Panavision Dolby Stereo
Director: David Lynch; *Prod. company*: Twin Peaks Productions; *Exec. Prod.*: David Lynch, Mark Frost; *Prod.*: Gregg Fienberg, John Wentworth; *Script*: David Lynch, Robert Engels; *Cinematography*: Ron Garcia; *Editor*: Mark Sweeney; *Prod. design:* Patricia Norris; *Special effects coordinator*: Robert E. McCarthy; *Music*: Angelo Badalamenti; *Music extract:* Luigi Cherubini's *Requiem* in C Minor; *Make-up*: Katharina Hirsch-Smith; *Sound design*: David Lynch; *Sound editor*: Douglas Murray.
Cast: Sheryl Lee (*Laura Palmer*), Ray Wise (*Leland Palmer*), Mädchen Amick (*Shelly Johnson*), Dana Ashbrook (*Bobby Briggs*), Phoebe Augustine (*Ronette Pulaski*), David Bowie (*Philip Jeffries*), Eric DaRae (*Leo Johnson*), Miguel Ferrer (*Albert Rosenfeld*), Pamela Gidley (*Teresa Banks*), Heather Graham (*Annie Blackburn*), Chris Isaak (*Special Agent Chester Desmond*), Moira Kelly (*Donna Hayward*), Peggy Lipton (*Norma Jennings*), David Lynch (*Gordon Cole*), James Marshall (*James Hurley*), Jürgen Prochnow (*Woodman*), Harry Dean Stanton (*Carl Rodd*), Kiefer Sutherland (*Sam Stanley*), Lenny Von Dohlen (*Harold Smith*), Grace Zabriskie (*Sarah Palmer*), Kyle MacLachlan (*Special Agent Dale Cooper*), Frances Bay (*Mrs Tremond*), Catherine E. Coulson (*Log Lady*), Michael J. Anderson (*Man from another place*), Frank Silva (*Bob*), Walter Olkewicz (*Jacques Renault*), Al Strobel (*Gerard, One-armed man*), Gary Hershberger (*Mike Nelson*), Sandra Kinder (*Irene*), Gary Bullock (*Sheriff Cable*), Calvin Lockhart (*Electrician*), Andrea Hays (*Heidi*), Julee Cruise (*Roadhouse singer*).

On The Air
USA 1991–2 7 episodes of 24' video col
Director: David Lynch; *Prod. company*: Lynch–Frost Productions, Twin Peaks Productions (ep. 1 only), Zoblotnick Broadcasting Corporation (eps. 2–7), Worldvision Entertainments.
First TX: 20 June 1992 at 21.30 on ABC (UK: 25 July 1993 at 01.55 on BBC 2)
Directors: David Lynch (ep. 1), Jack Fisk (eps. 2 and 6), Jonathan Sanger (ep. 3), Lesli Linka Glatter (eps. 4 and 7), Betty Thomas (ep. 6); *Exec. Prod.*: Mark Frost, David Lynch; *Series Co-Exec. Prod.*: Bob Engels;

Prod.: Gregg Fienberg and Deepak Nayak; *Scripts*: Mark Frost and David Lynch (ep. 1), Mark Frost (eps. 2, 4 and 7), Scott Frost (ep. 3), Robert Engels (ep. 5), David Lynch and Robert Engels (ep. 6); *Music*: Angelo Badalamenti; *Prod. design:* Okowita; *Cinematography*: Ron Garcia (ep. 1), Peter Deming;
Cast: Ian Buchanan (*Lester Guy*), Nancye Ferguson (*Ruth Trueworthy*), Miguel Ferrer (*Bud Budwaller*), Gary Grossman (*Bert Schein*), Mel Johnson Jr (*Micky*), Marvin Kaplan (*Dwight McGonigle*), David Lander (*Vladja Gochktch*), Kim McGuire (*Nicole Thorn*), Maria Jeanette Rubinoff (*Betty Hudson*), Tracey Walter (*Blinky*), Buddy Douglas (*Buddy Morris*), Raleigh and Raymond Friend (*Hurry Up Twins*), Bruce Grossberg (*Control booth technician*), Irwin Keyes (*Shorty the stagehand*), Everett Greenbaum (*ZBC announcer*); Guests ep. 1: Dorsay Alavi, Vanessa Angel, Reo Danzelle, Carolyn Lowry (*Chorus girls*), Susan Russell (*Announcer's assistant*), Angelo Badalamenti (*Piano player*), Walt Robles (*Flying stagehand*), Peter Rocca (*Stunt double*); Guests ep. 2: Diana Bellamy (*Ethel Thissle*), Richard Riehl (*Dr Winky*), Charles Tyner (*Prof. R. Answer*), Peter Pitofsky (*Worker*), Lorna Jones (*Executive*); Guests ep. 3: Freddie Jones (*Stan Tailings*), Bill Zuckert (*Crusty old stagehand*); Guests ep. 4: Anne Bloom (*Sylvia Hudson*), Chuck McCann (*Wally Walters*); Guests ep. 5: Robert Costanzo (*Mr Plumber*), I.M. Hobson (*Presidio*); Guests ep. 6: John Quade (*Billy 'The Ear' Mulkahey*), Bellina Logan (*Woman with no name*), Sydney Lassick (*Mr Zoblotnick*), Gregory Sporleder (*Sax player*); Guests ep. 7: Sydney Lassick (*Mr Zoblotnick*), Joseph Pecoraro (*Guiseppe*), Ben Kronen (*Waiter*).

Hotel Room
USA 1992 90' video col
First US TX: 8 January 1993 at 11.00 on HBO.
Directors: David Lynch ('Tricks' and 'Blackout'), James Signorelli ('Getting Rid Of Robert'); *Prod. company*: Asymmetrical Prods, Propaganda Films; *Exec. Prod.*: Monty Montgomery, David Lynch; *Prod.*: Deepak Nayar; *Scripts*: Barry Gifford ('Tricks' and 'Blackout'), Jay McInerney ('Getting Rid of Robert'); *Cinematography*: Peter Deming; *Music*: Angelo Badalamenti.
Cast: 'Tricks': Glenne Headly (*Darlene*), Freddie Jones (*Lou*), Harry Dean Stanton (*Mo*); 'Getting Rid of Robert': Griffin Dunne (*Robert*), Deborah Unger (*Sasha*), Mariska Hargitay (*Diane*), Chelsea Field (*Tina*); 'Blackout': Crispin Glover and Alcia Witt (*Tulsa Couple*), Clark Heathcliffe Brolly, Camilla Overbye Roos, John Solari, Carl Sundstrom.
A trilogy of television shorts set in Room 603 of the Railroad Hotel in New York City.

Advertising Spots:
Obsession for Calvin Klein, *Opium* for Yves Saint-Laurent, *Refuse Collection* for New York City.
Songs: co-author, with Angelo Badalamenti, of approx. 40 *Songs*, including material for Julee Cruise's album *Floating into the Night*.
David Lynch's comic strip, *The Angriest Dog in the World*, appears weekly in the *LA Reader*.

Television Programmes Featuring David Lynch:

Madelaine French's television interview with David Lynch for RPM Productions, first UK TX 23 January 1985 on Channel 4 Television at 21.00.

Helen Gallacher made an *Arena* programme for BBC2 in London entitled 'Ruth, Roses and Revolver', hosted and narrated by David Lynch; first UK TX: 20 February 1987.

Florence Dauman's television programme *Hollywood Mavericks*, produced by the American Film Institute and NHK Enterprises, focuses on David Lynch; first UK TX: 6 October 1990 at 21.00 by Channel 4 Television. The cast includes Martin Scorsese, Peter Bogdanovich and Paul Schrader.

Jonathan Ross Presents For One Week Only, made by Andy Harries, features David Lynch; first UK TX: 19 October 1990 at 23.05 on Channel 4 Television.

Behind The Screen: BBC programme about the making of *Twin Peaks*, 1st TX: 22 October 1990; produced by Catherine Elliott-Kemp.

An episode of *Entertainment UK*, produced by Mentorn Films, features David Lynch; first UK TX: 17 November 1992 at 00.30 on ITV.

Entertainment UK, produced by Mentorn Films, featuring David Lynch; first UK TX: 24 June 1993 at 01.30 on ITV.

Lucida Productions in Britain made a television programme with David Lynch: *Made In The USA Interviews – David Lynch*.

II. Annotated Bibliography

This bibliography is not exhaustive. Sections A to D include the items used for the writing of this book. The numbering corresponds to the numbering of the references given in the text.

For the English edition, some additional bibliographical material (sections E and F), not numbered and not directly used for the writing of this book, lists other substantial essays about the films and the director. The full credits of the features can be found in the *Monthly Film Bulletin* reviews.

A. Books and Dossiers

1. Jim Hoberman and Jonathan Rosenbaum, *Midnight Movies*, New York: Harper and Row, 1983. This is a study of the cult-film phenomenon and includes a very detailed essay on the genesis of *Eraserhead*.

2. *Ciné-Fantastique*, vol. 4, nos. 4–5, Special Double Issue, September 1984. This contains a dossier on the making of *Dune* by Paul M. Sammon and an essay on *Filming Lynch's Eraserhead* by George Godwin. This issue is a must for the Lynchmaniac.

3. Ed Naha, *The Making of Dune*, London: W.H. Allen, 1984. This is the official 'Making of' book released together with the film. It is understandably discreet about the difficulties that beset the film's production but contains a considerable amount of information and is well illustrated.

4. Mark Altman, *Twin Peaks: Behind The Scenes*, New York: Pioneer, 1991. Interviews and anecdotes about the first part of the serial, up to the arrest of Leland Palmer.

5. *Positif*, no. 356, October 1990. This issue contains a special dossier on Lynch, with contributions from Laurent Vachaud, Christophe Libilbehety and Philippe Rouyer on *Wild At Heart*, an interview conducted by Michel Ciment and Hubert Niogret, unpublished materials taken from the documentary *Hollywood Mavericks*, a filmography compiled by Michael Henry and Hubert Niogret. An elaborate dossier in a journal whose first essays on Lynch (on the release of *Eraserhead* and *The Elephant Man*) had been severely criticised.

6. *Génération Séries*, nos. 2–3, January and Summer 1992. Their *Dossier Spécial Twin Peaks* in two parts 'for fans of the serial' contains lots of information aiding viewer-orientation. It is distributed in Paris by the Librairie Huitième Art, 5 rue Cochin, 75005

Paris, France. It offers a genuine and serious documentation of the serial.

7. Federico Chiacchiari, Demetrio Salvi, Stefano Sorbini (eds.), *David Lynch*, Rome: Sentieri Selvaggi, 1991. An illustrated book containing essays on Lynch's various films, a succinct mini-biography and a compilation of the director's press statements.

B. Essays and Reviews in Journals

8. Cahiers du cinéma, no. 319, January 1981; a note on *Eraserhead* by Charles Tesson.

9. *Cahiers du cinéma*, no. 322, April 1981; a dossier on David Lynch, including a fine essay by Serge Daney on *The Elephant Man* and Jonathan Rosenbaum's '*Eraserhead*: Un film culte'.

10. *Starfix*, no. 22, January 1985; interview with Lynch.

11. *Première*, no. 95, February 1985; interview with Lynch.

12. *L'Ecran fantastique*, no. 53, February 1985; dossier about *Dune* with several interviews, including one with Lynch.

13. *Cahiers du cinéma*, no. 368, February 1985; contains Michel Chion's 'Les visages et les noms' about *Dune*, 'Une année sur Arrakis' and extracts from the report published in *L'Ecran fantastique*.

14. *La Revue du cinéma*, no. 403, March 1985; with a dossier on Lynch compiled by Guy Gauthier and Jacques Valot.

15. *L'Ecran fantastique*, no. 76, January 1987; about *Blue Velvet*.

16. *La Revue du cinéma*, no. 424, February 1987; essay by Jacques Zimmer and an interview conducted by Marie-José Simpson.

17. *Cahiers du cinéma*, no. 391, February 1987; essay on *Blue Velvet*: 'Ce que couve l'immobilité des plantes' by Michel Chion.

18. *Premiere* (USA), vol. 4, no. 1, September 1990; on *Wild at Heart*: 'David Lynch and Laura Dern Cut Loose' by Ralph Rugoff, and an interview with Laura Dern.

19. *Starfix*, no. 84, May–June 1990; dossier on *Wild at Heart*.

20. *Cahiers du cinéma*, no. 433, June 1990; essay by Nicolas Saada and an interview with Lynch.

21. *Starfix*, no. 87, September 1990; dossier with essays by, for instance, François Cognard, and reproductions of paintings, comic strips, etc.

22. *Revue du cinéma*, no. 484, October 1990; interview with Willem Dafoe and essays by Jacques Zimmer and Gérard Lenne.

23. *Le Monde*, 26 October 1990; interview with Lynch by Henry Béhar; essay by Jean-Michel Frodon.

24. *La Revue du cinéma*, no. 464, October 1990; dossier on *Wild at Heart* with an interview with Willem Dafoe and a Lynch-alphabet by Gérard Lenne.

25. *Max*, November 1990; interview with Lynch.

26. *Studio*, no. 43, November 1990; essay by Jean-Hugues Anglade and portrait of Laura Dern.

27. *Mad Movies*, no. 70, March 1991; *Twin Peaks* dossier.

28. *Télérama*, no. 2163, 26 June 1991; contains Alain Rémond's 'Sauce hollandaise'.

29. *Andere Sinema*, no. 107. Contains Stephen Sarrazin's 'Where did Laura Palmer go and how did she get there?'

30. *Elle*, no. 2406, 17 February 1992; interview with Isabella Rossellini.

31. *Glamour*, no. 43, May 1992; interview with Sherilyn Fenn.

32. *Mad Movies Ciné-Fantastique*, no. 77, April–May 1992; dossier on *Fire Walk With Me*.

33. *Studio*, Special Issue, May 1992; interview with Kyle MacLachlan about Lynch.

34. *Le Monde*, 3–10 May 1992, Radio–Television Supplement; with Colette Godard's essay on *Industrial Symphony No. 1*.

35. *Le Monde*, 7 May 1992; interview with Lynch by Henry Béhar.

36. *L'Ecran fantastique*, no. 2, New Formula, April–May 1992.

37. *Cinéphage*, no. 6, May–June 1992; interview with Lynch on *Fire Walk With Me*.

38. *Max:* 'Twin Peaks le film', promotional supplement with no. 37, includes an interview with Lynch.

39. *Première*, no. 183, June 1992; interview with Lynch.

40. *Studio Magazine*, no. 63, June 1992; comments by Lynch.

41. *Libération*, 5 June 1992; interview with

Lynch by Arnaud Viviant about the director's relationship with television.
42. *Ciné-News*, no. 37, June–July 1992; interview with Lynch.

C. Press Kits
on *The Elephant Man* (43), *Wild at Heart* (44) and *Twin Peaks: Fire Walk with Me* (45).

D. Source Materials
46. *The Dune Story Book: Adapted from a Screenplay by David Lynch*, by Joan D. Vinge, London and Sydney: Sphere Books, 1984.
47. Barry Gifford, *Wild at Heart: The Story of Sailor and Lula*, London: Paladin, 1990.

E. About *Twin Peaks*
Richard Saul Worman, Mark Frost, David Lynch, *Welcome To Twin Peaks, Access Guide to the Town*, Harmondsworth: Penguin Books, 1991.
The Secret Diary of Laura Palmer: As seen by Jennifer Lynch, New York: Simon and Schuster, 1990/ London: Penguin Books, 1990.
David Lavery, *Critical Approaches to 'Twin Peaks'*, Detroit: Wayne State University Press, 1994.

F. Additional Essays, Credits and Interviews
'The Alphabet' and 'The Grandmother', *Monthly Film Bulletin*, vol. 54, no. 639, April 1987, p. 127.
'Eraserhead', *Variety*, 23 March 1977, p. 24.
'Eraserhead', *Monthly Film Bulletin*, vol. 46, no. 542, March 1979, p. 44.
'Eraserhead', *Film Quarterly*, vol. 39, no. 1, Autumn 1985, p. 31.
'The Elephant Man', *Variety*, 1 October 1980, pp. 20 and 22.
'The Elephant Man', *Monthly Film Bulletin*, vol. 47, no. 561, October 1980, p. 192.
'Dune', *Variety*, 5 December 1984, p. 16.
'Dune', *Monthly Film Bulletin*, vol. 52, no. 613, February 1985, pp. 46–7.
'Blue Velvet', *Variety*, 3 September 1986, p. 16.
'The Sound of *Blue Velvet*', Interview with Alan Splet, *Millimeter*, no. 14, pp. 121–4, November 1986.
'Blue Velvet', *American Cinematographer*, vol. 67, no. 11, November 1986, pp. 60–74.
'Blue Velvet', *Sight and Sound*, vol. 56, no. 1, Winter 1986–7, pp. 30–3.
'Blue Velvet', *Cinématographe*, no. 126, January 1987.
'Blue Velvet', *Cinema Papers*, no. 62, March 1987, pp. 16–17 and 51.
'Blue Velvet', *Monthly Film Bulletin*, vol. 54, no. 639, April 1987, pp. 99–100 and 128.
'Blue Velvet', *Starburst*, no. 104, April 1987, pp. 13–14.
'Blue Velvet', *Film Quarterly*, vol. 41, no. 1, Autumn 1987, pp. 44–9.
'Blue Velvet', *Cineaste*, vol. 15, no. 3, 1987, pp. 38–41.
'Blue Velvet', *Literature/Film Quarterly*, vol. 16, no. 2, 1988, pp. 82–90.
'A Journey through *Blue Velvet*: Film, Fantasy and the Female Spectator', Barbara Creed, *New Formations*, no. 6, 1988.
'Blue Velvet', *Post Script*, vol. 8, no. 3, Summer 1989, pp. 2–17.
'Blue Velvet', *Literature/Film Quarterly*, vol. 18, no. 3, 1990, pp. 160–78.
'A Small Boy and Others: Sexual Dis-orientation in Henry James, Kenneth Anger and David Lynch', Michael Moon, in Hortense J. Spillers (ed.), *Comparative American Identities: Race, Sex and Nationality in the Modern Text*, New York: Routledge, 1991.
'Blue Velvet', *Genders*, no. 13, Spring 1992, pp. 73–89.
'Home Fires Burning: Family Noir in *Blue Velvet* and *Terminator 2*', Fred Pfeil, in Joan Copjec (ed.), *Shades of Noir: A Reader*, London: Verso, 1993, pp. 227–60.
'Wild at Heart', *Variety*, 23 May 1990, pp. 32 and 68.
'Wild at Heart', *Monthly Film Bulletin*, vol. 57, no. 680, September 1990, pp. 271–3.
'Wild at Heart', *Cinema Papers*, no. 80, August 1990, pp. 16–17.
'Wild at Heart', *Film Comment*, vol. 26, no. 6, November/December 1990, pp. 59–62.
'Wild at Heart', *Sight and Sound*, vol. 59, no. 4, Autumn 1990, p. 277.
'Wild at Heart', Film Comment, vol. 27, no. 1, January/February 1991, pp. 49–51.

'Wild at Heart', *Film Quarterly*, vol. 45, no. 2, Winter 1991–2.
'Wild at Heart', *Cineaste*, vol. 18, no. 2, 1991, pp. 39–41.
'Twin Peaks', *Variety*, 4 April 1990, p. 48.
'Twin Peaks', *Variety*, 8 October 1990, p. 63.
'Twin Peaks', *Film Comment*, vol. 26, no. 2, March/April 1990, pp. 73–5.
'Twin Peaks', *Film Comment*, vol. 27, no. 1, January/February 1991, pp. 18–21.
'Twin Peaks', *Primetime*, no. 16, Winter 1990–1, pp. 20-2.
'Twin Peaks', *Starburst*, no. 149, January 1991, p. 41.
'Twin Peaks', *Critical Studies in Mass Communication*, vol. 8, no. 4, December 1991, pp. 389–403.
'Twin Peaks', *CineAction*, no. 24/5, August 1991, pp. 50–9.
'Twin Peaks', *Film Quarterly*, vol. 46, no. 2, Winter 1991–2, pp. 22–34.
'Twin Peaks', *Spectator*, vol. 12, no. 2, Spring 1992, pp. 64–71.
'Twin Peaks: Fire Walk with Me', *Variety*, 18 May 1992, pp. 43–4.
'Twin Peaks: Fire Walk with Me', *Sight and Sound*, vol. 2, no. 7, November 1992, p. 416.
'Twin Peaks: Fire Walk with Me', *Cinema Papers*, no. 89, August 1992, pp. 26–31.
'Twin Peaks: Fire Walk with Me', *Starburst*, no. 169, September 1992, p. 38.
'(Why) Is David Lynch Important?', *Parkett*, no. 28, 1991.